D1454261

THE SUBALTERN

A Chronicle of the Peninsular War

THE SUBALTERN
A Chronicle of the Peninsular War

George Robert Gleig

Edited, and with an Introduction by
Ian C. Robertson

LEO COOPER

First reprinted in 1969 by Leo Cooper

Reprinted in this format 2001 by
LEO COOPER
an imprint of Pen & Sword Books Limited
47 Church Street, Barnsley, South Yorkshire S70 2AS

© Ian Campbell Robertson, 2001

ISBN 0 85052 830 5

A catalogue record for this book is available from
the British Library

Typeset in 10.5/12pt Sabon by
Phoenix Typesetting, Ilkley, West Yorkshire

Printed in England by
CPI UK

Contents

Maps and Plans

Chronology

1813

21 June	The French, commanded by King Joseph Bonaparte and Marshal Jourdan, are defeated and scattered by Wellington at the battle of Vitoria
25	Pamplona is blockaded
28	San Sebastián is invested
21 July	General Rey, commanding the garrison, refuses Sir Thomas Graham's summons to surrender San Sebastián
25	The first assault on San Sebastián fails. Soult starts his counter-offensive in the Pyrenees at the passes of Maya and Roncesvalles
28 and 30	The battles of Sorauren
	The French retreat to the frontier, and Wellington establishes his Headquarters at Lesaka, south-west of Bera/Vera
19 August	Additional consignments of artillery landed at Pasajes
31	The French are repulsed by the Spaniards at San Marcial. San Sebastián is taken, although the citadel did not surrender until 8 September
7 October	Wellington crosses the Bidasoa and enters France
31	Pamplona surrenders
10 November	The battle of the Nivelle
8 December	Wellington receives confirmation of Napoleon's defeat at Leipzig (16–19 October)
9–10	The battle of the Nive
13	The battle of St Pierre; Bayonne is invested

1814

26 February	Hope crosses the bridge of boats west of Bayonne, now surrounded
27	The battle of Orthez. Soult retired east towards Toulouse
20 March	French rearguard action at Tarbes
10 April	The battle of Toulouse

12 April	Wellington receives news of Napoleon's abdication (on the 6th)
14	The sortie from Bayonne, which surrenders on the 27th
30	The Treaty of Paris signed
23 June	Wellington reaches Dover after a continuous absence from Britain of five years and two months
8 August	Wellington leaves for Paris as Ambassador

1815

24 January	Wellington leaves Paris to attend the Congress of Vienna
26 February	Napoleon escapes from Elba, the news reaching Wellington on 7 March
29 March	Wellington leaves Vienna for Brussels, arriving 5 April
18 June	The battle of Waterloo

Introduction

The first book on the Peninsular War I acquired was a copy of the first edition of Gleig's *The Subaltern*. That was over forty years ago, before the demand for such narratives caused them to rise in prices beyond the pocket of most of us. My interest in the subject had been excited by the fact that the families of my in-laws were from San Sebastián and Sare respectively, both close to the Franco-Spanish frontier, and our holidays were often spent in the vicinity of the battlefields so vividly described in this little book. Oman, the great historian of that war, when commenting on military memoirs of the period, remarked that not only was it charmingly written, but it had the additional merit of being trustworthy for matters of detail, sticking closely to personal experience and avoiding second-hand stories. Richard Ford, author of the *Hand-Book for Travellers in Spain* (1845), when referring to military authorities, observed that of the minor works of the period, among the most entertaining were those of Gleig, Sherer, and Kincaid. As *The Subaltern* was published three years prior to the appearance of the first volume of Napier's monumental *History*, on which too many later writers relied – an understandable foible – its author cannot be accused of plagiarism, whatever minor faults it may contain.

George Robert Gleig was born at Stirling on 20 April 1796 to Janet, the youngest daughter of Robert Hamilton of Kilbrackmont, and George Gleig (1753–1840), a pillar of the Scottish Episcopalian Church, who contributed frequently to the *Gentleman's Magazine*, among other periodicals. He also wrote several articles for the third edition of *The Encyclopaedia Britannica*, the last six volumes of which he edited from 1793. In October 1808 he was consecrated Bishop of Brechin.

Late in 1807 Napoleon's troops under General Junot had crossed Spain to occupy Portugal, then allied to Britain; by the following Spring the French had also occupied Madrid. In May 1808 the Spaniards rebelled, uprisings taking place throughout the country. Envoys were sent to England to seek military support and, in August, an expeditionary force commanded by Sir Arthur Wellesley landed at Figuera da Foz on the west coast of Portugal some distance north of Lisbon, to win the battles of Roliça and Vimeiro. After the Convention of Sintra, by which the remaining French troops in Portugal were repatriated, Wellesley himself returned to England. It was during the following winter that the army, now under Sir John Moore, was forced to retreat to Corunna, in what might be described as 'the Dunkirk of its day'. Wellesley then returned to the Peninsula and, after the battle of Talavera (July 1809), he was known as Viscount Wellington. He was able to delay Marshal Masséna's advance on Lisbon at Busaco in the September of the following year and frustrated his capture of the capital by the Lines of Torres Vedras, secretly constructed during previous months, before pushing the invaders back to the Spanish frontier in the spring of 1811.

Like many other boys of his age, young Gleig must have followed the fortunes of the army with a lively interest, although so delicate was his health that his life was at one time despaired of, and he was taught at home by his father. He was then sent to the Stirling Grammar School, the rigours of which he survived, followed by studies under Dr Russell at Leith prior to attending Glasgow University. In 1811 – the year in which the battles of Fuentes de Oñoro and La Albuera were fought – Gleig proceeded to Oxford, having gained a Snell exhibition to Balliol.

However, it was not long before he resigned this scholarship, finding himself unable to resist the urge to join Wellington's victorious army in the Peninsula. Gleig obtained an ensigncy in the 85th Regiment of Light Infantry (the Bucks Volunteers), and joined his company at the Cove of Cork. Within a few months he was promoted Lieutenant, and thus we find him at the commencement of his chronicle at Hythe, impatiently awaiting orders to embark for Spain, delayed by bad weather until late July 1813.

First mentioned in Orders on 23 July, the 85th formed part of Lord Aylmer's brigade, which took its place in the 1st Division, with which it always acted. On the resignation of Sir Thomas Graham due to his deteriorating eyesight, this Division was commanded by Sir John Hope (4th Earl of Hopetoun from 1816; he died in 1823). By the following January the 2/67th and 77th had joined Aylmer's brigade, the 2/84th having been withdrawn, and soon afterwards the brigade's strength was further increased by the arrival of the 1/37th.

Gleig's narrative ends early in May 1814, when his regiment struck its tents prior to marching to Bordeaux. It had remained with the 1st Division on the left flank of the Allied army encircling Bayonne, not having taken part in the final advance into France, in which Soult's army had been worsted at Orthez (27 February) on its retreat towards Toulouse, where the last battle of the war was fought on 10 April.

The 85th Regiment then sailed to America, where it saw action at Bladensburg, Baltimore, New Orleans, and at the capture of Washington and Fort Bowyer, during which engagements Gleig was wounded on three occasions. Apparently he was wounded also – maybe only slightly – in the battles of the Nivelle and the Nive, although his name does not appear in

INTRODUCTION

The Biographical Dictionary of British Officers Killed and Wounded, 1808–1814 (1998), compiled by John A. Hall as a supplementary volume to Greenhill Books' reprint of Oman's *A History of the Peninsular War*. After the peace, Gleig went on half-pay and returned to Oxford in 1816, taking his B.A. at Magdalen Hall in 1818 and his M.A. three years later. Meanwhile, in 1819, he had married a ward of his father, the daughter of Captain Cameron the younger of Kinlochleven, and prepared to take Holy Orders. In the following year Gleig was ordained by the Archbishop of Canterbury, Dr Manners Sutton, and appointed to the curacy of Westwell, near Ashford in Kent. During his time here he wrote *Campaigns of the British Army at Washington and New Orleans*. His income was increased on receiving the perpetual curacy of Ash (west of Sandwich) and the rectory of Ivychurch (near New Romney).

The Subaltern first appeared as a series of anonymous contributions to *Blackwood's Magazine*. These were so well received that it was proposed to publish the narrative as a separate volume, which came out in 1825. This attracted the attention of the Duke of Wellington, who made enquiries as to the identity of the author. Gleig took the opportunity of seeking permission to dedicate the next edition to him, but this the Duke would not allow, at least formally, however much he admired its simplicity and truth; but by way of an indirect sanction, in replying to the request, he added: 'If, however, you should think proper to dedicate your Second Edition to me, you are at perfect liberty to do so; and you cannot express in too strong terms my approbation and admiration of your interesting work' [letter of 9 November, 1826]. Gleig's success was such that Mr Constable of Edinburgh suggested that he should write a military life of Wellington. This was a task which he would undertake only with the full collaboration of the Duke, who declined the proposal on the grounds that he would only agree to publish the truth, and did not wish for the remainder of his life to be 'engaged in controversies of a nature most unpleasant, as they will be with the wounded vanity of individuals and nations'.

Eventually, in the summer of 1829, when composing a biography of Sir Thomas Munro, Gleig was invited to Walmer Castle – only eight miles from his living – to discuss with Wellington the publication of letters which had passed between the Duke and Munro. He was to become a frequent visitor both at Walmer and at Stratfield Saye, while, on 11 November 1831, Wellington attended the christening of one of Gleig's children at Ash. The Duke may well have been responsible for putting forward Gleig's name for the vacant Chaplaincy of Chelsea Hospital, offered to him by Lord John Russell in 1834; he certainly knew all about it.

It is curious that some of the more interesting diaries or accounts of the late war were those by men who later took Holy Orders, among them Alexander Dallas of the Commissariat, and Captain Charles Boothby of

the Royal Engineers. Gleig was fortunate in being able to follow his vocation while at the same time continuing to interest himself in the profession
he loved, namely military affairs, or at least in the welfare of veterans
maimed in the war. By this time he had published a number of soldiers'
tales, entitled *The Chelsea Pensioners*, and *Chelsea Hospital and its
Traditions* came out in 1838.

From 1830, in addition to ministering to an extensive parish, he wrote
incessantly to support his growing family and was one of the first con-
tributors to *Fraser's Magazine*. Several of these papers, together with those
written for *The Quarterly*, *The Edinburgh*, and *Blackwood's* formed his
Essays, published in 1858. Although his output was great, the quality
was uneven. Among books which came from his pen, apart from volumes
of theology and sermons, were 'Lives' of Clive, of Warren Hastings, and of
Military Commanders; a *History of India*, *India and its Army*, and *Sale's
Brigade in Afghanistan*; also descriptions of both the Waterloo and Leipzig
campaigns, etc. Norbert Landsheit's *The Hussar* and George Farmer's *The
Light Dragoon*, military reminiscences retold by Gleig in his inimitable
style, were published in 1837 and 1844 respectively, while the result of his
experiences on an extensive continental tour, undertaken on his doctor's
recommendation, appeared under the title *Germany, Bohemia and
Hungary visited in 1837*.

In 1844 Gleig was appointed Chaplain-General of the Forces, a position
he held until 1875, while from 1846 until his resignation in 1857 he was
also Inspector-General of Military Schools. Although conservative as far
as politics were concerned – he had attacked the Reform Bill in 1832 –
Gleig's friendship with Wellington may have cooled at this time, for the
Duke was opposed to his more liberal views on education in military estab-
lishments. John Wilson Croker, who had also spoken against the Reform
Bill, noted that the Duke had commented with some vexation that Gleig
talked 'too much of his personal comforts, and too little of his men'.
Gleig's *Personal Recollections of the First Duke of Wellington*, published
posthumously, at his own request and edited by his daughter Mary in
1904, quotes the Duke as saying, when schemes for educating NCOs and
other ranks were proposed in the 1840s: 'By Jove! If there is a mutiny in
the army – and in all probability we shall have one – you'll see that these
new-fangled schoolmasters will be at the bottom of it'.

In 1862, ten years after the Duke's death, Gleig's *Life of Arthur, First
Duke of Wellington* appeared, but it was largely founded on Brailmont's
biography. It seems likely that at some time in the 1860s Gleig may have
visited the scenes of his youthful campaigning, for the 1872 edition of *The
Subaltern* contained a new 30-page preface, much of it taken up with a
description of the countryside between Bayonne and San Sebastián, which,
in spite of the advent of the railway, had 'undergone fewer changes,
whether physical or social, than might perhaps have been anticipated in

the course of six long and very busy decades'; continuing, 'Of the works thrown up by the English during the last siege [of Bayonne], not a vestige remains. The Blue House, as we used to call the château standing in the suburb of St Pierre [an error – St Etienne, surely], and in the garden of which we established our most formidable mortar-battery, retains no trace of the fire to which it was then exposed. The shot-holes are all filled up, the walls are white-washed, and the avenue by which it was approached has been replanted. Nobody could tell that our axes cut down trees as umbrageous as those that now flank the roadway on either side, that their stems might be converted into platforms, and their tops and stouter branches into stockades and *abattis*'. He remarked that 'The graves of the British officers who fell in the sortie are well kept up'. (They still survive in two small railed-off cemeteries standing amidst fields on the north-western perimeter of the town, of Coldstream and Scots Guards respectively.) Biarritz in particular had grown, 'which in 1813 was little better than a seaside hamlet', had 'expanded into a gay and luxurious watering place'. On passing the Château d'Urtubie at Urrugne, Gleig remembers his Spanish Grammar, and he admitted also to having plundered it on his previous visit of a 'prettily-enamelled pair of bellows', which had proved invaluable in bivouac during that bitter winter of 1813.

On 9 July 1888 Gleig died at the advanced age of ninety-two at Stratfield Turgis, near Winchfield, Hampshire, almost until his last days in full control of his faculties. Seventy-four years had passed since he had fought the French at Bayonne. Although in the evening of his life his recollections of the Peninsula may have become dim, when he composed *The Subaltern* his memory was fresh and he had diaries to hand, to which he could refer. At the outset of the campaign he had formed a close friendship with Charles Gray, who was killed at New Orleans, and from him had developed the habit 'of noting down, at the close of every day, brief notices of the most memorable of the events that might have distinguished it'. A little memorandum book, with a pencil attached, was his constant companion, and by the light of a flickering bivouac fire he would jot down a couple of lines, writing it up in ink at the next convenient opportunity.

Without entering into the complexities of the series of actions taking place during the penultimate year of the Great War in the Peninsula, the following outline of events may help to set the scene.

Radical changes had taken place in the military situation during the months prior to the point where Gleig takes up the story. The seat of war, which was entering its fifth year, had moved rapidly from the parched central plateau of Castile to the thickly wooded foothills of the Western Pyrenees. After his great victory at Salamanca in July 1812, when the British had entered Madrid briefly, Wellington had chosen to lead a high proportion of his army north in an attempt to take Burgos. Unfortunately, he was singularly unsuccessful in capturing this important bastion on the highway to France, largely due to his lack of siege guns and adequately trained sappers and miners. Frustrated, he was obliged to retreat south-west in appalling weather towards his former base near the Portuguese frontier, losing some 3,000 men in the process, mostly from exposure or by their straggling. Having recuperated in the shelter of their winter cantonments, and after being re-clothed, re-shod, well-fed, and rigorously drilled, with their morale restored, the reinforced army was soon in readiness for Wellington's planned spring offensive. Meanwhile, in mid-February, he had received confirmation of the disaster which had overwhelmed Napoleon in Russia.

In mid-May took place one of the more spectacular movements of the entire war. Within a month, by a series of brilliant manoeuvres, Wellington had crossed the Duero, which forced the French to give up Madrid and retire north. Having outflanked Burgos, he had then driven Joseph Bonaparte and Marshal Jourdan from the field of Vitoria in confusion (21 June). They left behind them virtually all their artillery and immense quantities of equipment and booty. At Tolosa, Sir Thomas Graham fought a minor action with Foy, but the French general had been able to extricate himself from a precarious position in rugged country. Herding together all detachments in the area, he had pulled them back across the border, leaving only General Rey's garrison to defend San Sebastián, which remained a thorn in the flesh of the Allied army for the next two months. Joseph and Jourdan were replaced by Marshal Soult – 'the only military brain in the Peninsula', in Napoleon's opinion – who, commanding all French units in the Western Pyrenees, was to concentrate and re-equip his scattered and demoralized forces within a remarkably short time.

Meanwhile, Wellington consolidated his position on the frontier, being formed from Fuenterrabía at its estuary by the river Bidasoa as far as Bera, and then inland to the Pass of Roncesvalles. His main port of communication and supply was the inlet of Pasajes, between Fuenterrabía and San Sebastián, now invested. Pamplona, some forty miles south-east as the crow flies, also held a French garrison, similarly blockaded. The Allies were strung out along an irregular and discontinuous line across exceedingly broken and mountainous country. Wellington could not prevent a breakthrough, for the French, based on Bayonne, their strongest fortress in the south-west, could make a concentrated thrust either at Irún to relieve San Sebastián; or across the pass at Maya into the Baztan valley; or south-west from St Jean Pied-du-Port and up through Roncesvalles to relieve beleaguered Pamplona. These three sectors were defended respectively by Sir Thomas Graham on the coast, by Sir Rowland Hill in the Baztan, and by Sir Galbraith Lowry Cole, whose troops were comparatively isolated on the eastern flank. In the event, at dawn on 25 July, attacked simultaneously and with overwhelming numbers by both General D'Erlon's troops at Maya, and those of Soult and General Clausel at Roncesvalles, the Allies found themselves being pressed back towards Pamplona.

On that same afternoon, after conversing with Graham at San Sebastián, Wellington had ridden back to his headquarters in the village of Lesaka where, on arrival, he received conflicting accounts of the fighting further east, but it was very obvious that a powerful French offensive was well under way. Having made his dispositions, taking into consideration the possibility that it was a feint, and that the enemy might also make an additional thrust towards San Sebastián, Wellington galloped on south to meet his retreating troops, which had converged near Sorauren in the valley of the Ulzama not far north of Pamplona. His presence put new heart into the Allied lines, and here, along a ridge rising steeply from the village, they tenaciously held their ground. The outcome of the ensuing battles (on the 28th and 30th July) were determined by an irresistable Allied counter-attack, after which Soult, who had run out of rations and with no food at hand in those hostile mountains, had little alternative but to accept defeat and retreat north, stumbling through wild and tortuous country, with Wellington at his heels. His nine-day offensive had failed to relieve either San Sebastián or Pamplona, which would now be starved into submission; it eventually surrendered in late October – and the remnants of his reconstituted army re-crossed the frontier entirely destitute, having lost *en route* an immense amount of their recently-assembled *materiél*. Philip Stanhope, in his *Notes of Conversations with the Duke of Wellington*, refers to a conversation at Walmer on 12 November 1831, in which the Duke had remarked to Gleig that Soult was not the ablest general ever opposed to him; the ablest after Napoleon was Masséna. Soult, in his opinion, 'did not quite understand a field of battle; he was an excellent tactician – knew very well how to bring his troops to the field, but not so well how to use them, when he had brought them up'. When discussing the action at San Marcial, Gleig had observed how odd it was that the Spaniards, such fine and brave men as individuals, should make such indifferent troops, to which the Duke replied: 'That happens from want of confidence in their officers. And how should they have any? Their officers had seen no service and knew nothing'.

Wellington was determined to have San Sebastián in his hands before pushing into France. Reinforcements were expected daily. The First Brigade of Guards sailed into Pasajes from an enforced leave in Oporto, due to an epidemic of sickness, and were marched to Oyarzún on 18 August. Ordnance transports entered the harbour on the following day and commenced unloading, but were found to have been sent with an insufficient quantity of shot. However, this was made good by the arrival of another fleet on the 23rd. Between the 15th and the end of the month additional troops disembarked, among them a new brigade under the command of Lord Aylmer, consisting of the 76th, 2/84th, and 85th

Regiments. With the latter was Lieutenant Gleig. *The Subaltern* is his chronicle of the actions in which he was to take part during the ensuing eight months.

It is the text of the first edition which is reproduced – the changes made in later editions were very slight – and no orthographical corrections have been made, but the reader should not have much difficulty in recognizing topographical names: in most cases they are not dissimilar to the current spelling, and both are given in the index. Modern maps may also include variant Basque names. Brief explanatory paragraphs have been included at the head of each chapter, and their bald numeration has been replaced by chapter headings. A complement of maps and plans and illustrations – mostly contemporary – have been incorporated.

In addition to the more comprehensive histories of the war to which one may refer, the actions taking place during the period in question are described in numerous narratives and diaries, among the more notable being Thomas Henry Browne's, and John Cooke's, apart from those by Costello, Hennell, Kincaid, Leach, Simmonds, Thomas Bunbury, *et al.* Of particular interest, as concentrating almost entirely on the area concerned, are: Robert Batty, *Campaign of the Left Wing of the Allied Army, in the Western Pyrenees and South of France* (1832); Sir John Thomas Jones, *Journal of the Sieges . . . in Spain, during the years 1811 to 1814* (3rd. edition, 1846); Francis Seymour Larpent, *The Private Journal of Judge-Advocate Larpent* (1853; reprinted 2000); Sir Augustus Simon Frazer, *Letters* (1859); W. Hill James, *Battles around Biarritz* (1896); F.C. Beatson, *Wellington: The Bidassoa and the Nivelle* (1931); Edmund Wheatley, *The Wheatley Diary* (1964); for the regiment, Henry Stooks Smith, *An Alphabetical list of the officers of the Eighty-Fifth Bucks Volunteers . . . from 1800 to 1850* (1851); Anon., *The History of the Corps of the King's Shropshire Light Infantry*, volume 2 (of four); 85th (1759–1881), and C.R.B. Barrett's *The 85th King's Light Infantry* (1913). Also of interest is Philip A. Hurt, *The Guards' Cemeteries, St Etienne, Bayonne* (2nd edition, 1887).

For the cartography of the area, either the French Institut Géographique National (I.G.N.) map of the *Pyrénées Occidentales*, *serie rouge* no. 113 at 1:250,000, or *serie verte* no. 69 at 1:100,000 give an overall view; nos. 1245 OT (Hendaye/St Jean-de-Luz) and 1344 OT (Bayonne/Anglet/Biarritz), both at 1:25,000, provide more detailed coverage.

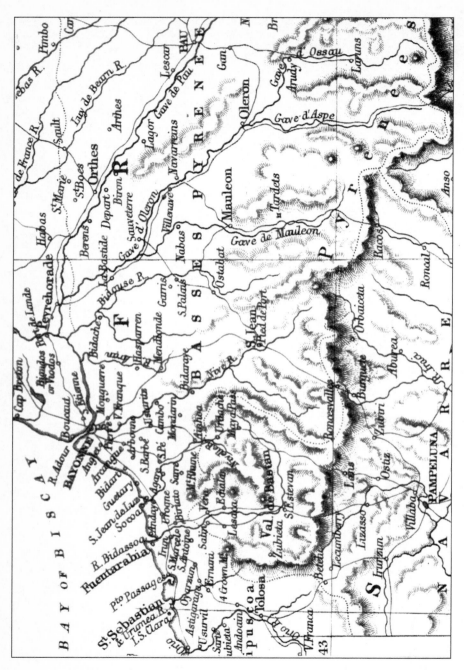

1. Detail of a mid 19th Century map of the frontier area

Chapter 1

Preparing for the Peninsula

The 85th Regiment, assembling at Hythe, in Kent, had been badly depleted by serving in the West Indies from 1803 to 1808; its rank and file numbered only 581 when it set out on the disastrous Walcheren expedition in 1809. The survivors were then sent to Ireland to recruit and recuperate before sailing to Spain, where they fought at Fuentes de Oñoro in May 1811 in Sontag's Brigade of Houston's 7th Division, and in the assault on Fort San Cristóbal at Badajoz that June. The Regiment was then sent home to build up its strength before returning to Spain. Gleig and his brother officers are found busily occupied in packing their portmanteaus prior to marching to the transports awaiting them at Dover. Gleig describes the harrowing scene of casting lots to decide which wives might accompany their husbands, and relates the tragic but not untypical story of Duncan and Mary Stewart.

It is now something more than twelve years ago since the [85th] regiment of infantry, in which I bore a commission, began to muster one fine May morning, on the parade ground at Hythe. An order had reached us two days before, to prepare for immediate service in the Peninsula; and on the morning to which I allude, we were to commence our march for that purpose. The point of embarkation was Dover, a port only twelve miles distant from our cantonments, where a couple of transports, with a gun-brig as convoy, were waiting to receive us.

The short space of time which intervened between the arrival of the route, and the eventful day which saw its directions carried into effect, was spent by myself, and by my brother officers, in making the best preparations which circumstances would permit for a campaign. Sundry little pieces of furniture, by the help of which we had contrived to render our barrack-rooms somewhat habitable, were sold for one tenth part of their value; a selection was made from our respective wardrobes, of such articles of apparel, as, being in a state of tolerable preservation, promised to continue for the longest time serviceable; canteens were hastily fitted up, and stored with tea, sugar, and other luxuries; cloaks were purchased by those who possessed them not before, and put in a state of repair by those

1

who did; in a word, everything was done which could be done by men similarly situated, not even forgetting the payment of debts, or the inditing of farewell letters in due form to absent friends and relations. Perhaps the reader may be curious to know what stock of necessaries the generality of British officers were wont, in the stirring times of war, to be contented. I will tell him how much I myself packed up in two small portmanteaus, so formed as to be an equal balance to each other, when slung across the back of a mule; and as my kit was not remarkable, either for its bulk or scantiness, he will not greatly err, if he esteem it a sort of medium for those of my comrades.

In one of those portmanteaus, then, I deposited a regimental jacket, with all its appendages of wings, lace, etc.; two pair of grey trowsers; sundry waistcoats, white, coloured, and flannel; a few changes of flannel drawers; half a dozen pairs of worsted stockings, and as many of cotton. In the other were placed six shirts, two or three cravats, a dressing-case competently filled, one undress pelisse, three pairs of boots, two pairs of shoes, with night-caps, pocket-handkerchiefs, etc. etc. in proportion. Thus, whilst I was not encumbered by any useless quantity of apparel, I carried with me quite enough to load a mule, and to ensure myself against the danger of falling short, for at least a couple of years to come; and after providing these and all other necessary articles, I retained five-and-twenty pounds in my pocket. This sum, indeed, when converted into bullion, dwindled down to £17, 18s.; for in those days we purchased dollars at the rate of six shillings a-piece, and doubloons at five pounds; but even £17, 18s. was no bad reserve for a subaltern officer in a marching regiment; at least I was contented with it, and that was enough.

It will readily be imagined that I was a great deal too busy, both in body and mind, to devote to sleep many of the hours of the night which preceded the day of our intended departure. My bodily labours, indeed, which had consisted chiefly in packing my baggage, and bidding adieu to the few civilians with whom I had formed an acquaintance, came to a close two hours before midnight; but my body was no sooner at rest, than my mind began to bestir itself. "So," said I, "to-morrow I commence my military career in real earnest." Well, and had this not been my most ardent desire from the first moment that I saw my name in the Gazette? Had it not been the most prominent petition in my daily prayers, for nearly a twelve-month past, not to be kept idling away my youth in the various country-towns of England, but to be sent, as speedily as possible, where I might have an opportunity of acquiring a practical knowledge of the profession which I had embraced? The case is even so. And without meaning to proclaim myself a fire-eater, I will venture to say, that no individual in the corps experienced greater satisfaction than I did at the prospect before me. But there were other thoughts which obtruded themselves upon me that night, and they savoured a good deal of the melancholy.

2

PREPARING FOR THE PENINSULA

I thought of home – of my father, my mother, and my sisters. I thought of the glorious mountains, and the fertile plains, of my native country, and could not help asking myself the question, whether it was probable that I should ever behold them again. The chances were, that I should not; and as my home had always been to me a scene of the purest and most perfect happiness, as I loved my relatives tenderly, and knew that I was tenderly beloved by them in return, it was impossible for me not to experience a pang of extreme bitterness at the idea, that in all human probability I should see their faces no more.

On the other hand, curiosity, if I may call it by so feeble a term, was on full stretch respecting the future. Now at length I was about to learn what war really was; how hostile armies met, and battles were decided; and the resolutions which I consequently formed as to my own proceedings, the eagerness with which I longed for an opportunity to distinguish myself, and the restlessness of my imagination, which persisted in drawing the most ridiculous pictures of events which never were, and never could be realized, created altogether such a fever in my brain, as rendered abortive every attempt to sleep. I went to bed at ten o'clock, for the purpose of securing a good night's rest, and of being fresh and vigorous in the morning; but eleven, twelve, and one, found me tossing about, and quite awake; nor could I have lain in a state of unconsciousness much above an hour, when the sound of the bugle restored me to my senses.

At the first blast I sprang from my bed, and, drawing aside the curtain of my window, I looked out. The day was just beginning to break; the parade ground, into which I gazed, was as yet empty, only two or three figures, those of the trumpeters, who were puffing away with all their might, being discernible upon it; and not a sound could be distinguished, except that which their puffing produced. The moon was shining brightly over-head – not a breath of air was astir – in short, it was just half past three o'clock, and the time of parade was four. I dropped the curtain again, and addressed myself to my toilette.

Having completed this, I waited for the second summons, when I walked forth. Were I to live a hundred years, I shall never forget that morning. Day had dawned, that is to say, the light of the moon was overpowered by the increasing brilliancy of the twilight; but a thick haze, rising from the low grounds, rendered objects even more indistinct and obscure than they had been half an hour before. When I opened my door, therefore, though a confused hum of voices, a clattering of canteens, the tread of footsteps, and occasionally the clash of arms, struck upon my ear, I could see nothing. This did not, however, last long. The rising sun gradually dispelled the fog, and in a few moments I beheld companies mustering in all form. Mingling in the ranks, I could likewise distinguish the dress of females; and as the noise of assembling gradually subsided into the stillness of order, the half-suppressed shriek, and the half-stifled sob, became more and more audible.

There are not many scenes in human life more striking or more harrowing to the feelings of him who regards it for the first time, than the departure of a regiment upon foreign service. By the customs of the army only six women for each company are allowed to follow their husbands, who are chosen by lot out of perhaps twenty or thirty. The casting of lots is usually deferred till, at least, the evening previous to the marching of the corps, probably with the humane design of leaving to each female, as long as it can be left, the enjoyment of that greatest of all earthly blessings, hope. The consequence then is, that a full sense of her forlorn condition coming all at once upon the wretched creature who is to be abandoned, produces, in many instances, a violence of grief, the display of which it is impossible to witness with any degree of indifference. Many were the agonizing scenes of the kind which it was my fortune this day to witness; but there was one so peculiarly distressing, so much more affecting in all its points than the rest, that I am tempted to give a detail of it, even at the risk of being thought the writer of a romance. I recollect having read in that amusing work, "The Hermit in the Country", an anecdote very similar in many respects, to the one which I am now going to relate. The reader is not, however, to suppose, that the two stories bear a common origin, namely the imagination of those by whom they are told. The worthy Hermit's tale probably rests upon no better foundation; but mine is a true story, and its truth will no doubt be attested by several of my readers: that is, supposing me to have any readers in the [85th] regiment of foot.

About three months previous to the day of embarkation, a batch of recruits had joined the regiment from Scotland. Among them was a remarkably fine young Highlander; a native, if I recollect right, of Balquidder, called Duncan Stewart. Duncan was in all respects a good soldier; he was clean, sober, orderly, and well behaved; but he seemed to be of a singularly melancholy temper; never mixing in the sports and amusements of his comrades, nor even speaking except when he was obliged to speak. It so happened that the pay-serjeant of Duncan's company was likewise a Highlander; and Highlanders being of all description of persons the most national, he very soon began to interest himself about the fate of the young recruit. At first Duncan shrunk back even from his advances, but it is not natural for the human heart, especially during the season of youth, to continue long indifferent to acts of kindness; so Duncan gradually permitted honest M'Intyre to insinuate himself into his good graces; and they became, before long, bosom friends.

When they had continued for some weeks on a footing of intimacy, Duncan did not scruple to make his friend the serjeant acquainted with the cause of his dejection. It was simply this:–

Duncan was the son of a Highland farmer, who, like many of his

4

countrymen in that situation, cultivated barley for the purpose of making whisky; in plain language, was a determined smuggler. Not far from the abode of Stewart, dwelt an exciseman of the name of Young, who, being extremely active in the discharge of his duty, had on various occasions made seizure of his neighbours' kegs as they were on their march towards the low-countries. This was an offence which the Highlander, of course, could not forgive; and there accordingly subsisted between the smuggler and the gauger, a degree of antipathy far surpassing anything of which it is easy for us to form a conception. It must, however, be confessed, that the feeling of hatred was all on one side. Stewart hated Young for presuming to interfere with his honest calling; and despised him, because he had the misfortune to be born in the shire of Renfrew; whereas Young was disposed to behave civilly to his neighbour, on every occasion except when his whisky casks happened to come in the way.

Gauger Young had an only and a very pretty daughter, a girl of eighteen years of age, with whom Duncan, as a matter of course, fell in love. The maiden returned his love, at which I am by no means surprised, for a handsomer or more manly-looking youth one would not desire to see; but alas! old Stewart would not hear of their union; absolutely commanding his son, under penalty of his heaviest malediction, not to think of her again. The authority of parents over their children, even after they have grown up to the age of manhood, is in Scotland very great; so Duncan would not dispute his father's will, and finding all entreaty to alter it useless, he determined to sacrifice inclination to duty, and to meet his pretty Mary no more.

To this resolution he adhered for several days, but, to use his own words, "Gang where I would, and do what I liket, I aye saw her before me. I saw her once, to tell her what my father had said; indeed, we were baith gay sure how it would be, before I spak to him ava; and oh! the look she gae me, M'Intyre, I ne'er forgot it, and I never can forget it. It haunted me like a ghaist baith night and day."

The consequence of constantly beholding such a vision may easily be imagined. Duncan forgot his determination and his duty, and found himself one evening, he scarce knew how, once more walking with Mary by the loch side. This occurred again and again. The meetings were the more sweet because they were secret, and they ended – as such stolen meetings generally end among persons of their station in life. Duncan was assured of becoming a father, before he was a husband.

This, however, was not to be permitted; Duncan was too tenderly attached to Mary, to suffer disgrace to fall upon her, even though he should incur the threatened penalty of a father's curse by marrying, so he resolved, at all hazards, to make her his wife. The reader is no doubt aware, that marriages are much more easily contracted in Scotland, than on the south side of the Tweed. An exchange of lines, as it is called, that is to say, a mutual agreement to live as man and wife, drawn up and signed by a young man and a young woman, constitutes as indisputable a union in North Britain, as if the marriage ceremony had been read or uttered by a clergyman; and to this method of uniting their destinies Duncan and Mary had recourse. They addressed a letter, the one to the other, in which he acknowledged her to be his wife, and she acknowledged him to be her husband; and, having made an exchange of them, they became to all intents and purposes a married couple.

Having thus gone in direct opposition to the will of his father, Duncan was by no means easy in his own mind. He well knew the unforgiving temper of the man with whom he had to deal; he knew likewise that his disobedience could not be long kept a secret, and the nearer the period approached which would compel a disclosure, the more anxious and uncomfortable he became. At length the time arrived when he must either acknowledge his marriage, or leave Mary to infamy. It was the season of Doun Fair, and Duncan was intrusted with the care of a drove of sheep which were to be disposed of at the market. Having bid farewell to his wife, he set out, still carrying his secret with him, but determined to disclose it by letter, as soon as he should reach Doun. His object in acting thus was, partly, to escape the first burst of his father's anger, and partly with the hope, that, having escaped it, he might be received at his return with forgiveness; but alas! the poor fellow had no opportunity of ascertaining the success of his scheme.

When he reached Doun, Duncan felt himself far too unhappy to attend to business. He accordingly intrusted the sale of his sheep to a neighbour; and sitting down in one of the public houses, wrote that letter which had been the subject of his meditations ever since he left Balquidder. Having completed this, Duncan bravely determined to forget his sorrows for a while, for which purpose he swallowed a dose of whisky, and entered into conversation with the company about him, among whom were several soldiers, fine, merry, hearty fellows, who, with their corporal, were on the look-out for recruits. The leader of the party was a skilful man in his vocation; he admired the fine proportions of the youth before him, and determined to inlist him if he could. For this purpose more whisky was ordered, – funny histories were told by him and his companions, – Duncan was plied with dram after dram, till at length he became completely inebriated, and the shilling was put into his hand. No time was given him to recover from his surprise; for, long ere the effects of intoxication had evaporated, Duncan was on his way to Edinburgh. Here he was instantly embarked with a number of young men similarly situated; and he actually reached head-quarters without having had an opportunity so much as to inform his relations of his fate.

The sequel of Duncan's story is soon told. Having obtained permission from the commanding officer, he wrote to Scotland for his wife, who joyfully hastened to join him. Her father did what he could, indeed, to prevent this step; not from any hatred towards his daughter, to whom he had behaved with great kindness in her distress, but because he knew how uncomfortable was the sort of life which she must lead as the wife of a private soldier; but Mary resisted every entreaty to remain apart from Duncan; she had been in a state of utter misery during the many weeks in which she was left in ignorance of his situation; and, now that she knew where he was to be found, nothing should hinder her from following him. Though far gone in a state of pregnancy, she set out instantly for the south of England; and having endured with patience all inconveniences attendant upon her want of experience as a traveller, she succeeded in reaching Hythe, just one week previous to the embarkation of the regiment.

This ill-fated couple were hardly brought together when they were once more doomed to part. Poor Mary's name came up among the names of those who should remain behind the regiment, and no language of mine can do justice to the scene which took place. I was not present when the women drew their tickets; but I was told by M'Intyre, that when Mary unrolled the slip of paper, and read upon it the fatal words, "To be left", she looked as if Heaven itself were incapable of adding one additional pang to her misery. Holding it with both hands, at the full stretch of her arms from her face, she gazed upon it for some minutes without speaking a word, though the rapid succession of colour and deadly paleness upon her cheeks, told how severe was the struggle which was going on within; till at length, completely overpowered by her own sensations, she crushed it between her palms, and fell senseless into the arms of a female who stood near.

That night was spent by Duncan and his wife exactly as it was to be supposed that it would be spent. They did not so much as lie down; but the moments sped on in spite of their watchfulness, – and at last the bugle sounded. When I came upon the ground, I saw Duncan standing in his place, but Mary was not near him. The wives of the few soldiers who were left behind to form a depot, having kindly detained her in the barrack-room. But, just before the column began to move, she rushed forth; and the scream which she uttered, as she flew towards Duncan, was heard throughout the whole of the ranks. – "Duncan, Duncan!" the poor thing cried, as she clung wildly round his neck: "Oh, Duncan, Duncan Stewart, ye're no gawn to leave me again, and me sae near being a mother! O, Serjeant M'Intyre, dinna tak' him awa'! if ye hae ony pity, dinna, dinna tak' him! – O, sir, ye'll let me gang wi' him?" she added, turning to one of the officers who stood by; "for the love of Heaven, if ye hae ony pity in ye, dinna separate us!"

Poor Duncan stood all this while in silence, leaning his forehead upon the muzzle of his firelock, and supporting his wretched wife upon his arm. He shed no tears – which is more than I can say for myself, or indeed for almost any private or officer upon the parade – his grief was evidently beyond them. "Ye may come as far as Dover, at least," he at length said, in a sort of murmur; and the poor creature absolutely shrieked with delight at the reprieve.

The band now struck up and the column began to move, the men shouting, partly to drown the cries of the women, and partly to express their own willingness to meet the enemy. Mary walked by the side of her husband; but she looked more like a moving corpse than a living creature. – She was evidently suffering acutely, not only in mind but in body; indeed, we had not proceeded above three miles on our journey, before she was seized with the pains of labour. It would have been the height of barbarity to have hindered her unfortunate husband, under these circumstances, from halting to take care of her; so having received his promise to join the regiment again before dark, we permitted him to fall out of the ranks. Fortunately, a cottage stood at no great distance from the road side, into which he and his friend M'Intyre removed her; and while there, I have reason to believe, she was received with great humanity, and treated with kindness; indeed, the inhabitants of the cottage must have been devoid of everything human except the form, had they treated a young woman so situated, otherwise than kindly.

A four hours' march brought the regiment in high spirits, and in good order, into Dover. As a matter of course, the inhabitants filled their windows, and thronged the streets, to witness the embarkation of a body of their countrymen, of whom it was more than probable that few would return; nor have I any cause to doubt the sincerity of the good wishes which they expressed, for our success and safety. It is only during the dull times of peace, or, which amounts to the same thing, when troops are lying idly in a garrison town, that feelings of mutual jealousy arise between the inhabitants and the soldiers.

As the men came in fresh, and, which by no means invariably follows, sober, little more than half an hour was spent in embarking. The transports, fortunately, lay along-side the pier; consequently, there was no need to employ boats for the removal of the troops and baggage; but boards being placed as bridges from the pier to the deck, the companies filed easily and regularly into their respective ships. We were not, however, to sail till the following morning, the remainder of that day being allowed for laying in sea-stock; and hence, as soon as they had seen the men comfortably housed, the officers adjourned to the various inns in the place.

Like my companions, I returned again to shore as soon as I had attended to the comforts of my division; but my mind was too full of the image of poor Mary, to permit my entering with gusto into the various amusements of my friends. I preferred walking back in the direction of Hythe, with the hope of meeting M'Intyre, and ascertaining how the poor creature did. I walked, however, for some time, before any traveller made his appearance.

At length, when the interest which I had felt in the fate of the young couple was beginning in some degree to moderate, and I was meditating a return to the inn, I saw two soldiers moving towards me. As they approached, I readily discovered that they were Duncan and his friend; so I waited for them. "Duncan Stewart," said I, "how is your wife?" – The poor fellow did not answer, but, touching his cap, passed on. "How is his wife, M'Intyre?" said I to the serjeant, who stood still. The honest Scotchman burst into tears; and as soon as he could command himself, he laconically answered, "She is at rest, sir." From this I guessed that she was dead; and on more minute inquiry, I learned that it was even so; – she died a few minutes after they removed her into the cottage, without having brought the child into the world. An attempt was made to save the infant, by performing the Cæsarean operation, but without effect; it hardly breathed at all.

Though the officer who commanded the depot was sent for, and offered to take the responsibility upon himself, if Duncan wished to remain behind for the purpose of burying his wife, the poor fellow would not avail himself of the offer. All that he desired was a solemn assurance from the officer that he would see his dear Mary decently interred; and as soon as the promise was given, the young widower hastened to join his regiment. He scarcely spoke after; and he was one of the first who fell after the regiment landed in Spain.

Chapter 2

The Disembarkation at Pasajes

After being buffeted by gales in the Channel, and then lying becalmed in the Bay of Biscay, the transports belatedly sailed into the inlet of Pasajes, first passing within gun-shot of the fortress of San Sebastián, which had been blockaded since 28 June. Although the Convent of San Bartolomé had been stormed on 17 July, and parallels approaching the town were completed by the 23rd, the first assault, undertaken far too hurriedly two days later, failed.

I have seldom witnessed a more beautiful summer's day than that on which our ships cast loose from their moorings, and put to sea. It was past noon before the tide arose, consequently the whole town of Dover was afoot to watch our departure. Crowds of well-dressed people stood upon the pier, bidding us farewell with hearty cheers, and waving of their hats and hand-kerchiefs – salutes which we cordially answered, by shouting and waving ours in return. But the wind was fair, and the tide in our favour. Objects on shore became gradually more and more indistinct; the shouts grew fainter and fainter, and at length were heard no more. All the sail was set which our frail masts were capable of carrying; and long before dark, nothing could be distinguished of Dover, or its magnificent cliffs, except a faint and vapouring outline.

The favourable breeze which carried us so rapidly beyond the straits of Dover, did not, however, last long. We had just caught sight of the low-lying point of Dungeness, when it suddenly chopped round, and blew a perfect hurricane in our teeth. It was, indeed, with the utmost difficulty that we succeeded in getting so near the head-land, as to obtain some shelter from the rolling sea which came up Channel; and here we had the misery to remain, consuming our sea-stock for no purpose, and growling over the inconsistancy of the windy element for a space of time consider-ably exceeding a week. I have spent many disagreeable weeks – that is, many weeks which might have been more profitably and more pleasantly spent; but one more utterly insipid than this – more galling to the spirits, or more trying to the temper, I cannot recollect. Even now, at the distance of twelve long years, I remember it, and the very name of Dungeness is abomination in mine ears. There is, indeed, one association connected with that week, which serves to render it somewhat tolerable. On the last day of its continuance, myself, with two others, landed upon the shingly beach, and received from the families of Mrs Denn and Benjamin Cobb, Esq. of Lydd, a degree of attention, such as we had no right to expect, and which will not soon pass away from our memories.

At length the gale moderated, and we once more put to sea; but only to be driven hither and thither by the most provokingly adverse weather to which men thirsting for military glory were ever exposed. Hastings, Eastbourne, Brighton, Worthing, all made their appearance in succession, and all remained so long in sight that we cordially wished them engulphed in the ocean. At the same tedious rate we moved onwards till Plymouth harbour lay before us; into which we were necessitated to put, for the purpose of renewing our fresh provisions and water.

In this place nearly another precious week was wasted; consequently July was far advanced ere we could be said to have commenced our voyage in earnest, nor was it till the 13th day of August, 1813, that the bold out-line of the Spanish coast became discernible. In crossing the Bay of Biscay we had been baffled by continual calms, and tossed about by the swell which always prevails there; our sails were, for the most part, perfectly useless, flapping indolently upon the masts; and though we did our best to keep up a good heart, we were all, both officers and men, beginning to wish ourselves anywhere rather than cooped up in a transport, when a cry of land, from the mast-head, attracted our attention.

We had kept our direct course so well, notwithstanding the frequent calms and adverse breezes to which we had been exposed, that the only coast we made, after losing sight of the Scilly Isles, was that of Biscay. The province of Biscay is in general rugged and mountainous, the Pyrenees extending, in some places, to the water's edge – and hence the voyager who beholds that coast for the first time is apt to imagine himself near the conclusion of his voyage long before the situation of the vessel authorises him to do so. Such was precisely the case with us on the present occasion. Turning our eyes in the direction to which the look-out seaman pointed, and beholding a line of coast so bold, as that almost all its features were clearly distinguishable, we fondly flattered ourselves that this evening, or the next morning at latest, would see us on shore; but hour after hour passed by without bringing us any sensible degree nearer to the object of our gaze. The wind, too, which had hitherto blown against us, was now in our favour; yet day-light departed, and we could not so much as tell whether we had gained upon the land, or otherwise.

Next morning, when I ascended the deck, I was delighted to perceive that we were not more than three or four miles from shore, and that we were moving steadily along at the rate of five miles and a half in the hour. Soon after, a merchant vessel hailed us, by which we were informed of the issue of the battle of the Pyrenees, and of the investiture of St Sebastian's; and I had the further gratification of beholding the gun-brig, under whose convoy we sailed, make prize of a tight-built American privateer schooner: but I could see nothing as yet of the harbour of Passages, towards which we were bound, and this day, accordingly, passed on as the other had done, under the galling pressure of hope deferred.

On the 17th of August, the first decisive indication of our approach to the seat of war was discovered, in the sound of a heavy cannonade, heard at first indistinctly, but becoming every hour more and more audible. This, we had little doubt, proceeded from the town of St Sebastian's, and from the batteries of its besiegers; but it was in vain that we turned our glasses in the direction of the sound, with the hope of ascertaining whether or not our supposition was correct. Though we strained our eyes with the utmost anxiety as long as day-light lasted, nothing could be descried which we desired to behold, and we were once more compelled to contemplate with resignation the prospect of spending another night in the extreme confinement of a cabin. The dawn of the following day, however, excited new and livelier feelings within us, when we found ourselves within a few hours' sail of the landing-place, and in a situation perhaps as interesting as can well be imagined to the mind of a soldier.

On ascending the deck of our ship at six o'clock in the morning of the 18th, I perceived that we were lying, under the influence of a dead calm, within range of the guns of the Castle of St Sebastian's, and at a distance of perhaps a mile and a half, or two miles, from shore. This fortress is built upon the summit of a perpendicular rock, of the height of perhaps two or three hundred feet, the foot of which is washed on three sides by the sea, and when viewed, as we then viewed it, from the water, presents as formidable appearance as any fortified place need to present. Its works, owing to the great height, are placed completely beyond the reach of molestation from a hostile squadron; whilst powerful batteries, rising tier above tier, wherever any platform in the rock has permitted them to be erected, threaten with inevitable destruction any vessel which may rashly venture within reach of their fire.

On the right of the castle is a small bay, which forms an extremely commodious harbour, and which is sheltered from the weather by a little island or mole, so placed, as that only one ship at a time can pass between it and the fort; whilst on the left, again, the river Gurumea, passing close under the walls of the town, joins the sea at the base of the castle rock. At the distance of perhaps a mile and a half, or two miles, several high hills enclose the place on every side, between which and the ramparts the country is flat, and the soil sandy and unfruitful.

The reader has not, I dare say, forgotten, that after the battle of Vittoria, Sir Thomas Graham, at the head of the 5th division of the British army, achieved a succession of petty victories over detached bodies of the enemy, and finally sat down before the town of St Sebastian's. On the 17th of July, the convent of St Bartholome, which is built upon one of the heights just alluded to, and which the French had fortified with great diligence and care, was taken by assault, and on the same night the ground for the trenches was broken. As the troops worked for their lives, blue lights being thrown out from the city, and a smart fire kept up upon them all the while, they laboured with such assiduity, as to effect a pretty secure cover for themselves before morning, and the sandy soil of the place being highly favourable to such operations, the first parallel was drawn within a moderate space of time. The trenches, indeed, were completed, and breaching batteries erected by the 21st, on the morning of which day upwards of forty pieces of ordnance opened their fire upon the place; and so incessant and so effectual was their practice, that, on the evening of the 24th, a breach was effected.

As the breach seemed practicable, and as Sir Thomas was aware that the advance of the whole army was delayed only till this important place should fall, he determined to lose no time in bringing matters to the issue of a storm, and orders were accordingly given that the troops should form in the trenches after dark, and be ready to commence the assault as soon as the state of the tide would permit the river to be forded. This occurred about two o'clock in the morning of the 25th, when the storming party advanced with great gallantry to the attack; but whether it was that the breach was not sufficiently assailable, or that some panic seized the leading divisions, the attack entirely failed. A sudden cry of "Retreat, retreat!" arose just as the first company had gained the summit of the rampart; it spread with extraordinary rapidity through the column, and some houses, which were close to the wall of the town, taking fire at the instant, all became confusion and dismay. Those who were already on the breach, turned round, and rushed against those who were ascending; of these many missed their footing, and fell; and the enemy, keeping up a tremendous fire of grape, musketry, and grenades all the while, the whole column speedily lost its order and tractability. A retreat, or rather a flight, accordingly began in real earnest; and happy was he who first made his way once more across the Gurumea, and found himself sheltered from destruction by the trenches. The loss in this affair amounted on our part to nearly a thousand men, of whom many, who had been only wounded, and had fallen within high-water mark, were carried off by the returning tide, and drowned.

From the period of this failure till some days after our arrival in the country, no farther attempts were made upon St Sebastian's, and the besieged were consequently enabled to repair, in a great degree, the devastation which had been committed upon their fortifications. The causes of this inactivity on the part of the besiegers were, first, the want of ammunition, of which a supply had been long expected from England, but which adverse winds had detained; and secondly, sundry demonstrations on the part of the French army, of renewing offensive operations, and raising the siege. Whilst these were making, it was deemed unwise to land any fresh stores; indeed, most of those already landed, were removed, and hence, when we passed under the walls of the fort, the tri-coloured flag was displayed upon their battlements.

On the high grounds which begirt the town, the white tents of the besiegers were, however, discernible, and to the left the Portuguese standard was unfurled. But all was quietness there. The trenches were empty, except of the ordinary guards; the batteries were unprovided with artillery, and some even in ruins; the only mark of hostility, indeed, which was exhibited on either side, came from the town, from which, ever and anon, a single shot was fired, as the allied piquets or sentinels relieved one another, or a group of officers, more curious than wise, exposed themselves unnecessarily to observation. Nevertheless, the whole formed a spectacle in the highest degree interesting and grand, especially to my eyes, to whom such spectacles were new.

I was gazing with much earnestness upon the scene before me, when a shot from the castle drew my attention to ourselves, and I found that the enemy were determined not to lose the opportunity which the calm afforded, of doing as much damage as possible to the ships which lay nearest to them. The ball passed over our deck, and fell harmless into the water. The next, however, struck only a few feet from our bow, and the third would have been perhaps still better directed, had not a light breeze fortunately sprung up, and carried us on our course. By the help of it we contrived in a few minutes to get beyond range; and the enemy, perceiving his balls falling short, soon ceased to waste them.

By this time we had approached within a short distance of Passages; and at eight o'clock that wished-for harbour came in view. Perhaps there are few ports in the world more striking in every respect than that of Passages. As you draw near to it, you run along a bold rocky shore, in which no opening appears to exist, nor is it till he has reached the very mouth of the creek, that a stranger is inclined to suspect that a harbour is there. The creek itself cannot be more than fifty yards wide; it runs directly up between overhanging cliffs, and presents altogether the appearance rather of an artificial cut, than of a cut of nature's forming. From the bare faces of these cliffs different kinds of dwarf trees and shrubs grow out in rich luxuriance, whilst their summits are crowned with groves of lime and cork trees.

Passing through the creek, we arrived in a spacious basin or harbour, on the left of which is built the little town of Passages. Here the scene became highly picturesque and beautiful. The houses, though none of the whitest or most clean in external appearance, were striking from the peculiarity of their structure; having balconies projecting from the upper stories, and wooden staircases which lead to them from without. The absence of glass, too, from most of the windows, which were furnished only with wooden lattices, powerfully impressed upon my mind, that I was no longer in happy England. Nor did the general dress and appearance of both men and women fail to interest one, who beheld them now for the first time. The men, with their broad hats, swarthy visages, mustachoed lips, red, blue, or yellow sleeved waistcoats; their brown breeches, stockings, and shoes with coloured ties; their scarlet sashes fastened round the waist, and brown jacket slung over one shoulder, formed a remarkable contrast with the smock-frocked peasantry whom I had left behind. With the dress of the women, again, I was not so much struck, because I had seen dresses not dissimilar in Scotland. They wear, for the most part, brown or scarlet petticoats, with a handkerchief tied round the neck or bosom, so as to form a sort of stomacher. Their waists are long, and the head and feet bare; their hair being permitted sometimes to hang over their back in ringlets; whilst sometimes it is gathered up into a knot. But the expressive countenances of these females, their fine dark laughing eye, their white teeth, and brunette complexion, are extremely pleasing.

To complete the picture, the back-ground behind Passages is on all hands beautifully romantic. Hills rise, one above another, to a very considerable height, all of them covered with rich herbage, and the most ample foliage; whilst far away in the distance are seen the tops of those stupendous mountains, which form a barrier, and no imaginary barrier, between France and Spain.

Though we entered the harbour as early as nine o'clock in the morning, and were ready for disembarkation in ten minutes after, that event, so ardently desired and so long deferred, occurred not till a late hour in the evening. Soldiers are, as every person knows, mere machines; they cannot think for themselves or act for themselves in any point of duty; and as no orders had been left here respecting us, no movement could be made, till intelligence had been sent to the General commanding the nearest division, of our arrival. This having been effected, we were forthwith commanded to come on shore; and all the boats in the harbour, as well as those belonging to the vessels lying there, as to the native fishermen, were put in requisition to transport us. In spite of every exertion, however, darkness had set in ere the last division reached the land; and hence we were unable to do more than march to a little wooded eminence about a couple of miles from the town, where we bivouacked.

This was the first night of my life which I had ever spent in so warlike a fashion; and I perfectly recollect, to this hour, the impression which it made upon me. It was one of the most exquisite delight. The season chanced to be uncommonly mild; not a breath of air was stirring; everything around me smelt sweet and refreshing after a long imprisonment on board of ship; above all, I felt that soldiering was no longer an amusement. Not that there was any peril attending our situation, for we were at least ten miles from the garrison of St Sebastian's, and perhaps twenty from the army of Marshal Soult; but the very circumstance of being called upon to sleep under the canopy of heaven, the wrapping myself up in my cloak, with my sabre hanging on the branch of a tree over my head, and my dog couching down at my heels, – these things alone were sufficient to assure me, that my military career had actually begun.

When I looked around me again, I saw arms piled up, and glittering in the light of twenty fires, which were speedily kindled, and cast a bright glare through the overhanging foliage. I saw men, enveloped in their great-coats, stretched or sitting around these fires in wild groups; I heard their merry chat, their hearty and careless laugh; now and then a song or a catch chanted by one or two, – all these things, I recollect, were delightfully exciting. I leant my head against a tree, and putting my pipe in my mouth, I puffed away in a state of feeling which any monarch might envy, and which, in truth, I have never experienced since.

When regiments are employed upon actual service, everything like a general mess is laid aside. The officers then divide themselves into small coteries of two, three, or four, according as they happen to form mutual friendships, or find the arrangement attended with convenience. I was fortunate enough to have contracted an intimacy with one of my comrades, whose memory I have never ceased to cherish with fondest affection, and whose good qualities deserve that his memory should be cherished with affection, as long as the power of thinking and reflecting remains by me. He is now at peace, and lies beside two others of his companions in arms, at the bottom of a garden. But let that pass for the present. My friend was an old campaigner. He had served during the greater part of the Peninsular war, and was therefore perfectly acquainted with the course which soldiers ought to pursue, if they desire to keep their health, and to do their duty effectually. At his suggestion I had brought with me a fowling-piece; he too brought his; between us we mustered a couple of greyhounds, a pointer, and a spaniel; and were indifferently furnished with fishing-rods and tackle. By the help of these we calculated on being able, at times, to add something to the fare allowed us in the way of rations; and the event proved that our calculations had not been formed upon mistaken grounds.

With him I spent the greater part of this night in chatting, sometimes of days gone by, and sometimes of the probabilities of the future. Though several years older than myself, Gray had lost none of the enthusiasm of the boy, and he was a perfect enthusiast in his profession. He described to me other scenes in which he had taken part, other bivouacks in which he had shared; and effectually hindered me from losing any portion of that military excitement with which I first sat down. But, at length, our eyelids began to grow heavy, in spite of all the whispers of romance, and every one around us was fast asleep. We accordingly trimmed our fire to keep it burning till after daybreak; and, having drank our allowance of grog to the health of our friends and relations at home, we wrapped our cloaks about us, and lay down. In ten minutes I was in the land of forgetfulness.

Chapter 3

San Sebastián is Besieged

The 85th bivouacked a short distance inland. The view today towards Pasajes which Gleig describes, is not so enchanting. The 'Quatracrone' (Cuatro Coronas or four crowns mountain - known by the French as the 'Trois [sic] Couronnes') which, with La Rhune is one of the more conspicuous heights of the western Pyrenees near the coast, is known also as the Peñas de Haya. The successful assault on San Sebastián – at which the 85th Regiment was not present – took place at noon on 31 August. Casualties were heavy: over 2,300, with a high proportion of killed to wounded, largely caused by having to face grape fired at point-blank range. Perhaps as many as 1,200 additional Allied losses had been sustained throughout the siege; among the more serious, as far as Wellington was concerned, being that of Colonel Richard Fletcher of the Royal Engineers. Gleig is inaccurate when referring to 'sixty-four' pounder guns; these would have been either 24- or 68-pounders, a few of which had been added to Wellington's artillery. On 31 August also, took place Soult's attempt to relieve the beleaguered fortress by launching three divisions in an unsuccessful attack from below the hamlet of Biriatou against the ridge of San Marcial, dominating the left bank of the Bidasoa. This was held by Spanish troops under General Manuel Freire, whose urgent request for support was declined by Wellington. Reverting to the event years later in conversation to Stanhope, the Duke had remarked that he had replied that as the French were already in retreat, they – poor devils, who had never won a battle – might as well win the action for themselves and, 'So they accordingly did; and now I see that in their accounts this is represented as one of their greatest battles – as a feat that does them the highest honour'.

Day had fully dawned, when the general stir of the troops around me put an end to my repose. I opened my eyes, and remained for half a minute perfectly at a loss to conceive where I was, so new and so splendid was the prospect which met them. We had bivouacked upon a well-wooded eminence, standing, as it were, in the very centre of an amphitheatre of mountains. Behind us lay the beautiful little Bay of Passages, tranquil and

18

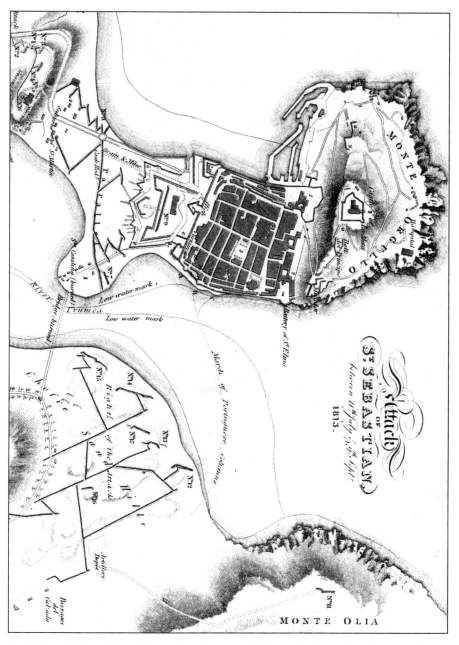

2. Plan of San Sebastián, when besieged. Plate 1 views the fortress from top right; plate 2 from lower centre

almost motionless, under the influence of a calm morning, though rendered more than usually gay by the ships and boats which covered its surface. In front, and to the right and left, rose, at some little distance off, hill above hill, not rugged and barren, like those among which we afterwards took up our abode, but shaggy with the richest and most luxuriant groves of plane, birch and mountain-ash. Immediately beneath was a small glen, covered partly with a stubble of last year's barley, and still loaded with an abundant crop of unreaped Indian corn; whilst a little to the rear from the spot where I had slept, stood a neat farm-house, having its walls hidden by the spreading branches of vines, and studded with clusters of grapes approaching rapidly to perfection. In a word, it was a scene to which the pencil might perhaps do justice, but which defies all the powers of language adequately to describe.

I arose in the same enthusiastic tone of mind with which I had gone to sleep, and assigned myself willingly to the task of erecting huts for our own accommodation and that of the men, no tents having, as yet, been issued out to us. This was speedily effected; large stakes were felled and driven into the earth, between which were twisted thinner and more leafy branches, by way of walls, and these being covered with twigs so closely wedged as to prove impervious to any passing shower, formed a species of domicile not perhaps very commodious, but extremely habitable. Such was our occupation during the hours of light, and at night the corps lay down comfortably sheltered against dews and damps.

The following day was spent chiefly in purchasing horses and mules, which were brought in great abundance by the country people to the camp. For these, we of course paid considerably more than their full value; but it was essentially necessary to procure them without delay, as we were in hourly expectation of a move. Nearly a week elapsed, however, and we still remained in the same situation; nor was it till the evening of the 27th that the long-expected route arrived.

In the meanwhile, I had not been idle, nor had I confined myself with any strictness within the bounds of the camp. Much of my time was spent in seeking for game of various kinds among the stupendous cliffs around, a quest in which I was not always unsuccessful. On other occasions, I mounted my newly-purchased horse, and rode about to different points which promised to afford the most extensive prospect of the glorious scenery of the Lower Pyrenees. Nor was the camp before St Sebastian's neglected; to it I paid repeated visits, and perhaps I cannot do better, in this stage of my narrative, than give some account of the state in which I found it.

In a former Chapter, I stated that St Sebastian's occupies a neck of land which juts into the sea, being washed on two sides by the waters of the Bay of Biscay, and on the third by the River Gurumea. This stream, though inconsiderable in respect of width, cannot be forded, at least near the town, except at the time of low tide; it therefore adds not a little to the general strength of the place. But the strength of the place consists far more in the great regularity and solidity of its fortifications, than in its natural situation. Across the isthmus, from the river to the bay, is erected a chain of stupendous masonry, consisting of several bastions and towers, connected by a well-sheltered curtain, and covered by a ditch and glacis, whilst the castle, built upon an high hill, completely commands the whole, and seems to hold the town, and everything in it, entirely at its mercy.

The scenery around St Sebastian's is, in the highest degree, interesting and fine. As has been already mentioned, the ground, beginning to rise on all sides about a mile and a half from the glacis, is soon broken into hill and valley, mountain and ravine. Numerous orchards are, moreover, planted upon the lowest of these heights, with here and there a vineyard, a chateau, and a farm-house; whilst far off, in the back-ground, are seen the rugged tops of the Quatracrone, and the other gigantic mountains which overhang the Bidaossa, and divide Spain from France.

The tents of the besiegers were placed upon the lower range of hills, about two miles and a half distant from the town. Of course, they were so pitched as that they should be, as far as possible, hidden from the enemy, and for this purpose the uneven nature of the country happily sufficed. They stood, for the most part, among the orchards just alluded to, and in the valleys and ravines with which the place abounded. Leading from them to the first parallel, were cut various covered ways, that is, roads sunk in the ground so far as that troops might march along without exposing themselves to the fire of the enemy; and the parallel itself was drawn almost upon the brow of the ridge. Here, or rather in the ruined convent of St Bartholeme, was established the principal magazine of powder, shot, working-tools, and other necessaries for the siege, and here, as a matter of course, the reserve, or main body of the piquet-guard, was stationed.

The first parallel extended some way beyond the town, on both sides, and was connected with the second, as that again was with the third, by other covered ways, cut in an oblique direction towards the enemy's works; but no sap had been attempted. The third parallel, therefore, completed the works of the besiegers, and it was carried within a few hundred yards of the foot of the rampart. In each of these batteries were built, as well as on the brows of all the surrounding heights; but as yet they were masked by slight screens of sand and turf, though the guns were placed once more in many of them, and the rest were rapidly filling.

There is no species of duty in which a soldier is liable to be employed, so galling, or so disagreeable, as a siege. Not that it is deficient in causes of excitement, which, on the contrary, are in hourly operation; but it ties him so completely down to one spot, and breaks in so repeatedly upon his hours of rest, and exposes him so constantly to danger, and that too at times and in places where no honour is to be gained, that we cannot greatly

21

wonder at the feelings of absolute hatred which generally prevail, among the privates at least of a besieging army, against the garrison which does its duty to its country, by holding out to the last extremity. On the present occasion, I found much of that tone of mind among the various brigades which lay before St Sebastian's. They could not forgive the French garrison, which had now kept them during six weeks at bay, and they burned with anxiety to wipe off the disgrace of a former repulse; there was, therefore, little mention made of *quarter*, whenever the approaching assault chanced to be alluded to.

The governor of St Sebastian's was evidently a man of great energy of mind, and of very considerable military talent. Everything which could be done to retard the progress of the siege, he had attempted; the breach which had been effected previous to the first assault, was now almost entirely filled up, whilst many new works were erected, and what was not, perhaps, in strict accordance with the rules of modern warfare – they were erected by British prisoners. We could distinctly see these poor fellows labouring at their tasks in full regimentals, and the consequence was, that they were permitted to labour on, without a single gun being turned against them. Nor was this all that was done to annoy the assailants – night after night, petty sorties were made, with no other apparent design than to disturb the repose, and to harass the spirits, of the besiegers; for the attacking party seldom attempted to advance farther than the first parallel, and it was uniformly beaten back by the piquets and reserve.

During the last ten days, the besieging army had been busily employed in bringing up ammunition, and in dragging into battery one of the most splendid trains of heavy ordnance which a British general has ever had at his command. On the evening of the 26th, these matters were completed; no fewer than sixty pieces of artillery, some of them sixty-four, and none of lighter metal than eighteen-pounders, were mounted against the town, whilst twenty mortars of different calibre prepared to scatter death among its defenders, and bid fair to reduce the place itself to a heap of ruins.

These arrangements being completed, it was deemed prudent, previous to the opening of the batteries, to deprive the enemy of a little redoubt which stood upon an island in the harbour, and in some degree enfiladed the trenches. For this service a detachment, consisting of an hundred men, a captain, and two subalterns, were allotted, who, filing from the camp soon after night-fall, embarked in the boats of the cruizers; here they were joined by a few seamen and marines, under the command of a naval officer, and having made good their landing under cover of darkness, they advanced briskly to the assault. The enemy were taken completely by surprise – only a few shots were fired on either side, and in the space of five minutes, the small fort, mounting four guns, with an officer and thirty men in its garrison, surrendered, or rather were taken possession of by the assailants.

So trifling, indeed, was the resistance offered by the French garrison, that it disturbed not the slumbers of the troops in camp. The night of the 26th, accordingly, passed by in quiet, but as soon as the morning of the 27th dawned, affairs assumed a very different appearance. Soon after day-break, a single shell was thrown from the heights on the right of the town, as a signal for the batteries to open, and then a most tremendous cannonade began. The first salvo, indeed, was one of the finest things of the kind I ever witnessed. Without taking the trouble to remove the slight covering of sand and turf which masked the batteries, the artillerymen, laying their guns by such observations as small apertures left for the purpose enabled them to effect, fired upon the given signal, and thus caused the guns to clear a way for themselves in their future discharges; nor were these tardy in occurring. So rapid, indeed, were the gunners in their movements, and so unintermitting the fire which they kept up from morning till night, during the whole of the 27th, the 28th, the 29th, and 30th, that by sun-set on the latter day, not only was the old breach reduced to its former dilapidated condition, but a new and a far more promising breach was effected.

In the meantime, however, the enemy had not been remiss in their endeavours to silence the fire of the besiegers, and to dismount their guns. They had, indeed, exercised their artillery with so much good will, that most of the cannon found in the place, after its capture, were unservice-able; being melted at the touch-holes, or otherwise damaged from too frequent use. But they fought, on the present occasion, under every imag-inable disadvantage; for, not only was our artillery much more than a match for theirs, but our advanced trenches were lined with troops, who kept up an incessant and deadly fire of musketry upon the embrasures. The consequence was, that the fire from the town became every hour more and more intermitted, till, long before mid-day, on the 28th, the garrison attempted no further resistance, than by the occasional discharge of a mortar from beneath the ramparts.

I have said, that by sun-set on the 30th, the old breach was reduced to its former dilapidated state, and a new and a more promising one effected. It will be necessary to describe, with greater accuracy than I have yet done, the situation and actual state of these breaches.

The point selected by Sir Thomas Graham as most exposed, and offering the best mark to his breaching artillery, was that side of the town which looked towards the river. Here there was no ditch, nor any glacis, the waters of the Gurumea flowing so close to the foot of the wall, as to render the one useless, and the other impracticable. The rampart itself was con-sequently bare to the fire of our batteries, and as it rose to a considerable height, perhaps twenty or thirty feet above the plain, there was every prob-ability of its soon giving way to the shock of the battering guns. But the consistency of that wall is hardly to be imagined by those who have never beheld it. It seemed, indeed, as if it were formed of one solid rock; and hence, the breach, which, to the eye of one who examined it only from without, appeared at once capacious and easy of ascent, proved, when attacked, to be no more than a partial dilapidation of the exterior face of the masonry. Nor was this all. The rampart gave way, not in numerous small fragments, such as might afford a safe and easy footing to those who were to ascend, but in huge masses, which, rolling down like crags from the face of a precipice, served to impede the advance of the column, almost as effectually as if they had not fallen at all. The two breaches were about a stone's-throw apart, the one from the other. Both were commanded by the guns of the castle, and both were flanked by projections in the town wall. Yet such was the path by which our troops must proceed, if any attempt should be made to carry the place by assault.

That this attempt would be made, and that it certainly would be made on the morrow, every man in the camp was perfectly aware. The tide promised to answer about noon; and noon was accordingly fixed upon as the time of attack, and the question, therefore, was, who by the morrow's noon would be alive, and who would not. Whilst this surmise very naturally occupied the minds of the troops in general, a few more daring spirits were at work, devising means for furthering the intended assault, and securing its success. Conspicuous among these was Major Snodgrass, an officer belonging to the 52nd British regiment, but who commanded on the present occasion a battalion of Portuguese. Up to the present night, only one ford, and that at some little distance from both breaches, had been discovered. By examining the stream, as minutely as it could be examined by a telescope, and from a distance, Major Snodgrass had conceived the idea, that there must be another ford, so far above the one already known, as to carry those who should cross by it at once to the foot of the smaller breach. Though the moon was in her first quarter, and gave a very considerable light, he devoted the whole of the night of the 30th to a personal trial of the river; and he found it, as he expected to find it, fordable at low water, immediately opposite to the smaller breach. By this ford he accordingly crossed, the water reaching somewhat above his waist. Nor was he contented with having ascertained this fact; he clambered up the face of the breach at midnight, gained its summit, and looked down upon the town. How he contrived to elude the vigilance of the French sentinels, I know not; but that he did elude them, and that he performed the gallant act which I have just recorded, is familiarly known to all who served at the siege of St Sebastian's.

So passed the night of the 30th, a night of deep anxiety to many, and of high excitement to all; and many a will was made, as soldiers make their wills, before morning. About an hour before day, the troops were, as usual, under arms – and then the final orders were given for the assault. The division was to enter the trenches about ten o'clock, in what is called light marching order; that is, leaving their knapsacks, blankets, etc., behind, and carrying with them only their arms and ammunition; and the forlorn hope was to prepare to move forward, as soon as the tide should appear sufficiently low to permit their crossing the river. This post was assigned to certain detachments of volunteers, who had come down from the various divisions of the main army, for the purpose of assisting in the assault of the place. These were to be followed by the 1st, or royal regiment of foot; that by the 4th; that by the 9th, and it again by the 47th; whilst several corps of Portuguese were to remain behind as a reserve, and to act as circumstances should require, for the support or cover of the assailing brigades. Such were the orders issued at day-break on the 30th of August, and these orders, all who heard them cheerfully prepared to obey.

It is a curious fact, but it is a fact, that the morning of the 31st rose darkly and gloomily, as if the elements themselves had been aware of the approaching conflict, and were determined to add to its awfulness by their disorder. A close and oppressive heat pervaded the atmosphere, whilst lowering and sulphureous clouds covered the face of the sky, and hindered the sun from darting upon us one intervening ray, from morning till night. A sort of preternatural stillness, too, was in the air; the birds were silent in the groves; the very dogs and horses in the camp, and cattle on the hill side, gazed in apparent alarm about them. As the day passed on, and the hour of attack drew near, the clouds gradually collected into one black mass, directly over the devoted city; and almost at the instant when our troops began to march into the trenches, the storm burst forth. Still, it was comparatively mild in its effects. An occasional flash of lightning, succeeded by a burst of thunder, was all of it which we felt, though this was enough to divert our attention.

The forlorn hope took its station at the mouth of the most advanced trench, about half past ten o'clock. The tide, which had long turned, was now fast ebbing, and these gallant fellows beheld its departure with a degree of feverish anxiety, such as he only can imagine, who has stood in a similar situation. This was the first time that a town was stormed by daylight since the commencement of the war, and the storming party were enabled distinctly to perceive the preparations which were making for their reception. There was, therefore, something not only interesting but novel, in beholding the muzzles of the enemy's cannon, from the castle and other batteries, turned in such a direction as to flank the breaches; whilst the glancing of bayonets, and the occasional rise of caps and feathers, gave notice of the line of infantry which was forming underneath the parapet. There an officer could, from time to time, be distinguished, leaning his telescope over the top of the rampart, or through the opening of an embrasure, and prying with deep attention into our arrangements.

Nor were our own officers, particularly those of the engineers, idle. With the greatest coolness they exposed themselves to a dropping fire of musketry which the enemy at intervals kept up, whilst they examined and re-examined the state of the breaches – a procedure which cost the life of as brave and experienced a soldier as that distinguished corps has produced. I allude to Sir Richard Fletcher, chief engineer to the army, who was shot through the head only a few minutes before the column advanced to the assault.

It would be difficult to convey to the mind of an ordinary reader anything like a correct notion of the state of feeling which takes possession of a man waiting for the commencement of a battle. In the first place, time appears to move upon leaden wings; every minute seems an hour, and every hour a day. Then there is a strange commingling of levity and seriousness within him – a levity which prompts him to laugh, he scarce knows why; and a seriousness which urges him ever and anon to lift up a mental prayer to the Throne of Grace. On such occasions, little or no conversation passes. The privates generally lean upon their firelocks – the officers upon their swords; and few words, except monosyllables, at least in answer to questions put, are wasted. On these occasions, too, the faces of the bravest often change colour, and the limbs of the most resolute tremble, not with fear, but with anxiety; whilst watches are consulted, till the individuals who consult them grow absolutely weary of the employment. On the whole, it is a situation of higher excitement, and darker and deeper agitation, than any other in human life; nor can he be said to have felt all which man is capable of feeling, who has not filled it.

Noon had barely passed, when the low state of the tide giving evidence that the river might be forded, the word was given to advance. Silent as the grave, the column moved forward. In one instant the leading files had cleared the trenches, and the others poured on in quick succession after them, when the work of death began. The enemy having reserved their fire till the head of the column had gained the middle of the stream, then opened with the most deadly effect. Grape, cannister, musketry, shells, grenades, and every species of missile, were hurled from the ramparts, beneath which our gallant fellows dropped like corn before the reaper; insomuch, that in the space of two minutes, the river was literally choked up with the bodies of the killed and wounded, over whom, without discrimination, the advancing divisions pressed on.

The opposite bank was soon gained, and the short space between the landing-place and the foot of the breach rapidly cleared, without a single shot having been returned by the assailants. But here the most alarming prospect awaited them. Instead of a wide and tolerably level chasm, the breach presented the appearance only of an ill-built wall, thrown considerably from its perpendicular; to ascend which, even though unopposed, would be no easy task. It was, however, too late to pause; besides, the men's blood was hot, and their courage on fire; so they pressed on, clambering up as they best could, and effectually hindering one another from falling back, by the eagerness of the rear-ranks to follow those in front. Shouts and groans were now mingled with the roar of cannon and the rattle of musketry; our front-ranks likewise had an opportunity of occasionally firing with effect; and the slaughter on both sides was dreadful.

At length the head of the column forced its way to the summit of the breach, where it was met in the most gallant style by the bayonets of the garrison. When I say the summit of the breach, I mean not to assert that our soldiers stood upon a level with their enemies, for this was not the case. There was an high step, perhaps two or three feet in length, which the assailants must surmount before they could gain the same ground with the defenders, and a very considerable period elapsed ere that step was surmounted. Here bayonet met bayonet, and sabre met sabre, in close and desperate strife, without the one party being able to advance, or the other succeeding in driving them back.

Things had continued in this state for nearly a quarter of an hour, when Major Snodgrass, at the head of the 13th Portuguese regiment, dashed across the river by his own ford, and assaulted the lesser breach. This attack was made in the most cool and determined manner; but here, too, the obstacles were almost insurmountable; nor is it probable that the place would have been carried at all, but for a measure adopted by General Graham, such as has never perhaps been adopted before. Perceiving that matters were almost desperate, he had recourse to a desperate remedy, and ordered our own artillery to fire upon the breach. Nothing could be more exact or beautiful than this practice. Though our men stood only about two feet below the breach, scarcely a single ball from the guns of our batteries struck amongst them, whilst all told with fearful exactness among the enemy.

This fire had been kept up only a very few minutes, when all at once an explosion took place, such as drowned every other noise, and apparently confounded, for an instant, the combatants on both sides. A shell from one of our mortars had exploded near the train, which communicated with a quantity of gunpowder placed under the breach. This mine the French had intended to spring as soon as our troops should have made good their footing, or established themselves on the summit; but the fortunate accident just mentioned, anticipated them. It exploded whilst three hundred grenadiers, the *elite* of the garrison, stood over it, and instead of sweeping the storming party into eternity, it only cleared a way for their advance. It was a spectacle as appalling and grand as the imagination can conceive, the sight of that explosion. The noise was more awful than any which I have ever heard before or since; whilst a brief flash, instantly succeeded by a smoke so dense, as to obscure all vision, produced an effect upon those who witnessed it, such as no powers of language are adequate to describe.

Such, indeed, was the effect of the whole occurrence, that for perhaps half a minute after, not a shot was fired on either side. Both parties stood still to gaze upon the havock which had been produced; insomuch, that a whisper might have caught your ear for a distance of several yards.

The state of stupefaction into which they were at first thrown, did not, however, last long with the British troops. As the smoke and dust of the ruins cleared away, they beheld before them a space empty of defenders, and they instantly rushed forward to occupy it. Uttering an appalling shout, the troops sprang over the dilapidated parapet, and the rampart was their own. Now then began all those maddening scenes, which are witnessed only in a successful storm, of flight, and slaughter, and parties rallying only to be broken and dispersed; till, finally, having cleared the works to the right and left, the soldiers poured down into the town.

To reach the streets, they were obliged to leap about fifteen feet, or to make their way through the burning houses which joined the wall. Both courses were adopted, according as different parties were guided in their pursuit of the flying enemy, and here again the battle was renewed. The French fought with desperate courage; they were literally driven from house to house, and street to street, nor was it till a late hour in the evening that all opposition on their part ceased. Then, however, the governor, with little more than a thousand men, retired into the castle; whilst another detachment, of perhaps two hundred, shut themselves up in a convent.

As soon as the fighting began to wax faint, the horrors of plunder and rapine succeeded. Fortunately, there were few females in the place; but of the fate of the few which were there, I cannot even now think without a shudder. The houses were everywhere ransacked, the furniture wantonly broken, the churches profaned, the images dashed to pieces; wine and spirit cellars were broken open, and the troops, heated already with angry passions, became absolutely mad by intoxication. All order and discipline were abandoned. The officers had no longer the slightest control over their men, who, on the contrary, controlled the officers; nor is it by any means certain, that several of the latter did not fall by the hands of the former, when they vainly attempted to bring them back to a sense of subordination.

Night had now set in, but the darkness was effectually dispelled by the glare from burning houses, which, one after another, took fire. The morning of the 31st had risen upon St Sebastian's, as neat and regularly built a town as any in Spain; long before midnight, it was one sheet of flame; and by noon on the following day, little remained of it, except its smoking ashes. The houses, being lofty like those in the Old Town of Edinburgh, and the streets straight and narrow, the fire flew from one to another with extraordinary rapidity. At first, some attempts were made to extinguish it; but these soon proved useless, and then the only matter to be considered, was, how personally to escape its violence. Many a migration was accordingly effected from house to house, till, at last, houses enough to shelter all could no longer be found, and the streets became the place of rest to the majority.

The spectacle which these presented was truly shocking. A strong light falling upon them from the burning houses, disclosed crowds of dead, dying, and intoxicated men, huddled indiscriminately together. Carpets, rich tapestry, beds, curtains, wearing apparel, and everything valuable to persons in common life, were carelessly scattered about upon the bloody pavement, whilst ever and anon fresh bundles of these were thrown from the windows above. Here you would see a drunken fellow whirling a string of watches round his head, and then dashing them against the wall; there another, more provident, stuffing his bosom with such smaller articles as he most prized. Next would come a party, rolling a cask of wine or spirits before them, with loud acclamations, which in an instant was tapped, and in an incredibly short space of time emptied of its contents. Then the ceaseless hum of conversation, the occasional laugh, and wild shout of intoxication, the pitiable cries, or deep moans of the wounded, and the unintermitted roar of the flames, produced altogether such a concert, as no man who listened to it can ever forget.

Of these various noises, the greater number began gradually to subside, as night passed on; and long before dawn there was a fearful silence. Sleep had succeeded inebriety with the bulk of the army, – of the poor wretches who groaned and shrieked three hours ago, many had expired; and the very fire had almost wasted itself by consuming everything upon which it could feed. Nothing, therefore, could now be heard, except an occasional faint moan, scarcely distinguishable from the heavy breathing of the sleepers; and even that was soon heard no more.

Chapter 4

The Advance to the Bidasoa

On 27 August the 85th had been marched east to join the rest of the 1st Division, by then placed not far south of Irún, facing the French across the Bidasoa (a fast-flowing river rising near the watershed some distance north of Pamplona: Gleig is incorrect in assuming that it rose in 'about the centre of the Peninsula'). The regiment was ordered forward on 5 September to a more dominating position, where Gleig first caught sight of Wellington. The veterans would have shouted 'Douro' as that river is called in Portugal, not 'Duro'.

In order not to interrupt the connexion of my narrative, I have detailed, in the preceding chapter, the events attendant upon the assault and capture of St Sebastian's, instead of drawing the reader's attention to the movements of the particular corps to which I chanced to be attached. These, however, are soon related. On the evening of the 26th, an order arrived, by which we were directed to march on the following, and to join that division of the army which occupied the pass of Irun. This order was promptly obeyed; and, after an agreeable journey of four hours, we took up our abode in a barren valley, surrounded on every side by steep and rugged mountains; where we found huts already erected for our accommodation.

We remained here in a state of quiet till the morning of the 30th, when, at three o'clock, an aide-de-camp arrived in the camp, with directions for us instantly to retrace our steps, and to join the army before St Sebastian's. We were perfectly aware that the town was to be stormed on the following day, and, of course, were not reluctant to obey a command, which led us to the assistance of our comrades. The ranks were immediately formed, and by seven o'clock we had reached our ground.

It was the design of Sir Thomas Graham to embark a detachment of troops in the boats of the fleet, who should assault the castle at the moment when the main body moved from the trenches. The corps to which I belonged was selected for this purpose. But, on reconnoitring the face of the cliff, it was at once perceived, that, to make any attempt of the kind, would only devote to certain destruction the luckless detachment which should be so employed. This part of the plan was accordingly abandoned, and a few boats only being manned, for the purpose of making a feint, and for causing, if possible, a diversion, the remainder, with the exception of such as were chosen to accompany the storming party, returned, by the morrow's dawn, to the front.

I have already stated, that the morning of the 31st rose darkly and gloomily, and that just as the besiegers had begun to fill the trenches, a storm burst forth. This went on increasing every minute; so that, at the moment when our leading files emerged from their cover, one of the most fearful thunder-storms to which I ever listened had attained its height. Nor was this the only circumstance which added to the terrors of that eventful day. Marshal Soult, aware of the importance of St Sebastian's, and full of that confidence which a late appointment to command generally bestows, made, on the 31st, a desperate effort to raise the siege. At the head of a column of fifteen thousand infantry, he crossed the Bidassoa near Irun, and attacked, with great spirit, the heights of St Marcial. These were defended only by Spanish troops, which gave way almost immediately, and were driven to the tops of the hills; but here, being joined by one or two brigades of British soldiers, they rallied, and maintained their ground with considerable resolution. By this means, it so happened, that whilst one division of the army was hotly engaged in the assault of St Sebastian's, the divisions in front were in desperate strife with the troops of Marshal Soult, whilst the heavens thundered in an awful manner, and the rain fell in torrents. In one word, it was a day never to be forgotten by those who witnessed its occurrence; it was a day which I, at least, shall never forget.

It is impossible to describe, with any degree of fidelity, the appearance which St Sebastian's presented, when the dawn of the 1st of September rendered objects visible. The streets, which had lately been covered with the living as well as the dead, were now left to the occupation of the latter; and these were so numerous, that it puzzled the beholder to guess where so many sleeping men could have found room to lie. The troops, however, returned not, with the return of light, to their accustomed state of discipline. Their strength being recruited by sleep, and their senses restored, they applied themselves, with greater diligence than ever, to the business of plunder. Of the houses, few now remained, except in a state of ruin; but even the ruins were explored with the most rapacious eagerness, not so much for jewels and other valuables, as for wine and spirits. Unfortunately, many cellars were this day discovered, which, in the hurry and confusion of last night, had escaped detection, and the consequence was, that, in the space of a very few hours, intoxication prevailed throughout the army. Then, too, such buildings as had escaped the flames of yesterday, were wantonly set on fire; and every species of enormity, which circumstances would admit of, was perpetrated.

Of St Sebastian's, and the proceedings within it, I can say no more from personal observation, my post being now with the advance of the army; but I may as well add, that the castle still held out, and continued to hold out, till the 8th of September. It was, however, as we afterwards discovered, wholly unprovided with shelter against the shells which were unintermittingly thrown into it; and hence, after suffering every possible misery during a whole week, the governor was at last obliged to surrender. About nine hundred men, the remains of a garrison of four thousand, became, by this measure, prisoners of war; and such British prisoners as had escaped the horrors of the siege, were recaptured; but the place itself was utterly valueless, being in a state of the most complete dilapidation.

The whole of the 1st of September was spent under arms, and in a state of deep anxiety, by the troops which occupied the pass of Irun, inasmuch as various movements in the French lines appeared to indicate a renewal of hostilities. Many bullock-cars, loaded with wounded Spaniards, passed, in the meanwhile, through our encampment; and the groans and shrieks of these poor fellows, as the jolting of their uneasy vehicles shook their wounds open afresh, by no means tended to elevate the spirits, or add to the courage of those who heard them. Not that there was any reluctance on our part to engage. I believe a reluctance to fight was never felt by Britons, when the enemy were in sight. But a view of the real effects of war, contemplated in a moment of coolness and inaction, seldom has the effect of adding fuel to the valorous fire, which is supposed at all moments to burn in the breast of a soldier. And, in truth, this was a piteous sight.

Of all the classes of men with whom I ever had intercourse, the Spanish surgeons are, I think, the most ignorant and the most prejudiced. Among the many amputations which, during the war, they were called upon to perform, about one-half, or more than half, proved fatal. Their mode of dressing other wounds was, moreover, at once clumsy and inefficient; and hence the mangled wretches who passed us this morning, were not only suffering acutely, from the natural effect of their hurts, but were put to more than ordinary torture, on account of the clumsy and rude manner in which their hurts had been looked to.

Though I have no intention of writing a regular memoir of the campaigns of 1813 and 1814, it is necessary, for the purpose of rendering my journal intelligible, to give, in this stage of it, some account of the relative situations of the British and French armies.

The two kingdoms of France and Spain are divided, towards the shores of the Bay of Biscay, by the river Bidassoa; an inconsiderable stream, which, rising about the centre of the Peninsula, follows the winding course of one of those many valleys with which the Pyrenees abound, and falls into the sea near the ancient town of Font-Arabia. The Bidassoa is perfectly fordable in almost all places, at the distance of ten miles from its mouth; whilst immediately opposite to Font-Arabia itself, there is one part where, at low tide, a passage may be effected, the water reaching only to the chest of him who crosses. About two or three miles from Irun, which is distant something less than a league from Font-Arabia, is another ford, across which a bridge had been built, but which, at the period of my narrative, was in ruins; consequently, there were two separate fords, leading to the pass of Irun, by both, or either of which, an army might advance with safety.

On either side of this little stream, the mountains, except at the passes of Irun, Roncesvalles, etc. rise so abruptly, as to form an almost impassable barrier between the one kingdom and the other. The scenery of the Bidassoa is, in consequence, romantic and striking in no ordinary degree; for not only are the faces of the hills steep and rugged, but they are clothed, here and there, with the most luxuriant herbage; whilst frequent streams pour down from the summits, forming, especially after rain, cascades exceedingly picturesque, and in some instances almost sublime. The river itself is clear, and rapid in its course; winding, as all mountain streams wind, where rocks ever and anon interpose to impede their progress; and it is not deficient in excellent trout, as I and my friend Gray found, to our frequent comfort and amusement.

At the period of which I am now speaking, the armies of Lord Wellington and Marshal Soult occupied the opposite banks of this little stream. Our piquets were stationed on the rise of the Spanish hills; those of the French on the faces of their own mountains; whilst the advanced sentinels were divided only by the river, which measured in many places not more than thirty yards across. But the French, whatever their faults may be, are a noble enemy. The most perfect understanding, consequently, prevailed between them and us, by which, not only the sentries were free from danger, but the piquets themselves were safe from wanton surprisal; no attack upon an outpost being under any other circumstances thought of, unless it was meant to be followed up by a general engagement.

For myself, my situation was, as I have already stated, in a bleak valley, distant nearly three miles from the river, and surrounded on every side by bold and barren precipices. In such a place, there was little either to interest or amuse, for of the French army we could see nothing; and of game, in quest of which I regularly proceeded, there was a woeful scarcity. There, however, we remained, till the morning of the 5th, without any event occurring worthy of notice, unless a fortunate purchase of two excellent milch goats, which I effected, from a Spanish peasant, be deemed such. But on that day our position was changed; and the glorious scenery to which the march introduced us, far more than compensated for the fatigues occasioned by it.

It is by no means the least pleasing circumstance in the life of a soldier upon active service, that he never knows, when he awakes in the morning, where he is to sleep at night. Once set in motion, and, like any other machine, he moves till the power which regulates his movements calls a halt; and wherever that halt may occur, there, for the present, is his home. Such a man has not upon his mind the shadow of a care; for the worst bed which he can meet with is the turf; and he seldom enjoys a better than his cloak or blanket. Give him but a tent – and with tents the commander of the forces had lately supplied us – and he is in luxury – at least as long as the summer lasts, or the weather continues moderate; nor had we, as yet, experienced any, against which our tents furnished not a sufficient shelter.

The sun was just rising on the morning of the 5th of September, when our tents were struck, the line of march formed, and we advanced towards the base of one of the highest hills, which hemmed us in on every side. Along the face of this mountain was cut a narrow winding path, for the accommodation, in all probability, of goatherds, or muleteers, who contrive to transport articles of luxury and clothing into the wildest districts, where human inhabitants are to be found. It was, however, so rough and so precipitous, as effectually to hinder our men from preserving anything like order in their ranks, and thus caused a battalion, of little more than six hundred bayonets, to cover an extent of ground, measuring, from front to rear, not less than three-quarters of a mile. Of course, the fatigue of climbing, loaded, as we were, with arms, ammunition, and necessaries, was very great; and, as the heat of the day increased, it became almost intolerable. But we toiled on in good spirits, hoping that each vale or level at which we arrived would prove the place of our rest; and not a little delighted with the romantic prospects, which every turning in the road placed before us.

We had continued this arduous journey during five hours, when, on reaching the summit of an isolated green hill, at the back of the ridge already described, four mounted officers crossed us, one of them riding a little ahead of the rest, who, on the contrary, kept together. He who rode in front was a thin, well-made man, apparently of the middle stature, and just passed the prime of life. His dress was a plain grey frock, buttoned close to the chin; a cocked hat, covered with oilskin; grey pantaloons, with boots, buckled at the side, and a steel-mounted light sabre. Though I knew not who he was, there was a brightness in his eye, which bespoke him something more than an aide-de-camp, or a general of brigade; nor was I long left in doubt. There were in the ranks many veterans, who had served in the Peninsula during some of the earlier campaigns; these instantly recognised their old leader; and the cry of "Duro, Duro!" the familiar title given by the soldiers to the Duke of Wellington, was raised. This was followed by reiterated shouts, to which he replied by taking off his hat and bowing; when, after commending the appearance of the corps, and chatting for a moment with the commanding officer, he advised that a halt should take place where we were, and rode on.

As I had never seen the great Captain of the day before, it will readily be imagined that I looked at him on the present occasion with a degree of admiration and respect, such as a soldier of seventeen years of age, who doats upon his profession, is likely to feel for the man whom he regards as its brightest ornament. There was in his general aspect nothing indicative of a life spent in hardships and fatigues; not any expression of care or anxiety in his countenance. On the contrary, his cheek, though bronzed with frequent exposure to the sun, had on it the ruddy hue of health, whilst a smile of satisfaction played about his mouth, and told, far more plainly than words could have spoken, how perfectly he felt himself at ease. How different is his appearance now! Of course, I felt, as I gazed upon him, that an army under his command could not be beaten; and I had frequent opportunities afterwards of perceiving, how far such a feeling goes towards preventing a defeat. Let troops only place perfect confidence in him who leads them, and the sight of him, at the most trying moment, is worth a fresh brigade.

In compliance with the recommendation of Lord Wellington, the corps halted on the beautiful green hill which it had attained; but two full hours elapsed ere the baggage came up. In the meantime, by far the greater number amongst us, myself included, threw ourselves down upon the grass, and fell fast asleep; from which we were not aroused till the arrival of the tents summoned us to the very agreeable occupation of boiling our kettles and preparing breakfast. This was quickly commenced; and having satisfied the cravings of hunger, we dispelled every source of annoyance to which we were subject.

Chapter 5

A Period of Inaction

Gleig ascends the Cuatro Coronas, although he exaggerates the extent of the view it commands, and continues his exploration to the ridge of San Marcial before his regiment encamped at a site nearer Irún. He also visits San Sebastián and describes its state of ruin.

I have seldom looked upon scenery more romantic than that which surrounded the spot where we were commanded to halt. For the last four or five hours, we had been gradually ascending the mountains, and now found ourselves on the top of a green hill, which, when contrasted with the bold heights that begirt it, might be deemed a valley, though itself many thousand feet above the level of the sea. One side of this grassy platform appeared perfectly perpendicular. In this direction it was separated from a steep ridge by a narrow ravine, so deep and so rugged, that all attempts to behold its base were fruitless. On another side, it connected itself with the Quatracone; on a third, that by which we had advanced, it sloped gradually downwards till the view became lost in hanging forests; whilst behind us, only a little green declivity divided it from other similar hills, which afforded a comparatively smooth passage to the Foundery of St Antonio.

It was here that, during the succession of battles which Soult had hazarded about a month before, one division of the French army made several daring efforts to break the allied line; and where, in truth, the line was for a time completely broken. To this, the appearance of all things around bore ample testimony. Not only the ground of our encampment, but the whole of the pass, was strewed with broken firelocks, pikes, caps, and accoutrements; whilst here and there a mound of brown earth, breaking in upon the uniformity of the green sod, marked the spot where some ten or twelve brave fellows lay asleep. In the course of my wanderings, too, I came upon sundry retired corners, where the remains of dead bodies – such remains as the wolves and vultures had left – lay still unburied; and these, by the direction in which they were turned towards one another, led me to conclude, that the contest had been desperate, and that the British troops had been gradually borne back to the very edge of

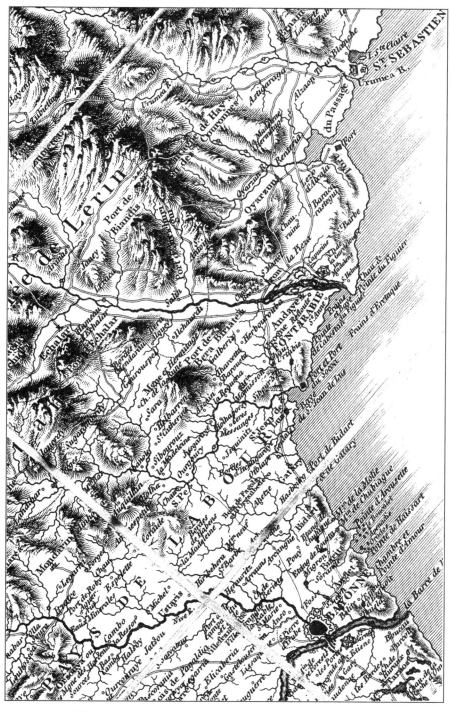

3. Detail from Arrowsmith's edition (1809) of Roussel & Blotière's
'Map of the Pyrenees', from San Sebastián to Bayonne

the precipice. That some of them were driven beyond its edge, is indeed more than probable; for, at one place in particular, I remarked a little group of French and English soldiers lying foot to foot, close beside it.

I need not inform my reader, that eagles, vultures, and kites, are faithful followers of an army. These were particularly abundant here – whether because a more than ordinary supply of food was furnished to them, or that their nests were built among the rocks of the Quatracone, I know not; but they wheeled and careered over our heads so daringly, as almost to challenge a pursuit. I took my gun accordingly, on the morning after our arrival, and clambered up the face of the mountain; but all my efforts to get within shot of these wary creatures, proved abortive. The fatigue of the excursion was, however, more than compensated by the glorious prospect which it opened to my gaze; and which, though it may, perhaps, be equalled, cannot, I firmly believe, be surpassed in any quarter of the world.

From the top of the Quatracone the traveller looks down, not only upon the varied scenery which all mountainous districts present, but upon the fertile plains of Gascony, the waters of the Bay of Biscay, and the level fields of the Asturias. The towns of Bayonne, St Jean de Luz, Fontarabia, Irun, St Sebastian's, Vittoria, and many others, lie beneath, diminished, indeed, into mere specks, but still distinguishable; whilst, southward, forests of pine, and groves of cork-trees, rugged precipices, and dark valleys, present a striking contrast to these abodes of man. The day on which I scaled the mountains chanced to be particularly favourable. There was not a cloud in the sky, nor the slightest haze in the atmosphere; and hence, though I failed in obtaining the object in quest of which I had quitted the camp, I returned to it in the evening more than usually delighted with the issue of my ramble.

We remained in this delightful position only two days, and on the morning of the 6th of September, once more struck our tents. Noon had passed, however, before we began to move; when taking the direction of the Foundery, we ascended the chain of green hills before us, till we had attained an eminence directly over the Bidassoa, and consequently within sight of the enemy's camp. Our march was by no means an agreeable one. We had scarcely left our ground when the rain began to fall in torrents, and as the baggage travelled more slowly than ourselves, we were doomed to wait a full hour upon the side of a bleak hill before any shelter against the storm could be procured. But such things in the life of a soldier are too common to be much esteemed. The baggage arrived at last. Our tent was speedily pitched; our segars lighted; our wine mulled; our cloaks and blankets spread upon the ground; and ourselves as snug and light-hearted as men could desire to be.

It is an invariable custom, when armies are in the field, for such corps as compose the advanced line to muster under arms every morning an hour before day-break. On the present occasion we formed the advance, a few piquets of the Spanish army being the only troops between us and the enemy; consequently we were roused from our comfortable lairs, and ordered under arms long before the dawn appeared. A close column was then formed, in which our men stood still as long as the darkness lasted; but when the eastern sky began to redden, they were permitted to pile their arms, and move about. And, in truth, the extreme chillness which, in these regions in particular, accompanies the first approach of daylight, rendered such an indulgence extremely acceptable. We could not, however, venture far from our arms, because, if an attack should be made at all, this was exactly the hour at which we might look for it; but we contrived, at least, to keep our blood in circulation, by running round them.

The approach of day among the Pyrenees, in the month of September, is a spectacle which it falls not to the lot of every man to witness; and it is one which can hardly be imagined by him who has not beheld it. For some time after the grey twilight breaks, you behold around you only one huge sea of mist, which, gradually rising, discloses, by fits, the peak of some rugged hill, and gives to it the appearance of a real island in a real ocean. By and by, the mountains become everywhere distinguishable, looming, as a sailor would say, large through the haze; but the valleys continue long enshrouded, the fogs which hang upon them yielding only to the rays of the noon-day sun. Along a valley immediately beneath our present position, a considerable column of French infantry made their way, during one of the late actions; and so perfect was the cover afforded by the mist, that, though the sun had risen some time, they penetrated, wholly un-observed, to the brow of the hill. On the present occasion no such attempt was made; but we were kept at our post till the fog had so far dispersed as to render objects half way down the gorge distinctly visible; as soon as this occurred, the column was dismissed, and we betook ourselves each to his favourite employment.

For myself, my constant occupation, whenever circumstances would permit, was to wander about, with a gun over my shoulder, and a dog or two hunting before me, not only in quest of game, but for the purpose of viewing the country to the best advantage, and making, if possible, my own observations upon the different positions of the hostile armies. For this purpose, I seldom took a direction to the rear, generally strolling on towards the advanced piquets, and then bending my course to the right or left, according as the one or the other held out to me the best prospect of obtaining an accurate survey of both encampments. On the present occa-sion, I turned my steps towards the heights of San Marcial. This was the point which Soult assailed with the greatest vigour, in his vain attempt to raise the siege of St Sebastian's, at the very time when the assault of that city was proceeding. It was defended on that day by Spaniards, and Spaniards only, whom Lord Wellington's dispatch represented to have repulsed the enemy with great gallantry; for my own part, I could not but admire the bravery of the troops who, however superior in numbers, ventured to attack a position so commanding. The heights of San Marcial rise so abruptly over the bed of the Bidassoa, that in many places it was only by swinging myself from bough to bough, that I managed to descend them at all; yet a column of fifteen thousand Frenchmen forced their way nearly to the summit, and would have probably succeeded in carrying even that, but for the opportune arrival of a brigade of British guards. These latter were not, indeed, engaged, but they acted as a reserve, and the very sight of them inspired the Spanish division with courage sufficient to maintain their ground, and check the farther progress of the assailants.

From the brow of these heights I obtained a tolerably distinct view of the French encampment for a considerable distance, both to the right and left. The range of hills which it occupied was in some points less lofty, in others even more rugged and more lofty than that on which I now stood. Between me and it flowed the Bidassoa, through a valley narrow, indeed, not more perhaps than a gun-shot across, but rich and beautiful in the extreme; not only on account of the shaggy woods which in a great measure overspread it, but because of the luxuriant corn-fields, meadows, and farm-houses which lay scattered along both banks of the river. The outposts of the French army occupied their own side of this vale, their sentinels being posted at the river's brink; ours, that is the Spanish piquets, were stationed about half way down the hill, and sent their videttes no farther than its base. For the white tents of the British army I looked round in vain. These were generally pitched in woody hollows, so as to screen them entirely from the gaze of the enemy, and to shelter their inmates as much as might be, from the storms; but the well-built huts of the French soldiers were, in many places, distinguishable. Certainly, a Frenchman is far more expert in the art of hutting himself than a soldier of any other nation. The domiciles upon which I now gazed were not like those lately occupied by us, composed of branches of trees only, covered over with twigs and withering leaves, and devoid of chimneys by which smoke might escape: on the contrary, they were good, substantial cottages, with clay walls and regularly thatched roofs, and erected in long straight streets; the camp of each brigade or battalion having more the appearance of a settled village, than of the temporary abiding place of troops on active service. By the aid of my telescope I could perceive the French soldiers, some at drill, others at play, near the huts, nor could I admire the perfect light-heartedness which seemed to pervade men who had been so lately beaten.

At this period, the right of the French army occupied the high ground above the village of Andaye, and rested upon the sea; while our left, taking in the towns of Irun and Fontarabia, rested upon the sea also. The French left was stationed upon a mountain called La Rhune, and was supported by a strongly fortified post, upon the hill, or rather the rock, of the

Hermitage. Our right, again, was posted in the pass of Roncesvalles, and along the mountains beyond it; but from the spot which I now occupied, it could not be descried. Thus the valley of the Bidassoa alone separated us from one another, though that may appear a barrier sufficient, when the extreme steepness of its banks is considered.

Having remained here long enough to satisfy my curiosity, I turned my steps homewards, taking the direction of the deep valley which lay beneath our camp. It was not without considerable difficulty that I succeeded in reaching its base; and when there I was particularly struck with the extreme loneliness, the more than usual stillness, of all things about me. I looked round in vain for game. Not a living creature seemed to tenant the glen, – there was not a bird of any kind or description among the branches, but a death-like silence prevailed, the very breezes being shut out, and the very leaves motionless. I sat down by the edge of a little stream, somewhat weary, and oppressed with thirst, yet I felt a strong disinclination to drink; the water looked so slimy and blue I could not fancy it. I rose again and pursued its course, hoping to reach some linn, where it might present a more tempting appearance. At length thirst overcame me, and though there was no improvement in the hue of the water, I had stooped down and applied my lips to its surface, when, accidentally casting my eye a little to the right, I beheld a man's arm sticking up from the very centre of the rivulet. It was black and putrid, and the nails had dropt from some of the fingers. Of course, I started to my feet without tasting the polluted element, nor could I resist a momentary squeamishness at the idea of having narrowly escaped drinking this tincture of human carcases.

In this manner I continued to while away four or five days, strolling about amid some of the wildest scenes which nature is capable of producing, whenever the weather would permit, and amusing myself the best way I could, under cover of the canvass, when the rains descended and the winds blew. Among other matters I discovered, in the course of these rambles, two remarkable caves, having the appearance rather of deserted mines, than of natural cavities; but I had not an opportunity of exploring them, for on the morning which I had intended to devote to that purpose, we once more abandoned our camp, and moved to a new position. This was a little hill, distant about two miles from Irun, a mile from the high road, at the foot of these mountains which we had so lately occupied, and it proved one of the most agreeable posts of any which had been assigned to us since our landing. There we remained stationary till the advance of the army into France, and as the business of one day very much resembled that of another, I shall not weary my reader by narrating it in regular order, but state, in few words, only some of the most memorable of the adventures which occurred.

In the first place, the main business of the army was to fortify its position, by throwing up redoubts here and there, wherever scope for a redoubt could be found. Secondly, frequent visits were paid by myself and others to Irun and Fontarabia, towns of which little can be said in praise at any time, and certainly nothing at present. They were both entirely deserted, at least by the more respectable of their inhabitants; the latter, indeed, was in ruins, crowded with Spanish soldiers, muleteers, followers of the camp, sutlers, and adventurers. The keepers of gaming-houses had, indeed, remained, and they reaped no inconsiderable harvest from their guests; but with the exception of these, and of other characters not more pure than these, few of the original tenants of houses now occupied them. Again, there was a capital trouting stream before us in the Bidassoa, of which my friend and myself made good use. And here I cannot but remark upon the excellent understanding which prevailed between the hostile armies, and their genuine magnanimity towards one another. Many a time have I waded half across the little river, on the opposite bank of which the enemy's piquets were posted, whilst they came down in crowds only to watch my success, and to point out particular pools or eddies where the best sport was to be had. On such occasions, the sole precaution which I took was to dress myself in scarlet, and then I might approach within a few yards of their sentries without risk of molestation.

It fell to my lot one morning, whilst the corps lay here, to go out in command of a foraging party. We were directed to proceed along the bank of the river, and to bring back as much green corn, or, rather, ripe corn, – for though unreaped, the corn was perfectly ripe, – as our horses could carry. On this occasion I had charge of twenty men, totally unarmed, and about fifty horses and mules; and, I must confess, that I was not without apprehension that a troop of French cavalry would push across the stream, and cut us off. Of course, I made every disposition for a hasty retreat, desiring the men to cast loose their led animals, should any such event occur, and to make the best of their way to the piquets; but happily we were permitted to cut down the maize at our leisure, and to return with it unmolested. But enough of these details, – as soon as I have related the particulars of an excursion which a party of us made to St Sebastian's, for the purpose of amusing, as we best could, the period of inaction.

I have already stated, that the citadel, after enduring all the miseries of a bombardment during a whole week, finally surrendered on the 8th of September. It was now the 15th, when myself, with two or three others – being desirous of examining the condition of a place which had held out so long and so vigorously against the efforts of its besiegers – mounted our horses soon after sunrise, and set forth. The road by which we travelled was both sound and level, running through the pass of Irun, a narrow winding gorge, overhung on both sides by rugged precipices, which, in some places, are hardly fifty yards apart. This we followed for about twelve miles, when, striking off to the left, we made our way, by a sort of cross-road, over hill and dale, till we found ourselves among the orchards which crown the heights immediately above the town. We had directed our course thither, because a medical friend, who was left in charge of such of the wounded as could not be moved, had taken up his quarters there in a large farm-house, which he had converted into a temporary hospital; and to him we looked for beds and entertainment. Nor were we disappointed; – we found both, and both greatly superior in quality to any which had fallen to our lot since we landed.

The reader will easily believe that a man who has spent some of the best years of his life amid scenes of violence and bloodshed, must have witnessed many spectacles highly revolting to the purest feelings of our nature; but a more appalling picture of war passed by – of war in its darkest colours, – those which distinguish it when its din is over – than was presented by St Sebastian's, and the country in its immediate vicinity, I certainly never beheld. Whilst an army is stationary in any district, you are wholly unconscious of the work of devastation which is proceeding – you see only the hurry and pomp of hostile operations. But, when the tide has rolled on, and you return by chance to the spot over which it has last swept, the effect upon your own mind is such, as cannot even be imagined by him who has not experienced it. Little more than a week had elapsed, since the division employed in the siege of St Sebastian's had moved forward. Their trenches were not yet filled up, nor their batteries demolished; yet the former had, in some places, fallen in of their own accord, and the latter were beginning to crumble to pieces. We passed them by, however, without much notice. It was, indeed, impossible not to acknowledge, that the perfect silence which prevailed was far more awful than the bustle and stir that lately pervaded them; whilst the dilapidated condition of the convent, and of the few cottages which stood near it, stripped as they were of roofs, doors, and windows, and perforated with cannon-shot, inspired us, now that they were deserted, with sensations somewhat gloomy. But these were trifling – a mere nothing, when compared with the feelings which a view of the town itself excited.

As we pursued the main road, and approached St Sebastian's by its ordinary entrance, we were at first surprised at the slight degree of damage done to its fortifications by the fire of our batteries. The walls and battlements beside the gateway appeared wholly uninjured, the very embrasures being hardly defaced. But the delusion grew gradually more faint as we drew nearer, and had totally vanished before we reached the glacis. We found the draw-bridge fallen down across the ditch, in such a fashion, that the endeavour to pass it was not without danger. The folding-gates were torn from their hinges, one lying flat upon the ground, the other leaning against the wall; whilst our own steps, as we moved along the arched passage, sounded loud and melancholy.

Having crossed this, we found ourselves at the commencement of what had once been the principal street in the place. No doubt it was, in its day, both neat and regular; but of the houses, nothing now remained except the outward shells, which, however, appeared to be of an uniform height and style of architecture. As far as I could judge, they stood five stories from the ground, and were faced with a sort of free-stone, so thoroughly blackened and defiled, as to be hardly cognizable. The street itself was, moreover, choked up with heaps of ruins, among which were strewed about fragments of household furniture and clothing, mixed with caps, military accoutrements, round shot, pieces of shells, and all the other implements of strife. Neither were there wanting other evidences of the drama which had been lately acted here, in the shape of dead bodies, putrefying, and infecting the air with the most horrible stench. Of living creatures, on the other hand, not one was to be seen, not even a dog or a cat; indeed, we traversed the whole city, without meeting more than six human beings. These, from their dress and abject appearance, struck me as being some of the inhabitants who had survived the assault. They looked wild and haggard, and moved about here and there, poking among the ruins, as if they were either in search of the bodies of their slaughtered relatives, or hoped to find some little remnant of their property. I remarked, that two or three of them carried bags over their arms, into which they thrust every trifling article of copper or iron which came in their way.

From the streets, each of which resembled, in every particular, that which we had first entered, we proceeded towards the breach, where a dreadful spectacle awaited us. We found it covered – literally covered – with fragments of dead carcases, to bury which it was evident that no effectual attempt had been made. I afterwards learned, that the Spanish corps which had been left to perform this duty, instead of burying, endeavoured to burn the bodies; and hence the half-consumed limbs and trunks were scattered about, the effluvia arising from which was beyond conception overpowering. We were heartily glad to quit this part of the town, and hastened, by the nearest covered way, to the Castle.

Our visit to it soon convinced us, that in the idea which we had formed of its vast strength, we were greatly deceived. The walls were so feebly built, that in some places, where no shot could have struck them, they were rent from top to bottom by the recoil of the guns which surmounted them. About twenty heavy pieces of ordnance, with a couple of mortars, composed the whole artillery of the place; whilst there was not a single bomb-proof building in it, except the Governor's house. A large bakehouse, indeed, was bomb-proof, because it was hollowed out of the rock; but the barracks were everywhere perforated and in ruins. That the garrison must have suffered fearfully during the week's bombardment, everything in and about the place gave proof. Many holes were dug in the earth, and covered with large stones, into which, no doubt, the soldiers had crept for shelter; but these were not capable of protecting them, at least in sufficient numbers.

A PERIOD OF INACTION

Among other places, we strolled into what had been the hospital. It was a long room, containing, perhaps, twenty truckle bedsteads, all of which were entire, and covered with straw palliasses; of these, by far the greater number were dyed with blood; but only one had a tenant. We approached, and lifting a coarse sheet which covered it, we found the body of a mere youth, evidently not more than seventeen years of age. There was the mark of a musket-ball through his breast; but he was so fresh – had suffered so little from the effects of decay, that we feared he had been left to perish of neglect. – I trust we were mistaken. We covered him up again, and quitted the place.

We had now gratified our curiosity to the full, and turned our backs upon St Sebastian's, not without a chilling sense of the horrible points in our profession. But this gradually wore off as we approached the quarters of our host, and soon gave place to the more cheering influence of a substantial dinner, and a few cups of indifferently good wine. We slept soundly after our day's journey, and, starting next morning with the lark, we returned to our beautiful encampment above Irun.

Chapter 6

Fording into France

While the troops continue throwing up a line of earthworks, Gleig occupies his time in shooting and fishing excursions. At dawn on 7 October, the 1st Division fords the Bidasoa between Fuenterrabía and Béhobie and ascends the far bank, driving the French from their defences along the hills above Hendaye and towards the Croix des Bouquets. Demoralized by the speed and surprise of the attack, Soult's troops retreated towards their fortified camp at Urrugne, leaving behind their forward artillery, most of their baggage, and their huts. Further east, from near Bera, the Light Division together with General Girón's Spaniards, after ascending the Bayonette Ridge, had thrust the French from the summit of La Rhune, which dominated the area. Gleig's memory appears to have been at fault, when referring to having only just heard of the disastrous result of Napoleon's Russian campaign, which had been known to Wellington several months earlier.

Thus passed nearly four weeks, the weather varying, as at this season it is everywhere liable to vary, and from storm to calm. The troops worked sedulously at the redoubts, till no fewer than seven-and-thirty, commanding and flanking all the most assailable points between Fontarabia and the Foundery, were completed. For my own part, I pursued my ordinary routine, shooting or fishing all day long, whenever leisure was afforded, or rambling about amid scenery, grand beyond all power of language to describe. In one of these excursions, I stumbled upon another cave, similar, in all respects, to those which I had before been hindered from exploring. Determined not to be disappointed this time, I returned immediately to the camp, where, providing myself with a dark lantern, and taking a drawn sword in my hand, I hastened back to the spot. As I drew near, the thought that very possibly it might be a harbour for wolves, came across me, and half tempted me to stifle my curiosity; but curiosity overpowered caution, and I entered. Like most adventures of the kind, mine was wholly without danger. The cave proved, as I suspected it would, to be a deserted mine, extending several hundred feet under-ground, and ending in a heap of rubbish, as if the roof had given way and choked up farther progress. I found in it only an old iron three-legged pot, which I brought away with me, as a trophy of my hardihood.

It was now the 5th of October, and in spite of numerous rumours of a movement, the army still remained quiet. Marshal Soult, however, appeared fully to expect our advance, for he caused a number of hand-bills to be scattered through the camp, by the market people, most of whom were in his pay, warning us, that Gascony had risen *en masse*; and that if we dared to violate the sacred soil, every man who ventured beyond the camp would undoubtedly be murdered. These hand-bills were printed in French and Spanish; and they came in, in increased quantities, about the time that intelligence of Buonaparte's disastrous campaign in Russia reached us. Of course, we paid to them no attention whatever, nor had they the most remote effect in determining the plans of our leader, who probably knew, as well as the French general, how affairs really stood.

I shall not soon forget the 5th, the 6th, or the 7th of October. The first of these days I had spent among the woods, and returned to my tent in the evening, with a tolerably well-stored game-bag; but though fagged with my morning exercise, I could not sleep. After tossing about upon my blanket, till near midnight, I rose, and pulling on my clothes, walked out. The moon was shining in cloudless majesty, and lighted up a scene such as I never looked upon before, and shall probably never look upon again. I had admired the situation of our camp during the day, as it well deserved; but when I viewed it by moonlight, – the tents moist with dew, and glitter-ing in the silver rays which fell upon them, with a grove of dwarf oaks partly shading them, and the stupendous cliffs distinctly visible in the back ground, I thought, and I think now, that the eye of man never beheld a scene more romantic or more beautiful. There was just breeze enough to produce a slight waving of the branches, which, joined to the unceasing roar of a little waterfall at no great distance, and the occasional voice of a sentinel, who challenged as anyone approached his post, produced an effect altogether too powerful for me to pourtray, at this distance of time, even to myself. I walked about for two hours, perfectly enchanted, though I could not help thinking, that thousands who slept securely under that moon's rays, would sleep far more soundly under the rays of another.

I returned to my couch of fern about two in the morning, and slept, or rather dosed, till daybreak; then, having waited the usual time under arms with the men, I set off again, with my dog and gun, to the mountains. But I was weary with last night's watching, and a friend, in something of my own turn of mind, overtaking me, we sat down to bask in the sun, upon a lofty rock which overlooked the camp. There we remained till the collecting clouds warned us of a coming storm; when, hurrying home, the information so long expected was communicated to us, namely, that we were to attack on the morrow.

I am no fire-eater, nor ever professed to be one; but I confess that the news produced in me very pleasurable sensations. We had been stationary, in our present position, so long, that all the objects around had become familiar, and variety is everything in the life of a soldier. Besides, there was the idea of invading France, an idea which, a few years before, would have been scouted as visionary; this created a degree of excitement highly animating. Not that I was thoughtless of what might be my own fate; on the contrary, I never yet went into action without making up my mind beforehand, for the worst. But you become so familiarized with death, after you have spent a few months amid such scenes as I had lately witnessed, that it loses most of its terrors, and is considered, only as a blank is considered in the lottery of which you may have purchased a ticket. It may come, and if so, why, there is no help for it; but you may escape, and then there are new scenes to be witnessed, and new adventures to go through.

As the attack was to be made at an early hour, the troops were ordered to lie down as soon after dark as possible, in order that they might be fresh, and in good spirits for the work of to-morrow. In the meanwhile, the clouds continued to collect over the whole face of the sky, and the extreme sultriness of the atmosphere indicated an approaching thunder-storm. The sun went down, lowering and ominously, but it was not till the first night-relief had been planted, that is, about eight or nine o'clock in the evening, that the storm burst upon us. Then indeed it came, and with a degree of sublimity which accompanies such a storm, only amid such scenery. The lightning was more vivid than any which I recollect ever to have seen, and the peals of thunder, echoed back as they were by the rocks and mountains around, sounded more like one continued rending of the elements, than the intermitted discharges of an electric cloud. Happily, little or no rain fell, at least for a time, by which means I was enabled to sit at the door of my tent and watch the storm, nor have I been frequently more delighted than with its progress.

Immediately opposite to where I sat, was a valley or glen, beautifully wooded; at the bottom of which flowed a little rivulet, which came from the waterfall already alluded to. This was completely laid open to me at every flash, as well as the whole side of the mountain beyond it; near the summit of which, a body of Spanish soldiers were posted in a lonely cottage. It was exceedingly curious to catch sight of this hut, with warlike figures moving about it, and arms piled beside it; of the bold heights around, with the stream tumbling from its rocky bed, and the thick groves, and the white tents – and then, to have the whole hidden from you in a moment. I sat and feasted my eyes, till the rain began to descend; when the storm gradually abating, I stretched myself on the ground, and without undressing, wrapt myself in my cloak, and fell asleep.

It was, as nearly as I can now recollect, about four o'clock next morning, when I was roused from my slumber by the orderly serjeant of the company. By this time the storm had completely passed away, and the stars were shining in a sky perfectly cloudless. The moon had, however, gone down, nor was there any other light except what they afforded, to aid the red glare from the decaying fires, which, for want of fuel, were fast dying out. The effect of this dull light, as it fell upon the soldiers, mustering in solemn silence, was exceedingly fine. You could not distinguish either the uniform or the features of the men; you saw only groups collecting together, with arms in their hands; and it was impossible not to associate in your own mind the idea of banditti, rather than of regular troops, with the wild forest scenery around. Of course, I started to my feet at the first summons; and having buckled on my sabre, stowed away some cold meat, biscuit, and rum, in a haversack, and placed it, with my cloak, across the back of my horse, and swallowed a cup or two of coffee, I felt myself ready and willing for any kind of service whatever.

In little more than a quarter of an hour, the corps was under arms, and each man in his place. We had already been joined by two other battalions, forming a brigade of about fifteen hundred men; and about an hour before sun-rise, just as the first streaks of dawn were appearing in the east, the word was given to march. Our tents were not, on this occasion, struck. They were left standing, with the baggage and mules, under the protection of a guard, for the purpose of deceiving the enemy's piquets, in whose view they were exposed, into the belief that nothing was going forward. This measure was rendered necessary, because the state of the tide promised not to admit of our fording the river till past seven o'clock; long before which hour broad day-light would set in; and hence, the whole object of our early movement was to gain, unobserved, a sort of hollow, close to the banks of the Bidassoa, from which, as soon as the stream should be passable, we might emerge.

As we moved in profound silence, we reached our place of ambuscade without creating the smallest alarm; where we laid ourselves down upon the ground, for the double purpose of more effectually avoiding a display, and of taking as much rest as possible. Whilst lying here, we listened, with eager curiosity, to the distant tread of feet, which marked the coming up of other divisions, and to the lumbering sound of artillery, as it rolled along the high road. The latter increased upon us every moment, till at length three ponderous eighteen-pounders reached the hollow, and began to ascend the rising ground immediately in front of us. These were placed in battery, so as to command the ford, across which a stone bridge, now in ruins, was thrown; and by which we knew, from the position which we now occupied, that we were destined to proceed. By what infatuation it arose, that all those preparations excited no suspicion among the enemy, whose sentinels were scarcely half musket-shot distant, I know not; but the event proved, that they expected this morning anything rather than an attack.

Before I proceed to describe the circumstances of the battle, I must endeavour to convey to the minds of my non-military readers something like a clear notion of the nature of the position occupied by the right of the French army. I have already said, that its extreme flank rested upon the sea. Its more central brigades occupied a chain of heights, not, indeed, deserving of the name of mountains, but still sufficiently steep to check the progress of an advancing force, and full of natural inequalities, well adapted to cover the defenders from the fire of the assailants. Along the face of these heights is built the straggling village of Andaye; and immediately in front of them runs the frith or mouth of the Bidassoa, fordable only in two points, one opposite to Fontarabia, and the other in the direction of the main road. Close to the French bank of the river, is a grove, or strip of willows, with several vineyards, and other enclosures, admirably calculated for skirmishers; whilst the ford beside the ruined bridge, the only one by which artillery could pass, was completely commanded by a fortified house, or *tete-du-pont*, filled with infantry. The main road, again, on the French side of the river, winds among over-hanging precipices, not, indeed, so rugged as those in the pass of Irun, but sufficiently bold to place troops which might occupy them in comparative security, and to render one hundred resolute men more than a match for a thousand who might attack them. Yet these were the most assailable points in the whole position, all beyond the road being little else than perpendicular cliffs, shaggy with pine and ash trees.

Such was the nature of the ground which we were commanded to carry. As day dawned, I could distinctly see that the old town of Fontarabia was filled with British soldiers. The fifth division, which had borne the brunt of the late siege, and which, since the issue of their labours, had been permitted to rest somewhat in the rear, had been moved up on the preceding evening; and reaching Fontarabia a little before midnight, had spent some hours in the streets. Immediately in rear of ourselves, again, and in the streets of Irun, about eight thousand of the Guards and of the German Legion were reposing; whilst a brigade of cavalry just showed its leading files, at a turning in the main road, and a couple of nine-pounders stood close beside them. It was altogether a beautiful and an animating sight, not fewer than fifteen or twenty thousand British and Portuguese troops being distinguishable at a single glance.

Away to our right, and on the tops of San Marcial, the Spanish divisions took their stations; nor could I avoid drawing something like an invidious comparison between them and their gallant allies. Half clothed, and badly fed, though sufficiently armed, their appearance certainly promised no more than their actions, for the most part, verified. Not that the Spanish peasantry are deficient in personal courage, (and their soldiers were, generally speaking, no other than peasants with muskets in their hands,) but their corps were so miserably officered, and their commissariat so miserably supplied, that the chief matter of surprise is, how they came to fight at all. Even at this period of the war, when their country might be said to be completely freed from the invader, the principal subsistence of the Spanish army consisted in the heads of Indian corn, which they gathered for themselves in the fields, and cooked by roasting them over their fires.

It will readily be imagined, that we watched the gradual fall of the river with intense anxiety, turning our glasses ever and anon towards the French lines, throughout which all remained most unaccountably quiet. At length a movement could be distinguished among the troops which occupied Fontarabia. Their skirmishers began to emerge from under cover of the houses, and to approach the river, when instantly the three eighteen-pounders opened from the heights above us. This was the signal for a general advance. Our column, likewise, threw out its skirmishers, which, hastening towards the ford, were saluted by a sharp fire of musketry from the enemy's piquets, and from the garrison of the *tete-du-pont*. But the latter was speedily abandoned as our people pressed through the stream, and our artillery kept up an incessant discharge of round and grape shot upon it.

The French piquets were driven in, and our troops established on the opposite bank, with hardly any loss on our part, though those who crossed by Fontarabia were obliged to hold their firelocks and cartouch-boxes over their heads, to keep them dry; and the water reached considerably above the knees beside the bridge. The alarm had, however, been communicated to the columns in rear, which hastily formed upon the heights, and endeavoured, but in vain, to keep possession of Andaye. That village was carried in gallant style by a brigade of the fifth division, whilst the first, moving steadily along the road, dislodged from their post the garrison of the hills which commanded it, and crowned the heights almost without opposition. A general panic seemed to have seized the enemy. Instead of boldly charging us, as we moved forward in column, they fired their pieces, and fled without pausing to reload them, nor was anything like a determined stand attempted, till all their works had fallen into our hands, and much of their artillery was taken. It was one of the most perfect, and yet extraordinary surprises, which I ever beheld.

There were not, however, wanting many brave fellows among the French officers, who exerted themselves strenuously to rally their terrified comrades, and to restore the battle. Among these I remarked one in particular. He was on horseback; and, riding among a flying battalion, he used every means which threat and entreaty could produce, to stop them; and he succeeded. The battalion paused, its example was followed by others, and in five minutes a well-formed line occupied what looked like the last of a range of green hills, on the other side of a valley which we were descending.

This sudden movement on the part of the enemy was met by a corre-sponding formation on ours; we wheeled into line and advanced. Not a word was spoken, not a shot fired, till our troops had reached nearly half way across the little hollow, when the French, raising one of their discord-ant yells, – a sort of shout, in which every man halloos for himself, without regard to the tone or time of those about him, – fired a volley. It was well directed, and did considerable execution; but it checked not our approach for a moment. Our men replied to it with a hearty British cheer, and giving them back their fire, rushed on to the charge.

In this they were met with great spirit by the enemy. I remarked the same individual, who had first stopped their flight, ride along the front of his men, and animate them to their duty, nor was it without very consider-able difficulty, and after having exchanged several discharges of musketry, that we succeeded in getting within charging distance. Then, indeed, another cheer was given, and the French, without waiting for the rush, once more broke their ranks and fled. Their leader was still as active as before. He rode among the men, reproached, exhorted, and even struck those near him with his sword, and he was once more about to restore order, when he fell. In an instant, however, he rose again and mounted another horse, but he had hardly done so when a ball took effect in his neck, and he dropped dead. The fall of this one man decided the day upon the heights of Andaye. The French troops lost all order and all discipline, and making their way to the rear, each by himself as he best could, they left us in undisputed possession of the field.

On the right of our army, however, and on the extreme left of the enemy, a much more determined opposition was offered. There Soult had added to the natural strength of his position, by throwing up redoubts and batteries upon every commanding point, and hence, it was not without suffering a very considerable loss, that the light division succeeded in turning it. All attempts, indeed, to carry the Hermitage, failed, though they were renewed with the most daring resolution, till a late hour in the night. But of the operations of the army in these quarters, I could see nothing, and therefore I will not attempt to describe them.

The day was far spent when our troops, wearied as much with the pursuit as with fighting, were commanded to halt, and to lie down in brigades and divisions along the heights which the enemy had abandoned. With us all was now perfectly quiet; but the roar of musketry, and the thunder of the cannon, still sounded on our right. As the darkness set in, too, the flashes became every moment more and more conspicuous, and produced, on account of the great unevenness of the ground, a remarkably beautiful effect. Repeated assaults being still made upon the Hermitage rock, the whole side of that conical hill seemed in a blaze, whilst every valley and eminence around it sparkled from time to time like the hills and valleys of a tropical climate, when the fire-flies are out in millions. Nor were other and stronger lights wanting. Our troops, in the hurry of the battle, had set fire to the huts of the French soldiers, which now burst forth, and cast a strong glare over the entire extent of the field. On the whole it was a glorious scene, and tended much to keep up the degree of excitement which had pervaded our minds during the day.

Our loss, I mean the loss of the corps to which I was attached, chanced to be trifling. No particular companion, or intimate acquaintance of mine at least, had fallen, consequently there was nothing to destroy the feeling of pure delight, which the meanest individual in an army experiences when that army has triumphed; nor do I recollect many happier moments of my life, than when I stretched myself this evening beside a fire, near my friend Gray, to chat over the occurrences of the day. The Quarter-master coming up soon after with a supply of provisions and rum, added, indeed, not a little to my satisfaction, for the stock which I had provided in the morning was long ago disposed of among those who had been less provident; and my meal was followed by a sleep, such as kings might envy, though the heavens were my canopy, and the green turf was my bed.

Chapter 7

Deserters are Shot

Pamplona having surrendered on 31 October, Wellington disposed his troops in readiness for crossing the Nivelle. Gleig speculates on the causes of desertion and witnesses the execution of two deserters. He dines with General Sir John Hope. The expected order to advance is cancelled, largely due to downpours having made the roads virtually impassable for artillery.

About an hour after sunrise, on the following morning, the tents and baggage, which had been left on the Spanish side of the river, came up; and we were once more enabled to shelter ourselves against the inclemency of the weather. And it was well that their arrival was not longer deferred, for we had hardly time to pitch the former, when a heavy storm of wind and rain began, which, lasting with little intermission during two whole days, rendered our situation the reverse of agreeable. The position which we occupied, was, moreover, exceedingly exposed, our camp stretching along the ridge of a bleak hill, totally bare of every description of wood; indeed, the only fuel now within our reach, consisted of furze, the green and prickly parts of which we chopped and gave as forage to our horses, whilst the stems and smaller branches supplied us with very indifferent material for our fires.

The left column of the army had not long established itself in France, when crowds of sutlers, and other camp-followers, began to pour in. These persons, taking possession of such of the enemy's huts as had escaped the violence of our soldiers, opened their shops in due form along the high road, and soon gave to the spot which they occupied the appearance of a settled village during the season of a fair, when booths, and caravans of wild beasts, crowd its little street. This village became, before long, a favourite resort of the idle, and of such as still retained a few dollars in their purses, and many were the bottles of nominal brown-stout which, night after night, were consumed at the sign of the "Jolly Soldier".

I hardly recollect any period of my active life more devoid of interesting occurrences, than that which intervened between the crossing of the Spanish border, and the advance of the army towards Bayonne. We continued on the heights of Andaye, from the 8th of October till the 9th

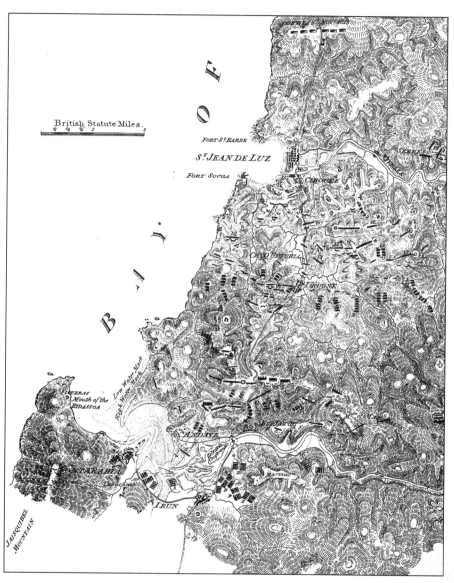

4. From Irún to St Jean-de-Luz (detail from Robert Batty's Map)

of November, during the greater part of which time the weather was uncommonly severe, cold showers of rain unceasingly falling, and tremendous gusts of wind prevailing; indeed, we began to fear at last, that nothing more would be done this season, and that we should either retire to the towns of Irun and Fontarabia, or spend the winter under canvass. That we were wantonly kept here, no one imagined. On the contrary, we were quite aware, that nothing but the protracted fall of Pampeluna hindered our advance, and joyful was the news which at length reached us, that that important city had surrendered.

Of course, I did not confine myself to my tent, or within the bounds of the camp, all this while. I shot and fished, as usual – made excursions to the rear and to the front, as the humour directed, and adopted every ordinary expedient to kill time. On these occasions adventures were not always wanting, but they were for the most part such as would excite but little interest were they repeated. I recollect one, however, which deserves narration, more perhaps than the others, and that I will detail.

Whilst the British army occupied its position along the Spanish bank of the Bidassoa, a vast number of desertions took place; insomuch as to cause a serious diminution of its strength. As this was an event which had but rarely occurred before, many opinions were hazarded as to its cause. For my own part, I attributed it entirely to the operation of superstitious terror on the minds of the men, and for this reason. It is generally the custom, in planting sentinels in the immediate presence of an enemy – to station them in pairs, so that one may patrol as far as the next post, whilst the other remains steady on his ground. Perhaps, too, the wish of giving greater confidence to the men themselves, may have some weight in dictating the measure; at all events, there can be no doubt that it produces that effect. Such, however, was the nature of the ground covered by our piquets among the Pyrenees, that in many places there was hardly room for a couple of sentinels to occupy a single post, whilst it was only at the mouths of the various passes that two were more desirable than one for securing the safety of the army. Rugged as the country was, however, almost every foot of it had been the scene of action, whilst the dead, falling among rocks and cliffs, were left, in various instances, from necessity, unburied; and exactly in those parts where the dead lay unburied, single sentinels were planted. That both soldiers and sailors are frequently superstitious, every person knows; nor can it be pleasant for the strongest-minded among them to spend two or three hours of a stormy night beside a mangled and half-devoured carcase; indeed I have been myself, more than once, remonstrated with, for desiring as brave a fellow as any in the corps, to keep guard near one of his fallen comrades. "I don't care for living men," said the soldier; "but, for Godsake, sir, don't keep me beside *him*;" and wherever I could yield to the remonstrance, I invariably did so. My own opinion, therefore, was that many of our sentries became so overpowered by superstition, that they could not keep their ground. They knew, however, that if they returned to the piquet, a severe punishment awaited them; and hence they went over to the enemy, rather than endure the misery of a diseased imagination.

As a proof that my notions were correct, it was remarked, that the army had no sooner descended from the mountains, and taken up a position which required a chain of double sentinels to be renewed, than desertion in a very great degree ceased. A few instances, indeed, still occurred, as will always be the case where men of all tempers are brought together, as in an army; but they bore not the proportion of one to twenty towards those which took place among the Pyrenees. To put a stop to this entirely, a severe order was issued, positively prohibiting every man from passing the advanced videttes; and it was declared, that whoever was caught on what is termed the neutral ground – that is, on the ground between the enemy's out-posts and our own, should henceforth be treated as a deserter.

I had ridden towards the front one morning, for the purpose of visiting a friend in the 5th division, when I learned, that three men had been seized a few days before, half-way between the two chains of posts, and that one of them had confessed that their intention was to desert. A court-martial was immediately ordered; the prisoners were condemned to be shot; and this was the day on which the sentence was to be carried into execution. I consequently found the division, on my arrival, getting under arms; and being informed of the circumstances, I determined, after a short struggle with my weaker feelings, to witness the proceeding.

It was, altogether, a most solemn and impressive spectacle. The soldiers took their stations, and formed their ranks, without speaking a word; and they looked at one another with that peculiar expression, which, without seeming to imply any suspicion of the impropriety of the measure, indicated great reluctance to become spectators of it. The same feeling evidently pervaded the minds of the officers; indeed you could almost perceive the sort of shudder which ran through the frames of all who were on parade.

The place appointed for the execution was a little elevated plain, a few hundred yards in front of the camp, and near the piquet from which the culprits had deserted. Hither the different battalions directed their steps, and the whole division being formed into three sides of a hollow square, the men grounded their arms, and stood still. At the vacant side of this square, a grave was dug, the earth, which had been excavated, being piled up on its opposite bank; and this, as the event proved, was the spot to be occupied by the prisoners.

We had stood thus about five minutes, when the muffled drums of the corps to which the culprits belonged, were heard beating the dead-march; and they themselves, handcuffed and surrounded by their guards, made their appearance. One was a fine young man, tall, and well-made; another was a dark, thick-set, little man, about forty years of age; and the third had nothing remarkable in his countenance, except an expression of deep cunning and treachery. They all moved forward with considerable firmness, and took their stations on the mound, when, attention being ordered, a staff-officer advanced into the centre of the square, and read aloud the proceedings of the Court. By these, sentence of death was passed upon all three, but the most villainous-looking among them was recommended to mercy, on the score of his having added the guilt of treachery to his other crimes.

As soon as the reading was finished, the prisoners were commanded to kneel down upon the ground, and a handkerchief was tied over the eyes of each. Whilst this was doing, I looked round, not so much from curiosity as to give a momentary relief to my own excited feelings, upon the countenances of the soldiers. They were, one and all of them, deadly pale, whilst the teeth of many were set closely together, and their very breaths seemed to be repressed. It was altogether a most harrowing moment.

The eyes of the prisoners being now tied up, the guard was withdrawn from around them, and took post about ten yards within their front. As soon as this was done, the same staff-officer who had read the proceedings of the trial, calling to the informer by name, ordered him to rise, for that the commander of the forces had attended to the recommendation of his judges, and spared his life. But the poor wretch paid no attention to the order; I question, indeed, whether he heard it; for he knelt there as if rooted to the spot, till a file of men removed him in a state of insensibility. What the feelings of his companions in crime must have been at this moment I know not, but their miseries were of short duration; for, a signal being given, about sixteen soldiers fired, and they were instantly numbered with the dead. The little man, I observed, sprang into the air when he received his wounds, the other fell flat upon his face; but neither gave the slightest symptom of vitality after.

The discharge of the muskets in the face of the culprits, was followed by a sound as if every man in the division had been stifled for the last five minutes, and now at length drew in his breath. It was not a groan, nor a sigh, but a sob, like that which you unconsciously utter after dipping your head under water; and now all excitement was at an end. The men were dead; they died by musket-shots; and these were occurrences, viewing them in the abstract, far too common to be much regarded. But in order to give to the execution its full effect, the division formed into open column of battalions, and marched round the grave, on the brink of which the bodies lay; after which each corps filed off to its tent, and long before dark the scene of the morning was forgotten. Not but that it produced a good effect, by checking the prevalence of the offence of which it was the punishment; but pity soon died away, and every feeling of disgust, if, indeed, any such feeling had at all arisen, was obliterated. The bodies were thrown into the hole and covered up, and I returned to my tent to muse upon what I had seen.

I have stated, that on the third of November intelligence of the fall of Pampeluna reached us. From that day we began to calculate, in real earnest, upon a speedy renewal of operations, and to speculate upon the probable extent of our progress ere a new halt should be ordered, or the troops placed in quarters for the winter. But so much rain had fallen during the preceding fortnight, that the cross-roads were rendered wholly impassable, and, what was worse, there appeared no promise of a change in the weather.

I had the honour to be personally acquainted with the distinguished officer, whose unlooked-for death caused, of late, so great a sensation of sorrow throughout Scotland; I mean the Earl of Hopetoun, at that period Sir John Hope. Sir John had lately joined the army, relieving Sir Thomas Graham in the guidance of the left column, and filling the office of second in command under Lord Wellington. Whilst our division occupied the heights of Andaye, I spent several agreeable evenings in his company; the particulars attending one of which, as they had, at the time at least, a more than ordinary degree of interest in them, I shall take the liberty to repeat.

On the seventh of November I dined with the General. We sat down to the table about six o'clock, and were beginning to experience as much satisfaction as good cheer and pleasant company can produce, when an orderly dragoon rode into the court-yard of the house at full speed. He was immediately admitted, and, being ushered into the room where we sat, he handed a sealed packet to our host. Sir John opened it, glanced his eye over its contents, put it into his pocket, and, motioning to the orderly to withdraw, renewed the conversation which had been interrupted. Though more than half suspicious that the packet contained intelligence of importance, we, I mean the General's guests and staff, soon returned to our usual lively chat, when the clattering of another horse's hoofs was heard, and Colonel Delancy entered. He was accompanied by an officer of the corps of guides, and requesting permission to hold a few minutes' private conversation with Sir John Hope, they all three retired together.

"We shall have something to do before twenty-four hours pass," said one of the aides-de-camp; "Delancy always brings warlike communications with him." – "So much the better," was the general reply. "Let us drink to our host, and success to to-morrow's operations." The toast was hardly finished, when Sir John returned, bringing with him only the officer of the corps of guides; Delancy was gone; but of the purport of the communication not a hint was dropped, and the evening passed on as if no such communication had been made.

About nine o'clock our party broke up, and we were wishing our friends good-night, when a French officer, who had deserted from his corps, was

brought in. He was civilly, but very coolly received. He had little information to give, except that a batch of conscripts had lately joined the army,
most of whom were either old men or boys; so thoroughly was the youth
of France by this time wasted through a continuance of wars. We, who
were guests, stayed not, however, to hear him out, but mounting our
horses, returned each to his tent.

On reaching the camp of my own corps, I found, as, indeed, I had
expected to find, that the order for an attack was issued, and that the
brigade was to be under arms by four o'clock next morning. Once more,
therefore, I made up my mind for the worst, and having instructed my
friend as to the manner in which I wished my little property to be disposed
of; having assigned my sword to one, my pelisse to another, and my
faithful dog to a third, I was, if you please, methodist enough to recommend my soul to the mercy of its Creator, and then lay down. For a while
Gray and myself chatted, as men, at least men of any reflection, so situated,
are wont to chat. We agreed, as, indeed, we always did on such occasions,
to act as executors the one to the other, and having cordially shaken hands,
lest an opportunity of so doing should not occur again, we fell fast asleep.

I had slept perhaps an hour and a half, when I was awoke by the voice
of the orderly serjeant, who came to inform us that the movement of the
army was countermanded. I will not say whether the intelligence was
received as acceptable, or the reverse; indeed, I question whether we
ourselves knew, at the moment, whether we were relieved by the reprieve
or the contrary. One thing, however, is certain, that I slept not the less
soundly from knowing, that at least to-morrow was secured to me, to be
passed in a state of vigour and vitality, though perfectly aware that the
peril of a battle must be encountered before long, and hence, that it was
really a matter of very little moment, whether it should take place now, or
a few days hence.

On mustering, next morning, upon the parade-ground, we learned that
our intended operations were impeded only by the very bad state of the
roads. Though the rain had ceased for some days past, such was the quantity which had fallen, that no artillery could, as yet, move in any other
direction than along the main road. The continuance of dry weather for
eight-and-forty hours longer, would, however, it was calculated, remove
this obstacle to our advance; and hence, every man felt that he had but a
couple of days to count upon. By good fortune, these days continued clear
and serene, and the justice of our calculations was, in due time, evinced.

Chapter 8

Urrugne is Captured

At dawn on 10 November Wellington advances his centre and right on a broad front towards the Nivelle, leaving Hope to demonstrate effectively enough to ensure that the 23,000 French opposing him remained in their fieldworks. As part of this demonstration in force, the 85th overrun Urrugne, beyond which they mingled with skirmishers of the King's German Legion, there commanded by Colonel Colin Halkett, before retiring to the protection of the solidly-walled village church after a day's heavy fighting.

The eighth and ninth of November passed over, without any event occurring worthy of recital. On the former of these days, indeed, we had the satisfaction to see a French gun-brig destroyed by one of our light cruizers, a small schooner, off the harbour of St Jean de Luz. She had lain there, as it appeared, for some time, and apprehensive of falling into our hands, had ventured, on that day, to put to sea. But being observed by a brig, and the schooner above alluded to, she was immediately followed, and, after an engagement of nearly an hour's duration with the latter, she blew up. Whether her crew had abandoned her previous to the explosion, I had no opportunity to discover.

Among ourselves, in the meanwhile, and throughout the different divisions contiguous to us, a silence, like that of a calm before a storm, prevailed. Each man looked as if he knew that an attack was impending, but few conjectures were hazarded touching the precise moment of its occurrence. On the evening of the ninth, however, all doubt was at length removed. We were assembled at parade, or rather the parade was dismissed; but the band continuing to play, the officers were waiting in groups about the tent of the colonel, when an aide-de-camp riding up, informed us that the whole army was to advance upon the morrow. The corps to which I belonged was appointed to carry the village of Urogne, a place containing perhaps an hundred houses and a church, by assault; for which purpose, we were to take post, an hour before day-break, on the high road, and close to the advanced sentinels. Of the disposition of other corps we knew nothing, and we were perfectly satisfied with the part allotted to ourselves.

As soon as the aide-de-camp departed, we began, as people so circumstanced generally begin, to discuss the propriety of our general's arrangements. On the present occasion, we were more than usually convinced of the sagacity and profound skill of the noble lord. Our corps had been selected, in preference to many others, for a service, perilous, it is true, but therefore honourable. This showed that he knew at least on whom he could depend, and we, of course, were determined to prove that his confidence had not been misplaced. Alas, the vanity of men in all callings and professions, when each regards himself as infinitely superior to those around him!

Having passed an hour or two in this manner, we departed, each to his own tent, in order to make the necessary preparations for the morrow. These were speedily completed. Our baggage was packed; our horses and mules, which, for the sake of shelter, had been kept, during the last ten days, at certain houses in the rear, were called in, and provisions enough for one day's consumption, were put up in a haversack. With this and our cloaks we directed a Portuguese lad – a servant of Gray, to follow the battalion, upon a little pony which we kept chiefly for such uses, and finally, having renewed our directions, the one to the other, respecting the conduct of the survivor in case either of us should fall, we lay down.

It was quite dark when I arose. Our fires had all burned out, there was no moon in the heavens, and the stars were in a great measure obscured by clouds; but we took our places instinctively, and in profound silence. On these occasions, I have been always struck with the great coolness of the women. You seldom hear a single expression of alarm escape them; indeed, they become, probably from habit, and from the example of others, to the full as indifferent to danger as their husbands. I fear, too, that the sort of life which they lead, after they have for any length of time followed an army in the field, sadly unsexes them, (if I may be permitted to coin such a word for their benefit,) at least, I recollect but one instance in which any symptoms of real sorrow were shown, even by those whom the fate of a battle has rendered widows. Sixty women only being permitted to accompany a battalion, they are, of course, perfectly secure of obtaining as many husbands as they may choose; and hence, few widows of soldiers continue in a state of widowhood for any unreasonable time; so far, indeed, they are a highly favoured class of female society.

The column being formed and the tents and baggage so disposed, as that, in case of repulse, they might be carried to the rear without confusion or delay, the word was given to march. As our route lay over ground extremely uneven, we moved forward for a while slowly, and with caution; till, having gained the high road, we were enabled to quicken our pace. We proceeded by it, perhaps a mile, till the watch-fire of a German piquet was seen; when the order to halt being passed quietly from rank to rank, we grounded our arms, and sat down upon the green banks by the road side. Here we were directed to remain, till a gun on our left should sound the signal of attack, and objects should be distinctly visible.

Men are very differently affected at different times, even though the situations in which they may be cast bear a strong affinity to one another. On the present occasion, for example, I perfectly recollect, that hardly any feeling of seriousness pervaded my own mind, nor, if I might judge from appearances, the minds of those around me. Much conversation, on the contrary, passed among us in whispers, but it was all of as light a character, as if the business in which we were about to engage was mere amusement, and not that kind of play in which men stake their lives. Anxiety and restlessness, indeed, universally prevailed. We looked to the east, and watched the gradual approach of dawn with eager interest; but it was with that degree of interest which sportsmen feel on the morning of the twelfth of August, – or rather, perhaps, like that of a child in a box at Covent-Garden, when it expects every moment to see the stage-curtain lifted. We were exceedingly anxious to begin the fray, but we were quite confident of success.

In the meanwhile, such dispositions were made as the circumstances of the case appeared to require. Three companies, consisting of about one hundred and fifty men, were detached, under the command of a field-officer, a little to the right and left of the road, for the purpose of surprising, if possible, two of the enemy's piquets, which were there posted. The remaining seven, forming again into column, as day broke, extended their front so as to cover the whole breadth of the road, and made ready to rush at once, in what is called double quick time, upon the village. That it was strongly barricaded, and filled with French infantry, we were quite aware; but, by making our first attack a rapid one, we calculated on reaching the barricade before the enemy should be fully aware of the movement.

We stood perhaps half an hour, after these dispositions were effected, before the signal was given, the dawn gradually brightening over the whole of the sky. Now we could observe that we had diverged in some degree from the main road, and occupied with our little column a lane, hemmed in on both sides by high hedges. Presently we were able to remark that the lane again united itself with the road about a hundred yards in front of us; then the church and houses of the village began to show through the darkness, like rocks, or mounds; by and by the stubble fields immediately around could be distinguished from green meadows; then the hedge-rows which separated one field from another became visible. And now the signal-gun was fired. It was immediately repeated by a couple of nine-pounders, which were stationed in a field adjoining to the lane where we stood; and the battle began.

The three detached companies did their best to surprise the French piquets, but without success, the French troops being far too watchful to be easily taken. They drove them in, however, in gallant style, whilst the little column, according to the preconcerted plan, pressed forward. In the meantime, the houses and barricade of Urogne were thronged with defenders, who saluted us as we approached with a sharp discharge of musketry, which, however, was more harmless than might have been expected. A few men and one officer fell, the latter being shot through the heart. He uttered but a single word – the name of his favourite comrade, and expired. On our part, we had no time for firing, but rushed on to the charge; whilst the nine-pounders, already alluded to, cleared the barricade with grape and cannister. In two minutes we had reached its base; in an instant more we were on the top of it; when the enemy, panic-struck at the celerity of our movements, abandoned their defences and fled. We followed them through the street of the place, as far as its extremity, but, having been previously commanded to proceed no farther, we halted there, and they escaped to the high grounds beyond.

The position now attacked was that famous one in front of St Jean de Luz, than which, Lord Wellington himself has said that he never beheld any more formidable. It extended for about three miles, along the ridge of a rising ground, the ascent of which was, for the most part, covered with thick wood, and intersected by deep ditches. In addition to these natural defences, it was fortified with the utmost care, Mareschal Soult having begun to throw up upon it redoubts and breast-works, even before our army had crossed the Bidassoa, and having devoted the whole of that month which we had spent above Andaye, in completing his older works and erecting new. Towards our left, indeed, that is, towards the right of the enemy, and in the direction of the village which we had just carried, these worked presented so commanding an appearance, that our gallant leader deemed it unwise to attempt any serious impression upon them; and hence, having possessed ourselves of Urogne, we were directed to attempt nothing farther, but to keep it at all hazards, and to make from time to time a demonstration of advancing. This was done, in order to deter Soult from detaching any of his corps to the assistance of his left, which it was the object of Lord Wellington to turn, and which, after twelve hours' severe fighting, he succeeded in turning.

As soon as we had cleared the place of its defenders, we set about entrenching ourselves, in case any attempt should be made to retake the village. For this purpose, we tore up the barricade erected by the French, consisting of casks filled with earth, manure, and rubbish, and rolling them down to the opposite end of the town, we soon threw up a parapet for our own defence. The enemy, in the meanwhile, began to collect a dense mass of infantry upon the brow of the hill opposite, and, turning a battery of three pieces of cannon upon us, they swept the street with round shot. These, whizzing along, soon caused the walls and roofs of the houses to crumble into ruins; but neither they, nor the shells which from time to time burst about us, did any considerable execution. By avoiding conspicuous places, indeed, we managed to keep well out of reach; and hence the chief injury done by the cannonade was that which befell the proprietors of houses.

We found in the village a good store of brown bread, and several casks of brandy. The latter of these were instantly knocked on the head, and the spirits poured out into the street, as the only means of hindering our men from getting drunk, and saving ourselves from a defeat; but the former was divided amongst them; and even the black bread, allowed to the French soldiers, was a treat to us, because we had tasted nothing except biscuits, and these none of the most fresh, for the last three months. We were not, however, allowed much time to regail ourselves.

It was now about eleven o'clock, and the enemy had as yet made no attack upon us. We could perceive, indeed, from the glancing of bayonets through the wood in front, that troops were there mustering; and as the country was well adapted for skirmishing, being a good deal intersected with ditches, hedges, and hollow ways, it was deemed prudent to send out three or four companies to watch their movements. Among the companies thus sent out was that to which I belonged. We took a direction to the left of the village, and being noticed by the enemy's artillery, were immediately saluted with a shower of round shot and shells. Just at this moment a tumbril or ammunition-waggon coming up, a shell from a French mortar fell upon it; it exploded, and two unfortunate artillery-drivers, who chanced to be sitting upon it, were hurled into the air. I looked at them for a moment after they fell. One was quite dead, and dreadfully mangled; the other was as black as a coal, but he was alive, and groaned heavily. He lifted his head as we passed, and wished us success. What became of him afterwards I know not, but there appeared little chance of his recovery.

Having gained a hollow road, somewhat in advance of the village, we found ourselves in connexion with a line of skirmishers thrown out by Colonel Halket from his corps of light Germans, and in some degree sheltered from the cannonade. But our repose was not of long continuance. The enemy having collected a large force of tirailleurs, advanced, with loud shouts and every show of determination. To remain where we were, was to expose ourselves to the risk of being cut to pieces in a hollow way, the banks of which were higher than our heads, and perfectly perpendicular; the question therefore was, should we retire or advance? Of course, the former idea was not entertained for a moment. We clambered up the face of the bank with some difficulty; and, replying to the shouts of the French with a similar species of music, we pressed on.

When I looked to my right and to my left at this moment, I was delighted with the spectacle which that glance presented. For the benefit of my more peaceable readers, I may as well mention, that troops sent out to skirmish,

65

advance or retire in files; each file, or pair of men, keeping about ten yards from the files on both sides of them. On the present occasion, I beheld a line of skirmishers, extending nearly a mile in both directions, all keeping in a sort of irregular order; and all firing, independently of one another, as the opportunity of a good aim prompted each of them. On the side of the French, again, all was apparent confusion; but the French tirailleurs are by no means in disorder when they appear so. They are admirable skirmishers; and they gave our people, this day, a good deal of employment, before they again betook themselves to the heights. They did not, however, succeed, as I suspect was their design, in drawing us so far from the village as to expose us to the fire of their masked batteries; but having followed them across a few fields only, we once more retired to our hollow road.

It was quite evident, from the numerous solid bodies of troops, which kept their ground along the enemy's line, that the plan of Lord Wellington had been perfectly successful; and that no force had been sent from the right of Soult's army to the assistance of his left. The continual roar of musketry and of cannon, which was kept up in that direction, proved, at the same time, that a more serious struggle was going on there than any to which we were exposed. It was no rapid, but intermitting rattle, like that which we and our opponents from time to time produced; but an unceasing volley, as if men were able to fire without loading, or took no time to load. At length Soult appeared to have discovered that he had little to dread upon his right. About three o'clock, we could, accordingly, observe a heavy column, of perhaps ten or twelve thousand men, beginning its march to the left; and at the same instant, as if to cover the movement, the enemy's skirmishers again advanced. Again we met them, as we had done before, and again drove them in; when, instead of falling back to the hollow way, we lay down behind a hedge, half-way between the village and the base of their position. From this they made several attempts to dislodge us, but without effect, and here we remained till the approach of darkness put an end to the battle.

The sun had set about an hour, when the troops in advance were everywhere recalled; and I and my companions returned to the village. Upon it we found that the enemy still kept up an occasional fire of cannon; and hence, that the houses, which were extremely thin, furnished no sufficient shelter for the troops. It was accordingly determined to canton the corps, for the night, in the church, the walls of that building being of more solid materials, and proof against the violence of at least field artillery. Thither, therefore, we all repaired, and here I had the satisfaction to find that our Portuguese follower had arrived before us, so that a comfortable meal was prepared. Provisions and grog were likewise issued out to the men, and all was now jollity and mirth.

The spectacle which the interior of the church or Urogne presented this night, was one which the pious founder of the fabric probably never calculated upon its presenting. Along the two side aisles, the arms of the battalion were piled, whilst the men themselves occupied the centre aisle. In the pulpit was placed the large drum and other musical instruments, whilst a party of officers took possession of a gallery erected at the lower extremity of the building. For our own parts, Gray and myself asserted a claim to the space around the altar, which, in an English church, is generally railed in, but which, in foreign churches, is distinguished from the rest of the chancel only by its elevation. Here we spread out our cold salt beef, our brown bread, our cheese, and our grog; and here we eat and drank, in that state of excited feeling which attends every man who has gone safely through the perils of such a day.

Nor was the wild nature of the spectacle around us diminished by the gloomy and wavering light, which thirty or forty small rosin tapers cast over it. Of these, two or three stood beside us, upon the altar, whilst the rest were scattered about, by ones and twos, in different places, leaving every interval in a sort of shade, which gave a wider scope to the imagination than to the senses. The buzz of conversation, too, the frequent laugh and joke, and, by and by, the song, as the grog began to circulate, all these combined to produce a scene too striking to be soon forgotten.

As time passed on, all these sounds became gradually more and more faint. The soldiers, wearied with their day's work, dropped asleep, one after another, and I, having watched them for a while, stretched out like so many corpses upon the paved floor of the church, wrapped my cloak round me, and prepared to follow their example. I laid myself at the foot of the altar, and though the marble was not more soft than marble usually is, I slept as soundly upon it as if it had been a bed of down.

Chapter 9

St Jean-de-Luz is Occupied

With their left flank turned, the French retire. Gleig's detachment enters the undamaged Château de Urtubie, recently Soult's Headquarters, which still stands adjacent to the old highway (now the N10) just north of Urrugne. Gleig admits to having 'borrowed' a book from its library, and is astonished to find a letter from his father there among those taken from an intercepted courier. Ciboure, on the Nivelle facing St Jean-de-Luz, is entered: by noon the Allied troops had crossed and occupied the small port, which was to remain Wellington's Headquarters for the next three months. The advance was halted on approaching the coastal village of Bidart, in the vicinity of which the 5th Division was later posted.

We had slept about four or five hours, and the short hours of the morning were beginning to be lengthened, when our slumbers were disturbed by the arrival of a messenger from the advanced piquets, who came to inform us that the enemy were moving. As we had lain down in our clothes, with all our accoutrements on, we were under arms, and in column, in five seconds. It was not, however, deemed necessary that any advance on our part should be instantly attempted. We remained, on the contrary, quiet in the church; but standing in our ranks, we were perfectly ready to march to any quarter where the sound of firing might bespeak our presence necessary.

We had stood thus about half an hour, when a second messenger from the out-posts came in, from whom we learned, that a blue light had been thrown up within the enemy's lines, and that their fires were all freshly trimmed. "Is it so?" said some of our oldest veterans; "then there will be no work for us to-day – they are retreating"; and so sure enough it proved. As soon as dawn began to appear, a patrole was sent forward, which returned immediately to state, that not a vestige of the French army was to be found. The outposts and sentries were withdrawn, their baggage was all gone, and the whole of the right wing had disappeared.

The fact was, that Lord Wellington's scheme had succeeded according to his expectations. The right of our army, after some very hard fighting, turned the enemy's left; took possession of most of his redoubts, and got into his rear; which compelled Marshal Soult, sorely against his inclination, to abandon a position more tenable than any which he had yet occupied. Towards his right, indeed, as I have already mentioned, it would have been little short of madness seriously to have attacked him; nor could his left have been broken, but for the skilful manoeuvring on our part, which hindered any reinforcements from being sent to it. This object being obtained, however, to remain, at least with safety, even for a single day longer, on his ground, was impossible, and hence Soult only showed his wisdom and sound judgment by seizing the first favourable opportunity to retire.

The intelligence of the enemy's retreat was received, as such intelligence is usually received, with great satisfaction. Not that we felt the smallest disinclination to renew the battle – quite the reverse; but there is something in the idea of pursuing a flying enemy, far more exhilarating than in any other idea to which the human mind gives harbour; and this we experienced, on the present occasion, to its full extent. We had scarcely learned that the French troops had deserted their works, when an order arrived to advance; and that we prepared to obey with the most hearty good will.

Whilst the men were swallowing a hasty meal, preparatory to the commencement of the march, I went, with two or three others, to visit the spot where we had deposited such of our messmates as fell in the battle yesterday. It is not often that a soldier is so fortunate – if, indeed, the thing be worth esteeming fortunate – as to be laid to his last rest in consecrated ground. Our gallant comrades enjoyed that privilege on the present occasion. The soldiers had collected them from the various spots where they lay, and brought them in, with a sort of pious respect, to the churchyard. Here they dug a grave – one grave, it is true, for more than one body; but what boots it? and here they entombed them, carefully tearing up the green sod, and carefully replacing it upon the hillock. For my own part, I had little time to do more than wish rest to their souls; for the corps was already in motion, and in five minutes we were in the line of march.

It was as yet quite dark, consequently objects could not be distinguished at any considerable distance; but the farther we proceeded, the more strongly the day dawned upon us. Having cleared the village, we came to a bridge thrown across a little brook, for the possession of which a good deal of fighting had taken place towards evening on the day before. Here we found several French soldiers lying dead, as well as one of our own men, who had ventured too far in pursuit of the enemy. A little way beyond the bridge, again, and to the left of the road, stood a neat chateau of some size. This our advanced party was ordered to search; and, as I chanced to be in command of the detachment, the office of conducting the search devolved upon me.

I found the house furnished after the French fashion, and the furniture in a state of perfect preservation; nor did I permit the slightest injury to be done to it by my men. The only article, indeed, which I was guilty of plundering, was a Grammar of the Spanish language, thus entitled, "Grammaire et Dictionnaire François et Espagnol – Nouvellement Revû, Corrigé et Augmenté par Monsieur de Maunory: Suivant l'Usage de la Cour d'Espagne". Upon one of the boards is written, *Appartient a Lassalle Briguette, Lassalee.* The book is still in my possession, and as our countries are now at peace, I take this opportunity of informing Mr Briguette, that I am quite ready to restore to him his property, provided he will favour me with his address.

The room from which I took the volume just alluded to was the library, and by no means badly stored with books. I had not, however, much time to decipher the title-pages, for, independently of the necessity under which I lay of pushing forward as soon as I had ascertained that none of the enemy were secreted here, my attention was attracted by a mass of letters scattered over the floor. The reader may judge of my surprise, when, on lifting one to examine its contents, I found it to be in the hand-writing of my own father, and addressed to myself. It was of a later date, too, than any communication which I had received from home; and beside it were lying about twenty others, directed to different officers in the same division with myself. This let me into a secret. The house in which I now stood had been the official head-quarters of Marshal Soult. A courier, who was bringing letters from Lord Wellington's head-quarters, had been cut off by a patrole of the enemy's cavalry; and hence all our epistles, including sundry *billets-doux* from fair maidens at home, had been subjected to the scrutiny of the French marshal and his staff.

Leaving other letters to their fate, I put my own in my pocket, and, stuffing my volume of plunder into my bosom, pushed on. About a hundred yards in the rear of the chateau we arrived at the first line of works, consisting of a battery for two guns, with a deep trench in front of it. It was flanked, both on the right and left, by farm-houses, with a good deal of plantation, and a couple of garden walls, and would have cost our people no inconsiderable loss had we been fool-hardy enough to attack it. This battery was erected just upon the commencement of the rising ground. On passing it, we found ourselves on the face of a bare hill, about the length, perhaps, of Shooter's Hill, and not dissimilar in general appearance, the summit of which was covered by three redoubts, connected the one with the other by two open batteries. As we passed these, we could not but remark to ourselves, how painful must have been the feelings of the French general, when he found himself compelled to abandon his works, without an opportunity being given of putting their utility to the proof; and we, of course, paid the compliments, which were his due, to our own leader, who, by his judicious arrangements, had rendered these works perfectly unprofitable.

We had just cleared the entrenchments, when a cry arose from the rear, "Make way for the cavalry!" Our men accordingly inclined to the right of the road, when the 12th and 16th light dragoons rode past at a quick trot, sending out half a troop before them to feel their way. The object of this movement, as we afterwards found, was to hinder, if possible, the destruction of the bridge at St Jean de Luz. But the attempt succeeded only in part, the enemy having already set fire to their train.

"Push on, push on," was now the word. We accordingly quickened our pace, and reached St Jean de Luz about nine o'clock; but we were too late to secure a passage of the Nivelle, the bridge being completely in ruins. Our cavalry had reached it only in time to see the mine exploded which the French troops had dug in its centre arch; and hence a halt became absolutely necessary, till the chasm thus created should be filled up. The effect was remarkably striking. The whole of the first and fifth divisions, with the King's German legion, several brigades of Portuguese, and two divisions of Spanish troops, came pouring up, till the southern suburb of St Jean de Luz was filled with armed men, to the number of perhaps twenty or thirty thousand.

It is probably needless for me to say, that we found St Jean de Luz, for the most part, abandoned by its inhabitants. A few indeed remained; and these consulting, as under such circumstances people are justified in consulting, their own safety only, welcomed us by waving their handkerchiefs from the windows, and shouting, *Vivent les Anglois!* Those who thus met us were, however, of the lowest description, all the gentry and municipality having fled; though they, too, returned after a few days, and placed themselves under our protection. They were faithfully guarded against insult; nor were our soldiers permitted to exact anything from the inhabitants without paying for it whatever was demanded.

Whilst we were waiting till the bridge should be so far repaired as to permit the infantry to cross, I happened to stray a little from the main street, and beheld, in a lane which ran parallel with the river, a spectacle exceedingly shocking. I saw no fewer than fifty-three donkeys standing with the sinews of the hinder legs cut through. On inquiring from an inhabitant the cause of this, he told me, that these poor brutes, being overloaded with the baggage of the French army, had knocked up; when the soldiers, rather than suffer them to fall into our hands in a serviceable condition, hamstrung them all. Why they were not merciful enough to shoot them, I know not; unless, indeed, they were apprehensive of causing an alarm among us by the report; but what their caution hindered we performed. The poor creatures were all shot dead ere we advanced.

The town of St Jean de Luz covers about as much ground, and, I should imagine, contains about as many inhabitants, as Carlisle or Canterbury. It is divided into two parts by the river Nivelle, which falls into the sea about a couple or three miles below, at a village, or rather port, called

Secoa. Like other French towns of its size, St Jean de Luz is not remarkable for its air of neatness; but there is a good market-place in it, two or
three churches, and a theatre. The Nivelle, where it flows through the city,
may be about the width of the Eden, or the Isis; it is rendered passable,
and the two quarters of the city are connected, by a stone bridge of three
arches; besides which, the stream itself is fordable, both for cavalry and
infantry, at low water. When we came in this morning the tide was up, but
it had been for some time on the turn; and hence, in about a couple of
hours, we were perfectly independent of the repairs. By this time, however,
the broken arch had been united by means of planks and beams of wood;
but as the junction was none of the most firm, it was deemed prudent to
send the troopers through the water, whilst the infantry only should cross
by the bridge. Along with the cavalry was sent the artillery also; and thus,
by noon, on the 11th of November, the whole of the left column had
passed the Nivelle.

We had hardly quitted St Jean de Luz, when the weather, which during
the entire morning had looked suspicious, broke; and a cold heavy rain
began to fall. This lasted without any intermission till dark; by which
means our march became the reverse of agreeable, and we felt as if we
would have given the enemy a safe-conduct as far as Bayonne, in return
for permission to halt, and dry ourselves before a fire. But of halting no
hint was dropped, nor was it till our advanced-guard came up with the
rear of the French army, posted in the village of Bedart, and the heights
adjoining, that any check was given to our progress. As it was now late,
the sun having set, and twilight coming on, it was not judged expedient to
dislodge the enemy till morning; in consequence of which our troops were
commanded to halt. There was, however, no cover for them. Only a few
cottages stood near the road, and the tents were at least fourteen miles in
the rear; this night was accordingly spent by most of us on the wet ground.

From the moment that the rain began to fall, we remarked that
the Spanish, and in some instances the Portuguese troops, setting the
commands of their officers at defiance, left their ranks, and scattered themselves over the face of the country. Whilst this was going on, I have good
reason to believe that several horrible crimes were perpetrated. Of the
French peasants, many, trusting to our proclamations, remained quietly in
their houses; these were in too many instances plundered and cruelly
treated by the marauders, who were, I suspect, urged on to the commission of numerous atrocities, by a feeling far more powerful than the desire
of plunder. Revenge – a strong and overwhelming thirst of vengeance,
drew, I am convinced, many to the perpetration of the most terrible deeds;
indeed, one case of the kind came under my own immediate notice, which
I shall here relate.

About three o'clock this afternoon, a temporary check took place in the
line of march, when the corps to which I belonged was about two miles

distant from Bedart. A brigade of cavalry alone was in front of us. A Portuguese brigade, including one regiment of caçadores, was in our rear. Whilst we were standing still in our places, the caçadore regiment, breaking its ranks, rushed in a tumultuous manner towards two or three cottages on the left of the road. The officers with the utmost difficulty recalled them, but a few individuals, as the event proved, succeeded in their effort of insubordination. These, however, were not noticed at the time, and it was thought that all were where they ought to be.

A little way, perhaps a couple of hundred yards in front, stood another French cottage, surrounded by a garden, and perfectly detached from all others. In about five minutes after order had been restored, we heard a female shriek come from that cottage. It was followed by the report of a musket, and ere we had time to reach the spot, another shot was fired. We ran up, and found a poor old French peasant lying dead at the bottom of the garden. A bullet had passed through his head, and his thin grey hairs were dyed with his own blood. We hastened towards the house, and just as we neared the door, a caçadore rushed out, and attempted to elude us. But he was hotly pursued and taken. When he was brought back, we entered the cottage, and to our horror, we saw an old woman, in all probability the wife of the aged peasant, lying dead in the kitchen.

The desperate Portuguese pretended not to deny having perpetrated these murders. He seemed, on the contrary, wound up to a pitch of frenzy. – "They murdered my father, they cut my mother's throat, and they ravished my sister," said he, "and I vowed at the time that I would put to death the first French family that fell into my hands. You may hang me, if you will, but I have kept my oath, and I care not for dying." It is unnecessary to add that the man was hanged; indeed, no fewer than eighteen Spanish and Portuguese soldiers were tucked up, in the course of this and the following days, to the branches of trees. But I could not at the time avoid thinking, that if any shadow of excuse for murder can be framed, the unfortunate Portuguese who butchered this French family, deserves the benefit of it.

I have said that the greater part of the left column spent this night in no very comfortable plight, upon the wet ground. For ourselves, we were moved into what had once been a grass field, just at the base of the hill of Bedart; but which, with the tread of men's feet and horses' hoofs, was now battered into mud. Here, with the utmost difficulty, we succeeded in lighting fires, round which we crowded as we best might. But the rain still came down in torrents, and though our lad arrived shortly after with the cloaks, and rations of beef, and biscuit, and rum, were issued out to us, I cannot enumerate this among the nights of pure enjoyment, which my life, as a soldier, has frequently brought in my way.

Chapter 10

'. . . lying in a puddle'

On 18 November the 85th retired to their cantonments, probably on higher ground inland from Guéthary (not Gauthong). 'Garret's House' refers to the Château d'Urdainz (skirted by the D932 between Bassussarry and the Nive), the property of the Revolutionary politician Dominique Garat (d. 1833). General Baron Alton refers to Count Karl (Charles) von Alten; he had commanded the 7th Division from October 1811 until transferred to the Light Division in the following May on the death of General Craufurd. Wellington considered Alten to be 'the best of the Hanoverians'.

When I awoke next morning, I found myself lying in a perfect puddle, beside the decaying embers of a fire. The rain had come down so incessantly, and with such violence during the night, that my cloak, though excellent of its kind, stood not out against it; and I was now as thoroughly saturated with water as if I had been dragged through the Nivelle. Of course, my sensations were not of a very pleasant nature; but I considered that I was far from singular in my condition, and, like my comrades, I laughed at an evil for which there was no remedy.

Having remained under arms till day had fully dawned, we began to make ready for a farther advance. When we lay down on the preceding evening, several brigades of French troops were in possession of the village of Bedart. These we naturally laid our account with attacking; but on sending forward a patrol, it was found that the village had been abandoned, and that Soult had fallen back to his entrenched camp, in front of Bayonne. Our parade was accordingly dismissed, and we remained in the same situation for about four hours; when the arrival of the tents and baggage invited us to make ourselves somewhat more comfortable. For this purpose the brigade was moved about a quarter of a mile to the left of the main road; and there, on a skirt of turf comparatively sound and unbroken, the camp was pitched.

In the immediate vicinity of the tents stood a small farm-house, or rather a large cottage, containing three rooms and a kitchen. Hither a good many of the officers, and myself among the number, removed their canteens and portmanteaus; till no fewer than forty-five individuals, including servants

74

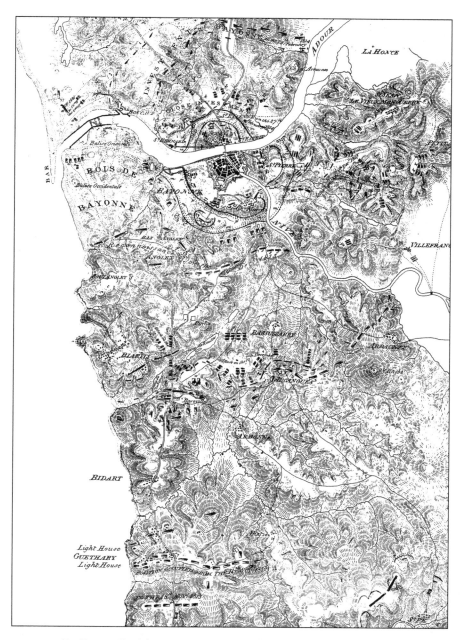

5. From Guéthary to Bayonne (detail from Batty's Map)

as well as masters, found a temporary shelter under its roof. I am sure, after all, that I was not more comfortable here than I should have been in my tent; but I fancied that to sleep upon a bed once more, even though that bed was a French one, would prove a luxury; and I made the experiment. It is needless to add, that the bed contained whole hordes of living occupants besides myself; and that I presumed not again to dispute with them the possession of their ancient domain.

From the 12th to the 17th November nothing occurred to myself, nor were any movements made by the left of the British army worthy of being repeated. The rain continued with hardly any interruption during the whole of that time, rendering the cross roads utterly impassable for artillery, and holding out no prospect of fresh battles or fresh adventures. It was, indeed, manifest, that the troops could not be kept much longer in the field, without material injury to their health, which began already to be threatened with dysentery and ague. Nor is it surprising, that the case should be so; for the tents were not proof against showers so heavy and so incessant as those which fell; and canvass, when once completely soaked, admits water to pass through it like a sieve. The consequence was, that our men were never dry, and many began to exhibit symptoms of the complaints above alluded to.

Under these circumstances we received, with sincere rejoicing, an order in the evening of the 17th, to strike our tents at dawn next morning, and to march into winter-quarters. The rain descended, however, in such torrents, that though a temporary inconvenience promised to lead to permanent comfort, it was deemed prudent to delay fulfilling that order, for at least some hours. We accordingly remained quiet till about one o'clock in the afternoon of the 18th, when the weather breaking up, and the sun shining out, our camp was struck, and we turned our faces towards the cantonments which had been allotted to us.

Having cleared the few fields which intervened between the situation of the camp and the high road, we left Bedart behind, and took a retrograde direction towards St Jean de Luz. We had not, however, proceeded about five or six miles, and were still a full league distant from the town, when, on reaching a cross road, which run in a direction to the left, we filed off by it, and made for a piece of elevated country, over which about half a dozen farm-houses were scattered. These were assigned to the corps to which I belonged. We accordingly halted on a sort of common, near the centre of them, and having cast lots as to which house should fall to the share of the different companies, Gray, myself, and two others, with about one hundred men, took possession of one, with which we were perfectly satisfied.

It would be difficult for an ordinary reader to form any adequate notion of the extreme satisfaction which soldiers experience, when first they establish themselves in winter-quarters. As long as the weather continues fine, and summer suns shed their influence over it, there are, indeed, few places more agreeable than a camp. But it is not so after the summer has departed. I have already hinted, that against heavy and continued rains, a tent supplies but a very inadequate shelter. A tent is, moreover, but a narrow chamber, in which it is not easy so much as to stand upright, excepting in one spot; and where all opportunity of locomotion is denied. It furnishes, moreover, little protection against cold, to light a fire within being impossible, on account of the smoke; and hence the only means of keeping yourself warm is, to wrap your cloak or a blanket about you, and to lie down. Occasionally, indeed, I have seen red-hot shot employed as heaters; but the kind of warmth which arises from heated iron is, at least to me, hardly more agreeable than that which is produced by charcoal. In a word, however enthusiastic a man may be in his profession, he begins, about the end of October or the beginning of November, to grow heartily tired of campaigning; and looks forward to a few weeks' rest, and a substantial protection against cold and damps, with almost as much pleasure as he experiences when the return of spring calls him once more into the field.

The farm-houses in the south of France, like those in the neighbouring country of Spain, are rarely provided with fire-places in any other apartment besides the kitchen. It is, indeed, customary for families to live, during the winter months, entirely with their servants; and hence the want of a fire-place in the parlour is not felt any more than in the bed-rooms. I observed, likewise, that hardly any maison of the kind was furnished with glazed windows; wooden lattices being almost universally substituted. These, during the summer months, are kept open all day, and closed only at night; and I believe that the extreme mildness of the climate renders an open window, at such seasons, very agreeable. On the present occasion, however, we anticipated no slight annoyance from the absence of these two essential matters, a chimney and a window in our room; and we immediately set our wits to work for the removal of both causes of complaint.

Both Gray's servant and my own chanced to be exceedingly ingenious fellows; the former, in particular, could, to use a vulgar phrase, turn his hand to anything. Under his directions we set a party of men to work, and knocking a hole through one corner of our room, we speedily converted it into a fire-place. To give vent to the smoke, we took the trouble to build an external chimney, carrying it up as high as the roof of the house; and our pride and satisfaction were neither of them trifling, when we found that it drew to admiration. I mean not to commend the masonry for its elegance, nor to assert that the sort of buttress now produced added in any degree to the general appearance of the house; but it had the effect of rendering our apartment exceedingly comfortable, and that was the sole object which we had in view.

Having thus provided for our warmth, the next thing to be done was to manufacture such a window as might supply us with light, and at the same time resist the weather. For this purpose we lifted a couple of lattices from their hinges; and having cut out four pannels in each, we covered the spaces with white paper soaked in oil. The light thus admitted was not, indeed, very brilliant, but it was sufficient for all our purposes; and we found, when the storm again returned, that our oil-paper stood out against it stoutly. Then, having swept our floor, unpacked and arranged the contents of our canteen, and provided good dry hay-sacks for our couches, we felt as if the whole world could have supplied no better or more desirable habitation.

To build the chimney, and construct the window, furnished occupation enough for one day; the next was spent in cutting wood, and laying in a store of fuel against the winter. In effecting this, it must be confessed, that we were not over fastidious as to the source from which it was derived; and hence a greater number of fruit trees were felled and cut to pieces, than, perhaps, there was any positive necessity to destroy. But it is impossible to guard against every little excess, when troops have established themselves in any enemy's country; and the French have just cause of thankfulness, that so little comparative devastation marked the progress of our armies. Their own, it is well known, were not remarkable for their orderly conduct in such countries as they overran.

I have dwelt upon these little circumstances longer, perhaps, than their insignificance in the eyes of my reader may warrant; but I could not help it. There is no period of my life on which I look back with more unmixed pleasure, than that which saw me, for the first time, set down in winter-quarters. And hence every trifling event connected with it, however unimportant to others, appears the reverse of unimportant to me. And such, I believe, is universally the case, when a man undertakes to be his own biographer. Things and occurrences which, to the world at large, seem wholly undeserving of record, his own feelings prompt him to detail with unusual minuteness, even though he may be conscious all the while that he is entering upon details which his readers will scarcely take the trouble to follow.

Having thus rendered our quarters as snug as they were capable of being made, my friend and myself proceeded daily into the adjoining woods in search of game; and as the frost set in, we found them amply stored, not only with hares and rabbits, but with cocks, snipes, and other birds of passage. We were not, however, so fortunate as to fall in with any of the wild boars which are said to frequent these thickets, though we devoted more than one morning to the search; but we managed to supply our own table, and the table of several of our comrades, with a very agreeable addition to the lean beef which was issued out to us. Nor were other luxuries wanting. The peasantry, having recovered their confidence, returned

San Sebastián, with the British artillery firing from the summit of Monte Ulia. *Published by Edward Orme.*

View of the fortress after the siege. The height of Monte Urgull – now more wooded – is somewhat exaggerated. *Edward Hawke Locker.*

An early 19th century view of the inlet at Pasajes.

The Guards fording the Bidasoa on 7 October 1813 (detail). *Robert Batty.*

Allied troops forded the estuary of the Bidasoa from a position in the foreground. Fuenterrabía is in the distance (detail). *Edward Hawke Locker.*

The Crown Mountain (top right of centre) from the heights of San Marcial (detail). *Robert Batty.*

Irún, with supplies being unloaded from mules of the commissariat (detail). *Robert Batty.*

The hutted encampment captured near Urrugne, looking west, with the mouth of the Bidasoa in the distance (detail). *Robert Batty.*

The quay at St Jean-de-Luz; Wellington's Headquarters were established in the right-hand mansion. *Robert Batty.*

The 85th attacking redoubts during the battle of the Nivelle. The line of hills would have been much steeper. *Richard Simkin.*

General Sir John Hope.
Detail from a portrait after Raeburn in a private Scottish collection.

The Château d'Urtubie (close to Urrugne).

A view of Bayonne from sandhills to the west, near which was the bridge of boats (detail). *Published by Edward Orme.*

The bridge of boats across the Adour below Bayonne. *Robert Batty.*

Detail of an early 19th century view of the citadel of Bayonne.

Looking south from the suburb of St Etienne towards the citadel, with La Rhune rising in the distance to the left (detail). *Robert Batty.*

in great numbers to their homes, and seldom failed to call at our mansion once or twice a-week, with wine, fresh bread, cyder, and bottled beer; by the help of which we continued to fare well as long as our fast-diminishing stock of money lasted. I say fast-diminishing stock of money, for as yet no addition had been made to that which each of us brought with him from England; and though the pay of the army was now six months in arrear, but faint hopes were entertained of any immediate donative.

It was not, however, among regimental and other inferior officers alone, that this period of military inaction was esteemed and acted upon as one of enjoyment. Lord Wellington's fox-hounds were unkennelled; and he himself took the field regularly twice a-week, as if he had been a denizen of Leicestershire, or any other sporting county in England. I need not add, that few packs, in any county, could be better attended. Not that the horses of all the huntsmen were of the best breed, or of the gayest appearance; but what was wanting in individual splendour, was made up by the number of Nimrods; nor would it be easy to discover a field more fruitful in laughable occurrences, which no man more heartily enjoyed than the gallant Marquis himself. When the hounds were out, he was no longer the commander of the forces, the General-in-Chief of three nations, and the representative of three sovereigns; but the gay, merry, country gentleman, who rode at everything, and laughed as loud when he fell himself, as when he witnessed the fall of a brother-sportsman.

Thus passed about twenty days, during the greater number of which the sky was clear, and the air cold and bracing. Occasionally, indeed, we varied our sporting life by visits to St Jean de Luz, and other towns in the rear; and by seeking out old friends in other divisions of the army. Nor were we altogether without military occupation. Here and there a re-doubt was thrown up, for the purpose of rendering our position doubly secure; whilst the various brigades of each division relieved one another in taking the outpost duty. A trifling skirmish or two tended likewise to keep us alive; but these were followed by no movement of importance, nor were they very fatal either to the enemy or ourselves.

The position which Lord Wellington had taken up, extended from the village of Bedart on the left to a place called Garret's House on the right. It embraced various other villages, such as that of Arcanques, Gauthong, etc. etc., between these points, and kept the extremities of the line at a distance of perhaps six or seven miles from each other. To a common observer it certainly had in it nothing imposing, or calculated to give the idea of great natural strength. On the left, in particular, our troops, when called into the field, occupied a level plain; wooded indeed, but very little broken; whilst at different points in the centre there were passes, easy of approach, nor defensible in any extraordinary degree. But its strength was well tried, as I shall occasion shortly to relate, and the issue of the trial proved that no error had been committed in its selection.

Of the manner in which the right and centre columns were disposed, I knew but little. The left column consisting of the first and fifth divisions; of two or three brigades of Portuguese infantry, one brigade of light and one of heavy cavalry, was thus posted: The town of St Jean de Luz, in which Lord Wellington had fixed his quarters, was occupied by three or four battalions of guards; its suburbs were given up to such corps of the German legion as were attached to the first division. In and about the town, the light cavalry was likewise quartered; whilst the heavy was sent back to Andaye and the villages near it, on account of the facility of procuring forage, which there existed. The Spaniards again had fallen back as far as Irun, and were not brought up during the remainder of the winter; but the Portuguese regiments were scattered, as we were scattered, among a number of detached cottages near the road. In the village of Bedart was posted the fifth division, with three or four pieces of field artillery, and the men and horses attached to them; and to it, the duty of watching the enemy, and keeping possession of the ground on which the piquets stood, was committed. Thus along the line of the high-road was housed a corps of about fifteen thousand infantry, twelve hundred cavalry, and a due proportion of artillery; all under the immediate command of Sir John Hope.

In direct communication with the head of this column, was the light division, under the command of Major-General Baron Alton. It consisted of the 52nd, 43rd, and 95th regiments, of a brigade or two of caçadores, and mustered in all about four or five thousand bayonets. These occupied the church and village of Arcanques, situated upon a rising ground, and of considerable natural strength. Beyond this division again lay the 4th; in connexion with which were the 3rd, the 7th, and the 2nd divisions, whilst the 6th took post a little in the rear, and acted as a reserve, in case a reserve should be wanting.

I have said that Lord Wellington's head-quarters were in the town of St Jean de Luz. Here also Sir John Hope, and several generals of division and of brigade, established themselves; and here all the general staff of the army was posted. Of course the place was kept in a place of warlike gaiety, such as it had not probably witnessed before, at least in modern times; but everything was done which could be done to conciliate the affections of the inhabitants; nor was the slightest outrage or riot permitted. Such is the manner in which the British army was disposed of, from the 18th of November, when it first went into cantonments, till the 9th of December, when it was found necessary once more to take the field.

Chapter 11

The Battle of the Nive

At dawn on 9 December the Allied army made a concentric advance towards Bayonne. Hill's 'Corps', forming the Right Wing, forded the Nive and thrust north towards the Adour river, while the 3rd and 6th Divisions under Marshal Beresford crossed the Nive further downstream. The French opposing them retired. The Left Wing had been ordered to make a reconnaissance in force only towards the entrenched camp of Beyris (between Anglet and Bayonne), but to remain out of range of enemy batteries and, after leaving a line of outposts, to pull back. Aylmer's Brigade and the 1st Division were then marched back to their quarters, which had been withdrawn far too distant – some ten miles – from the front. Only Campbell's and Bradford's Portuguese troops, together with units from Robinson's Brigade of the 5th Division had been left to withstand the French onslaught next day.

I had been out with my gun during the whole of the 8th of December, and returned at a late hour in the evening, not a little weary with wandering, when the first intelligence communicated to me was, that the corps had received orders to be under arms at an early hour next morning, when the whole of the army should advance. In a former chapter, I have hinted, that a continued tract of rainy weather drove Lord Wellington earlier than he had designed, and against his inclination, into winter-quarters. The consequence was, that the position of the army was not in every respect to his mind. The right, in particular, was too far thrown back; and the course of the Nivelle interfered in a very inconvenient degree with the communication between it and the left. We were accordingly given to understand, that the object of our present movement was merely to facilitate the crossing of that river by Sir Rowland Hill's corps, and that as soon as this object was attained, we should be permitted to return in peace to our comfortable quarters.

In consequence of this information, Gray and myself made fewer preparations than we had been in the habit of making on other and similar occasions. Instead of packing up our baggage, and ordering out our sumpter-pony and faithful Portuguese, as we had hitherto done, we left

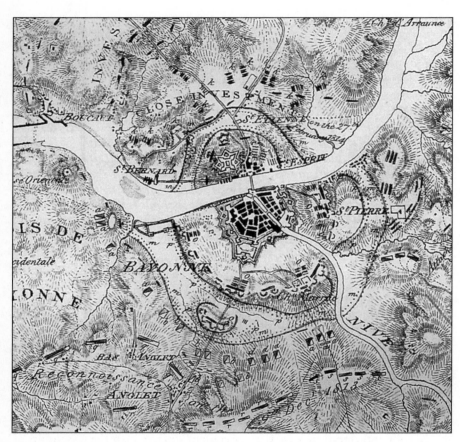

6. Bayonne (enlarged detail from Batty's Map)

everything in our apartment in its ordinary condition. Strict charges were indeed given to the servants, that a cheerful fire and a substantial meal should be prepared against our return in the evening; but we put up neither food nor clothes for immediate use, in full expectation that such things would not be required.

The night of the 8th passed quietly over, and I arose about two hours before dawn on the 9th, perfectly fresh, and, like those around me, in high spirits. We had been so long idle, that the near prospect of a little fighting, instead of creating gloomy sensations, was viewed with sincere delight; and we took our places, and began our march towards the high-road, in silence, it is true, but with extreme good will. There we remained stationary till the day broke; when the word being given to advance, we rushed forward in the direction of Bayonne.

The brigade to which I belonged took post at the head of the 1st division, and immediately in the rear of the 5th. This situation afforded to me, on several occasions, as the inequalities of the road placed me, from time to time, on the summit of an eminence, very favourable opportunities of beholding the whole of the warlike mass which was moving; nor is it easy to imagine a more imposing or more elevating spectacle. The entire left wing of the army advanced, in a single continuous column, by the main road, and covered, at the most moderate computation, a space of four miles. As far, indeed, as the eye could reach, nothing was to be seen except swarms of infantry, clothed not only in scarlet, but in green, blue, and brown uniforms; whilst here and there a brigade of four or six guns occupied a vacant space between the last files of one division and the first of another. In rear of all came the cavalry; but of their appearance I was unable accurately to judge, they were so distant.

We had proceeded about five miles, and it was now seven o'clock, when, our advanced guard falling in with the French piquets, a smart skirmish began. It was really a beautiful sight. The enemy made, it is true, no very determined stand, but they gave not up a rood of ground, without exchanging a few shots with their assailants; who pressed forward, vigorously indeed, but with all the caution and circumspection which mark the advance of a skilful skirmisher. The column, in the meanwhile, moved slowly but steadily on; nor was it once called upon, during the whole of the day, to deploy into line.

When the light troops of an army are engaged, as ours were this morning, the heavy infantry is necessitated to march at a slow rate; whilst, ever and anon, a short halt or check takes place. These halts occurred to-day with unusual frequency. The fact, I believe, was, that Lord Wellington had no desire to bring his left into determined action at all. His object was fully attained as long as he kept the right of the enemy in a state of anxiety and irresolution, but the ground which we gained was in no degree important to the furtherance of the sole design which he had in view. Of course, the tardiness of our motions gave a better opportunity of watching the progress of those connected with us; nor have I ever beheld a field-day at home more regularly and more elegantly gone through, than this trifling affair of the 9th of December.

It was getting somewhat late, perhaps it might be three or four o'clock in the afternoon, when our column, having overcome all opposition, halted on some rising ground, about three miles from the walls of Bayonne. From this point we obtained a perfect view of the out-works of that town, as well as of the formidable line of fortifications which Soult had thrown up, along the course of the Adour; but of the city itself we saw but little, on account of several groves of lofty elm and other trees which intervened. It will readily be imagined that we turned our glasses towards the entrenched camp with feelings very different from those which actuate an ordinary observer of the face of a strange country. That the French marshal had been at work upon these lines, not only from the moment of his last defeat, but from the very first day of his assuming the command of the army of Spain, we were quite aware; and hence we were by no means surprised at beholding such an obstacle presented to our farther progress in France. But I cannot say that the sight cast even a damp upon our usual confidence. We knew that whatever could be done to render these mighty preparations useless, our gallant general would effect; and perhaps we were each of us vain enough to believe, that nothing could resist our own individual valour. Be that as it may, though we freely acknowledged that many a brave fellow must find a grave ere these works could come into our possession, we would have advanced to the attack at the instant, not only without reluctance, but with the most perfect assurance of success.

The sound of firing had now gradually subsided; the enemy having withdrawn within their entrenchments, and our skirmishers being called in to join their respective corps. The left column, dividing itself according to its brigades, had taken post along a ridge of high ground; and our men, piling their arms, set about lighting fires in all directions; when I wandered from the corps, as my invariable custom was, in search of adventures. I had strolled forward for the purpose of obtaining, if possible, a more perfect view of the enemy's lines; and was stepping across a ditch on my return, when a low groan, as if from some person in acute pain, attracted my notice. I looked down into the ditch, which was, perhaps, four feet deep, and beheld three human beings lying at the bottom of it. They were all perfectly naked, and two of them were motionless. On farther examination, I found that they were three French soldiers, of whom only one was alive; and he lay bleeding from a severe wound in the face, a musket-ball having broken both cheek-bones. He was, however, sensible; so I ran for help, and he was carried by some of our people to a neighbouring house. Here the poor fellow, whom his own countrymen had stripped and deserted, was well taken care of by his enemies; but he had suffered so much from exposure to cold, that all attempts to preserve his life were vain, and he died in about a quarter of an hour after his wound was dressed.

In the meanwhile, Lord Wellington putting himself at the head of a small corps of cavalry, and attended by a few companies of light infantry, proceeded to the front, in order to reconnoitre the enemy's works. This he was permitted to do without any farther molestation than arose from the occasional discharge of a field-gun, as he and his party presented a favourable mark to the gunners. But neither he nor his followers received the slightest injuries from these discharges, and by six in the evening he had effected every object which he desired to effect. Orders were accordingly issued for the troops to fall back to their former quarters, and the main road was again crowded with armed men marching to the rear, in a fashion not perhaps quite so orderly as that which distinguished their advance.

A heavy rain had begun about an hour previous to this movement, accompanied by a cold wind, which blew directly in our faces. Darkness, too, set rapidly in; the road soon became deep and muddy from the trampling of the multitude of men and horses which covered it; and something like an inclination to grumble began to arise in our bosoms. Perhaps I need not tell the reader, that between the infantry and cavalry in the British army, a considerable degree of jealousy exists; the former description of force regarding the latter as little better than useless, the latter regarding the former as extremely vulgar and ungenteel. I was myself an officer of infantry; and I perfectly recollect the angry feelings which were excited at a particular period of the march, when the corps, weary, wet, and hungry, was rudely ordered by a squadron or two of light troopers, to "get out of the way, and allow them to pass".

Recollect, good reader, that the rain was falling as if it had come from buckets; that each infantry soldier carries a load of perhaps fifty pounds weight about his person; that our brave fellows had walked under this load upwards of fourteen miles, and were still six long miles from a place of rest; and you will not wonder that these troopers were saluted with "curses not loud but deep", as they somewhat wantonly jostled their less fortunate comrades into the deepest and dirtiest sides of the way. I must confess that I shared in the indignation of my men; though, of course, I exerted myself as much as possible to prevent its being more openly displayed.

Never has any saloon, when brilliantly lighted up, and filled with all the splendour and elegance of a fashionable assembly, appeared half so attractive to my eyes, as did our own humble apartment this evening, with its carpetless floor, its logs of wood arranged instead of chairs, and a few deals, or rather a piece of scaffolding, placed in the centre as a substitute for a table. A large fire was blazing on the rudely-constructed hearth, which shed a bright glare over the white walls; and our unpolished table being covered with a clean cloth, over which were arranged plates, knives, forks, and drinking-cups, gave promise of a substantial meal, and of an evening of real enjoyment. Nor were our hopes blighted. We had just time to strip off our wet and muddy garments, and to substitute others in their room, when a huge piece of roast-beef smoked upon the board, and summoned us to an occupation more agreeable than any which could have been at that moment proposed to us. Then our faithful valets had taken care to provide an ample supply of wine; a bottle or two of champaigne, with claret of no mean quality, which, with a little French beer, brisk, and weak, and well flavoured, served exceedingly well to wash down the more solid portions of our repast. To complete the thing, a few of our most intimate companions dropping in, soon after the fragments had been cleared away, our cigars were lighted, and the atmosphere of the apartment became speedily impregnated with the delicious fumes of tobacco; in sending forth the clouds of which, no other interruption took place than was produced by an occasional uplifting of the wine-cups to the lips, and an expression or short ejaculation, indicative of the perfect satisfaction of him who uttered it. I have seen many merry and many happy days and nights both before and since, but an evening of more quiet luxury than this, I certainly do not recollect at any period to have spent.

At length the fatigues of the day began to tell upon us in a degree somewhat too powerful for enjoyment. We had been under arms from four in the morning till nine at night, during the whole of which time, no opportunity of eating had been supplied to us; nor had we been permitted to unbend either our minds or bodies, in any effectual degree. Like other animals who have fasted long, we had all gorged ourselves as soon as the means of so doing were furnished; and hence, the sensation of absolute rest degenerated gradually into languor, and sleep laid his leaden fingers on our eyelids. I do not believe that half-a-dozen sentences of ordinary length had been uttered amongst us, when, about eleven o'clock, our last cup of wine was drained off; and our guests departing each to his own billet, we betook ourselves to our pallets. I need not add that our slumber was thoroughly unbroken.

Chapter 12

The Fighting at Arcangues

Early on the 10th the Allied piquets found themselves overrun by four French divisions. The Light Division retired on Arcangues, hastily forti- fying the château and church there. Meanwhile, Hope's troops further to the west near Barrouillet were equally hard pressed until the 5th Division with Hope in person, followed by Aylmer's Brigade, which after tramping along roads knee-deep in mud, belatedly reached the field, which tilted the precarious balance. The château owned by the Mayor of Biarritz, frequently referred to as 'the Mayor's House', is the Château Barrouillet/ Barroilhet, which survives not far south of the Lac de Mouriscot, between the motorway péage and the N10. In the subsequent confused fighting, partly taking place in woods, casualties among Hope's troops totalled almost 1,500 – of which one officer (Colonel Richard Lloyd of the 84th, who was to be buried upright in the village cemetery at Bidart) and thirty men were from Aylmer's Brigade. The Allies lost more prisoners this day – over 500 – than in any other day of the war, a high proportion of them when the piquets were overwhelmed. Oman has remarked that, 'if the 1st Division and Lord Aylmer's brigade had come up an hour later, the line would have been broken . . . [while] if Hope had kept his reserves at Bidart instead of at St Jean-de-Luz, Soult's attack . . . would never have had the least chance of success'. When writing to Torrens at the Horse Guards concerning Hope's personal rashness, Wellington remarked, 'We shall lose him if he continues to expose himself . . . He places himself among the sharp-shooters, without (as they do) sheltering himself from the enemy's fire. This will not answer . . .' Some 1,400 Germans in the French service deserted, led by Colonel Kruse (who was to command the Nassau con- tingent at Waterloo).

I arose next morning refreshed and vigorous, and prepared to follow my ordinary occupation of shooting. It was a clear frosty day, the sun was shining brightly over-head, and a thousand little birds were rejoicing in the warmth of his beams; my dogs were in high condition; my gun was clean and in good order; and myself big with determination, not to fire in too great a hurry, but to be sure of my aim before I pulled the trigger. Thus attended, and thus animated, I set forth after breakfast; and having previously ascertained the favourite haunt of a hare which had more than once escaped me, I turned my steps towards it. My faithful spaniel had just begun to give tongue, and my fowling-piece was already in a position to be lifted at once to my shoulder, when the report of a single cannon, coming from the front, attracted my attention. I stopped short, but had not time to call in my dog, when another and another discharge took place, mixed with an occasional rattle of musketry. This was warning enough. Though the hare started from her seat, I permitted her to depart in peace, and whistling loudly for my four-footed companions to follow, I ran back towards my quarters. As I proceeded, the firing became every moment more and more heavy, till at length it had increased into an uninterrupted roar.

On reaching the houses I found that the alarm was already given. The bugles were sounding to recall such as might be abroad, and the men were accoutring with all haste. For ourselves, Gray and I took care on the present occasion to make better provision against detention, than we had done the day before; but our baggage we were obliged to leave, to be packed and made ready for moving by our bat-men. Aide-de-camp after aide-de-camp passed in the meanwhile to and fro, one galloping from the front to urge an immediate advance, another galloping from the rear to ascertain how matters were going; whilst the various battalions, as each was equipped and ready, hurried down to the main road, to join its particular brigade.

A quarter of an hour had scarcely elapsed from the moment that the alarm was first given, when we found ourselves marching once more in the same direction, and nearly in the same order, in which we had marched yesterday. Our march had in it, however, even more of deep excitement, than that of the preceding day. We had not proceeded above a mile, when indications of what was going on in front began to present themselves, in the form of baggage, mules, and horses, pouring in all haste and confusion to the rear; whilst a wounded man or two, ever and anon, dragged himself with difficulty in the same direction, and gave, as the wounded invariably give, the most alarming account of the state of affairs. "Push on, push on, for God's sake," said one poor fellow who had been shot in the head, and was lying, rather than sitting, across a horse, "push on, or it will be all over. Forty thousand of the enemy are coming on, and there are not two thousand men up to oppose them." Of course, we quickened our pace with infinite good will.

A group of perhaps twenty wounded privates and officers had passed, when the next body which met us was a detachment of ten sound men and a serjeant, who were conducting to the rear about an hundred French prisoners. These were saluted with a cheer, but even these urged us forward, with the intelligence that the 5th division must soon be overpowered. And now the scene of action began to open upon us. We had passed through Bedart, and were descending the little eminence on which it is built, when the combatants became distinguishable; and a very magnificent, as well as gratifying, spectacle they presented. The merest handful of British troops were opposing themselves, in the most determined manner, to a mass of men, so dense, and so extended, as to cover the whole of the main road, as far as the eye could reach. Our people were, it is true, giving way. They had already maintained a most unequal contest for upwards of two hours, and their numbers, originally small, were fast diminishing. But no sooner had the head of our column shown itself, than their confidence completely returned, and they renewed the struggle with increased alacrity.

The same circumstance which gave fresh courage to our comrades, acted, as may well be supposed, in a directly contrary manner upon the enemy. Not that they fell into confusion, or exhibited any symptoms of dismay; but it was evident, from their mode of proceeding, that their general had lost his confidence of immediate success, and that he deemed it necessary to trust less to the weight of his single column, and to add manoeuvring and skill to brute violence. His attack was accordingly suspended, whilst a battery of ten or twelve guns being hastily brought to the front, opened, not upon the division with which he had been hitherto engaged, but upon us. And I must confess that the guns were well served. The gunners laying them for a particular turning in the road, mowed down some two or three out of each company as it came up, and caused us to suffer no inconsiderable loss long before we arrived within range of musketry.

As soon as we had passed this perilous spot, we abandoned the main road, and turning into an open green field on the right, we wheeled into line. In front of us was a thick wood, for the possession of which our people and the French were warmly struggling. On our side, it was garrisoned by a battalion of Portuguese, and a couple of British regiments, and it was assaulted by a perfect swarm of French tirailleurs; but neither did the latter succeed in driving their opponents through it, nor could the former deliver themselves from the annoyance of continual assaults. It was peculiarly the business of the corps to which I belonged, to give support to the defenders of that wood; for which purpose, company after company was sent forward, as a fresh supply of men became from time to time necessary; whilst two other corps, continuing steadily in line, prepared to use the bayonet with effect, in case our efforts to maintain our ground should prove unavailing.

Even the unwarlike reader will probably understand me, when I say, that the feelings of a man hurried into battle, as we were to-day, are totally different from those of the same man who goes gradually, and as it were preparedly into danger. We had dreamed of nothing less than a general action this morning; and we found ourselves bearing the brunt of it, before we could very well make up our minds as to the proximity of an enemy. Everything was accordingly done, every word spoken, and every movement made, under the influence of that species of excitement, which absolutely shuts out all ideas, except those which spring from the circumstances immediately about you; I mean an apprehension lest your own men shall give way, and an inexpressible eagerness to close with your adversary. Nor were sundry opportunities wanting, of gratifying the last of these desires. We fought, at least where I was stationed, in a thick wood; and more than once it occurred, that we fought hand to hand.

Affairs had continued in this state till about three in the afternoon; when the enemy, as if weary with their fruitless efforts, began to slacken in their exertions, and gradually to fall back. Not very far from the spot where I was posted, stood a chateau, the property of the Mayor of Bearitz; for the occupation of which the French had made, during the morning, several desperate, but unavailing efforts. Towards it, as soon as the firing began to wax faint, Sir John Hope, attended by three or four aides-de-camp and a few orderly dragoons, made his way. He had already mounted to an upper room, for the purpose of observing from thence the enemy's proceedings; his staff and orderlies were lounging about the court-yard, and the few skirmishers which lined the hedge in front were lying down to rest, when a mass of French infantry, which had formed in a hollow road a little to the left, dashed forward. The movement was so rapid, and the force employed so great, that all opposition on the part of the few British troops then up, was overcome; the house was surrounded. Instantly a cry was raised, "Save the general, Save the general," and a rush was made from all quarters towards the chateau; but our assistance was unnecessary. Sir John, seeing what had happened, threw himself upon his horse, and at the head of his mounted attendants charged from the doorway of the court-yard. He received, indeed, no fewer than three musket-balls through his hat, and his horse was so severely wounded, that its strength served only to carry him to a place of safety; but the charge was decisive. Many of the French were sabred, and the little party escaped – and now the fight was renewed on all sides with desperate resolution. Again and again the enemy pressed forward to empty the wood of its defenders and to secure the high-road; but all their efforts failed, and when the approach of darkness compelled the combatants to separate, the two armies occupied almost the same ground which they had occupied when the fighting began.

It were vain for me to attempt any description of the scene which now took place. So vigorous had been the last attack, and so determined our resistance, that when daylight disappeared, the French and allied troops found themselves completely mixed together. Instead of the roar of musketry, my ears were accordingly saluted by shouts and exclamations, delivered in almost every European tongue. French, English, German, Dutch, Spaniards, Portuguese, – the natives, in short, of almost every kingdom were here; and as each called out in his own language as loud as he could bawl, for the purpose of discovering his comrades, and giving evidence of his own situation, a jargon was produced, such as no man has probably listened to before, unless we except the artificers employed of yore in the erection of Babel. So complete, indeed, was the confusion, that neither the one party nor the other made the slightest attempt to avail itself of it for military purposes; on the contrary, we were each of us heartily glad to get rid of our troublesome neighbours, and not a little pleased when order became so far restored, as to permit our taking up a definite position for the night.

The enemy having gradually collected their scattered battalions, retired to the hollow way from which they last emerged. On our part, no movement of importance was made; except that the corps to which I belonged, leaving its original garrison to watch the wood during the hours of darkness, fell back as far as the green field, or rather common, where we had left the rest of the brigade. Here, with numbers considerably diminished, we drew up in line; when the arms being piled, we followed the example of our companions, and lighted large fires, round which men and officers indiscriminately crowded, in groups more or less numerous, according as each fire was capable of affording to them warmth.

I do not recollect to have witnessed, during the whole course of my military career, a more striking warlike spectacle than that which was now before me. Besides my own corps, three battalions of infantry lay stretched in a single green field round their watch-fires, amounting in all to about an hundred. Immediately behind them stood their arms, piled up in regular order, and glancing in the flames, which threw a dark red light across the common, upon the bare branches beyond; about twenty yards in rear, two regiments of cavalry were similarly disposed of, their horses being piqueted in line, and the men seated or lying on the ground. Looking farther back again, and towards the opposite side of the road, the fires of the whole of the fifth and first divisions met the eye; darkened ever and anon, as the soldiers passed between them, or a heap of wood was cast on to feed their brightness. By the light of these fires, I could farther perceive, that the road itself was thronged with artillery and tumbrils; whilst the glaring atmosphere above the wood showed that it too was fully tenanted, and that its occupants were, like ourselves, reposing in an attitude of watchfulness. To complete the picture, the night chanced to be uncommonly dark. Neither moon nor stars were out, and though no rain fell, a considerable fog was in the air, which, hindering the flames from ascending beyond a certain height, caused them to shed a stronger colouring upon the surrounding objects. Then the knowledge that the enemy was at hand, and that we only waited for the dawn of to-morrow, to renew the combat; the whole of these circumstances combined, gave so deep an interest to our situation, that it was long ere I was able to follow the example of my comrades, and lie down. Fatigue, however, at length prevailed over enthusiasm; and having heartily partaken of the meal which our faithful Francisco brought up, I wrapped my cloak about me, and taking my station, like the rest, with my feet towards the fire, I soon fell asleep.

It was still perfectly dark when the general stir among the troops put an end to my repose. The infantry stood to their arms; the cavalry mounted their horses; the artillery-men were at their guns with lighted matches; all in the space of one minute; nor was a single word uttered by any man beyond what was absolutely requisite in issuing orders. Early as it was, however, our fires had all but consumed themselves; they had become dull and red, and they threw not out heat enough to keep our blood greatly above the freezing point; but we bore the intense cold with exemplary patience, in the full assurance of warm work as soon as day-light should appear. Nor is there any hour in the four-and-twenty, as every out-side traveller by a stage-coach must know, so fruitful in intense cold, as that which immediately precedes the dawn. To-day, too, it chanced to freeze, with a cutting wind directly in our faces; nevertheless, our courage was high, and we counted the moments impatiently as they passed, not so much from a sense of our present uncomfortable situation, as from an eager desire to renew the battle.

Day dawned at length, but the enemy made no movement. They were before us as they had been all night, in countless numbers; but, like ourselves, they stood quietly in their ranks, as if they expected to be attacked, rather than to attack. For nearly two hours both armies continued stationary, till Lord Wellington coming up, ordered three Portuguese battalions to advance, with no other design than to bring matters to a crisis. Nor did this movement fail to lead the enemy into a renewal of offensive operations. The Portuguese brigade was gallantly met, and, after a good deal of firing, repulsed; and the repulse of it was followed by a determined assault upon such of our corps as defended the road, and occupied the wood.

Nothing can be more spirited or impetuous than the first attack of French troops. They come on, for a while slowly, and in silence; till, having reached within a hundred yards or two of the point to be assailed, they raise a loud but discordant yell, and rush forward. The advance of their columns is, moreover, covered by a perfect cloud of tirailleurs, who press on, apparently in utter confusion, but with every demonstration of courage; who fire irregularly, it is true, but with great rapidity and precision; and who are as much at home in the art of availing themselves of every species of cover as any light troops in the world. The ardour of the French is, however, admirably opposed by the coolness and undaunted deportment of Britons. On the present occasion, for instance, our people met their assailants exactly as if the whole affair had been a piece of acting, no man quitting his ground, but each deliberately waiting till the word of command was given, and then discharging his piece. Every effort of Marshal Soult to possess himself of the mayor's house, and of the enclosure and wood about it, accordingly proved fruitless; and hence his formidable column, which covered the high-road as far as the eye could reach, was, per force, obliged to halt, and to remain idle.

Matters continued in this state till towards noon, and yet a comparatively trifling number of our troops were engaged. The entire brigade to which I belonged, the brigade of light cavalry, as well as the greater proportion of the first division, had been mere spectators of the valour of others; when the enemy, as if worn out with fatigue, and disheartened by repeated failures, suddenly began to retire. His column of infantry having moved to the rear, till some rising ground in great degree concealed it, seemed to disperse; his guns were withdrawn, and his skirmishers falling back, left our advanced corps in possession of the disputed post. A retreat, indeed, appeared to have fairly commenced; and to many it was matter of surprise that no pursuit was on our side instituted. But our general, by keeping his soldiers steady in their places, showed that he was quite aware of his adversary's intentions; and that he was a far better judge of the measures which it behove him to adopt, than any of the numerous critics who presumed to pass censure upon him. The whole of this movement was no other than a manoeuvre on the part of the French Marshal, to draw our troops from their position, and to enfeeble the centre of our line, by causing the left to be too far advanced; but, although skilfully executed, it proved of no avail, thanks to the superior sagacity of Lord Wellington. Instead of being harassed by any useless change of ground, we were commanded to take advantage of the temporary truce, by cooking our dinners; a measure which the long fast of many of the soldiers, particularly of the Portuguese, who had eaten nothing during the whole of yesterday, rendered peculiarly desirable.

In a moment numerous fires were again lighted, and half of the men in each regiment, disencumbering themselves of their accoutrements, set to work, felling wood, boiling kettles, and preparing food for their comrades. In the meanwhile six or eight spring-waggons arriving, such of the wounded as were unable to crawl to the rear were collected from the various spots where they lay mingled with the dead, and lifted into them, with as much care as circumstances would permit. It was a sad spectacle this. The shrieks and groans of many of these poor fellows sounded horribly in our ears; whilst the absolute silence of the rest was not less appalling, inasmuch as it gave but too much reason to believe, that they were removed from the field only to die in the waggons. Nor were the muleteers, and other followers of the camp, idle. These harpies, spreading themselves in vast numbers over the face of the country, stripped and plundered the dead in an incredibly short space of time; and they were, withal, so skilful in their vocation, that they rarely afforded an opportunity of detecting them in the act. Nothing, indeed, has ever aston-ished me more, than the celerity with which these body-strippers execute their task. A man falls by your side, and the very next moment, if you chance to look round, he is as naked as he was when he came into the world, without your being able so much as to guess by whom his garments have been taken.

Whilst all these persons were engaged in their various occupations, I wandered towards the front, for the purpose of examining, in a moment of coolness, the nature of the ground on which we had yesterday fought. It was literally covered with the carcases of men and horses. Round the mayor's house, in particular, they lay in clusters, and not a few of the Frenchmen bore marks of having fallen by the sabre. One man, in particu-lar, I observed, whose head was cloven asunder, the sword of his adversary having fairly divided it as far as the eyes; whilst another lay upon his back, with his face absolutely split into two parts, across the line of the nose. The great majority had, however, been shot; and they were mixed indis-criminately together, English and French, as if each had been cut off by the hand of his next neighbour.

I was not, however, so fully occupied in contemplating the dead, but that I cast various anxious glances towards the living; nor was ground of anxiety wanting. The enemy had, indeed, fallen back; neither did he show any column upon the road, nor any masses in the woods. But I observed his men crossing the high-road towards our right by two and threes at a time, as if some formation were going on which he desired might escape notice. Nor was the circumstance lost upon my companions; "We shall have it again presently," said a veteran serjeant who stood near me; and the prediction was hardly uttered when it was fulfilled. As if they had risen from beneath the earth, two ponderous masses of infantry, covered by the fire of twelve pieces of cannon, rushed forward; one, a little to the right of where I was, and the other, upon the church and village of Arcanques; and such was the fury of their attack, that, for the instant, they carried every-thing before them. A Portuguese corps, which occupied the former of those parts, was broken, and gave way; a British regiment, stationed to support them, followed their example; and now, for the first time since the battle began, the head of a French column showed itself upon the common.

In the meanwhile, all was hurry and bustle in the rear. The plunderers, taking to their heels, fled in all directions; the waggons with the wounded set off at a pace by no means the most moderate, or the least likely to jolt those who filled them; our people, casting their half-dressed provisions into the fire, buckled on their accoutrements, and took their stations; whilst the artillery, which had begun to retire, came up again, at a hand gallop, to the front. Two squadrons of cavalry were next ordered out, partly to stop the fugitives in their flight, and partly to check a body of the enemy, which, at this moment, appeared upon the main road; and I must say, that our troopers executed both of these orders with great effect. Every man whom they met, no matter whether an English or a Portuguese soldier, they drove back, beating him with the flats of their swords over the head and shoulders; and then, suddenly rushing past a projecting copse which concealed their motions, they spread death and dismay among the French infantry. But we had not much time given to watch the operations of others. We were ourselves in line in a moment, and advancing to the charge.

It was a tremendous and an overwhelming rush. The enemy stood nobly, and fought with desperate resolution, but we bore them back, as I have seen one bull borne back by another, into the wood. And then again began the same ceaseless roar of musketry which had sounded in our ears last evening; whilst four or five pieces of cannon sent showers of grape and cannister amongst us, which, but for the shelter afforded by the trees, must have swept us all into eternity.

As soon as we were fairly in the wood, our compact order was, in spite of every effort, lost. We fought, however, with the same spirit as before, in detached parties, and pressed the enemy on all hands, who became as much divided as ourselves, – till not only was the ground recovered which had at first been abandoned, but we were considerably in advance of our original position. Nor was it practicable, even then, to check the ardour of the men. As fast as the enemy retired, our soldiers pushed on, till, at length, we found ourselves on the margin of a little lake, round the extremity of which the French were flying in great confusion. Such a sight added fuel to the fire of our eagerness; and we pursued in a state of little less confusion than that which prevailed among the fugitives.

We had already reached the farther end of the lake, and were in hot and heedless chase of a couple of field-pieces, when a cry was suddenly raised of "The cavalry! the cavalry!" Several troops of French dragoons were advancing. Their horses were already in speed, – and there was no time to collect or form a square; so we threw ourselves as we best could into compact circles, and stood to receive them. They came on with the noise of thunder; one circle wavered – some of the men abandoned their ranks – the cavalry rode through it in an instant. That in which I was stood more firm. We permitted them to approach, till the breasts of the horses almost touched our bayonets, when a close and well-directed volley was poured in, and numbers fell beneath it. But we knew that we had no business to remain where we were. Having, therefore, repelled this charge, we slowly retraced our steps, the cavalry hovering around us as we retired, till we had gained, once more, the shelter of the wood, and were safe from further molestation. There we stood fast, till a bugle sounding the recall, warned us to retire still farther, and we again united ourselves with the rest of the brigade.

The attack upon our post being thus defeated, we were commanded to lie down in a ditch, for the purpose of sheltering ourselves against a heavy cannonade with which the enemy still entertained us. A couple of brigades were, at the same time, marched towards the right, to support the light division, which had been very sorely pressed in its position at Arcanques. The French column had come on at a moment when a regiment of caçadores, which held the church, were in the act of cleaning their rifles, and hence one-half of the troops were virtually unarmed. But, though driven through the village and gardens, our people maintained themselves in the church, and the rising ground on which it stood; nor did the French succeed in making any lasting impression on that point. The loss, however, had, on our part, been so great, and the enemy still continued his exertions with so much ardour, that it was deemed requisite to send fresh regiments to relieve those which had been so long engaged; and hence five or six battalions were withdrawn from our rear, and the post which they had hitherto assisted in maintaining was left entirely to our protection.

Whether it was the intention of Soult to cause this movement, or whether he only hoped to avail himself of it, as soon as it had been made, I know not; but just as the bayonets of our detached troops began to glitter in the wood behind Arcanques, another most determined charge was made upon the corps in our immediate front. This corps was not only weak in point of numbers, but was absolutely worn out with hard fighting and want of food. It gave way almost immediately. Again the French were upon us; again we were hotly engaged, and, as it appeared to me, with a still denser and more numerous division than any which had yet attacked us. The wood and the mayor's house were now both of them carried – the French came on with loud shouts and great courage – our Portuguese allies fairly fled the field – one or two British regiments were overpowered; and even we, whose ranks had hitherto been preserved, began to waver, when Lord Wellington himself rode up. The effect was electrical. "You must keep your ground, my lads," cried he; "there is nothing behind you. – Charge! Charge!" Instantly a shout was raised. Many fugitives, who had lost their own corps, threw themselves into line upon our flank; we poured in but one volley, and then rushed on with the bayonet. The enemy would not stand it; their ranks were broken, and they fled in utter confusion. We followed without giving them a moment to recover from their panic; and having suffered hardly any loss in killed and wounded, we once more took possession of the chateau and the thicket. This was the last effort on either side, darkness having already set in; and hence we found ourselves, for the second time, at the close of a day of carnage and fatigue, occupying exactly the spot of ground which we had occupied when that day began. The same wild and outlandish tumult ensued; men of all countries bawling and hollowing to each other, and the same arrangements of lighting fires, and lying down to sleep around them, were entered into by the weary combatants. The corps to which I belonged was, indeed, turned about a quarter of a mile to the right, where the charge of the outposts was committed to it; and those who had hitherto kept them being called in, were permitted to repose more securely in the rear. But with this exception, everything which had been done during the night before was repeated; and such as were not actually employed on piquet, slept soundly beside their watch-fires.

Chapter 13

Soult Withdraws

The lake referred to is that of Mouriscot. Both adversaries spent the 11th waiting for the other to make the next move, but Wellington correctly assumed that Soult would probably attack Hill's 'Corps' on the triangle of land between the Nive and Adour and, after placing a pontoon bridge across the Nive south-west of Villefranque, began to transfer the 4th and 7th Divisions to his Right Wing. Meanwhile, Soult had unobtrusively withdrawn troops from opposite the 1st Division. Crossing the Nive on bridges within Bayonne during the night of the 12th, the French assailed Hill next morning at St Pierre (d'Irube) and Mouguerre (where a monument now commemorates Soult!). Having received reinforcements just in time, Hill was able to hold his own against heavy odds. Allied casualties were 1,775, light compared with those of Soult's, which were about 3,300 (not 5,000 as assumed by Gleig).

From an unwillingness to interrupt my narrative of the sanguinary operations of this day, I have omitted to notice an event, perhaps more important in its general consequences, than even the successful resistance of one British corps to the attack of almost the whole French army. The reader will, no doubt, recollect, that at the period of time respecting which I am now writing, the various states of Germany which had lain so long under the French yoke, were beginning once more to assert their independence, – many, indeed, had taken up arms against the common enemy. The battle of Leipsic had been fought; the Confederation of the Rhine was dissolved; Holland and the Netherlands were, in a great measure, restored to their legitimate sovereign, and all in rear of the allied line, extending from Hunengen to the Low Countries, was free. Attached to the army of Marshal Soult were several brigades of German and Dutch troops, from whom the intelligence of the real state of their respective countries could not be concealed. Of these, about four thousand men, through the instrumentality of their commanding officers, had for some time back been in secret communication with Lord Wellington. All, indeed, which was wanting to withdraw them from the ranks of the enemy, was a convenient opportunity to desert; and against this the French general appeared studiously to strive. One brigade he had already sent to the rear on suspicion, and he had thrown out various hints that the rest must speedily follow; nor can it be doubted, that these hints would have been acted upon, but for the events of the last three days. The extreme fatigue of his French battalions compelled him to assign the advanced station, this morning, to a corps of Germans, who had no sooner taken up their ground, than they proposed to carry into execution a plan which their officers had long matured. Collecting their baggage, and carrying with them their arms, ammunition, and accoutrements, they marched in regular order within our lines, and were instantly shipped, as they had previously desired, for their own country. Thus, independently of his loss in killed and wounded, which, on the most moderate computation, could not amount to less, during the late operations, than four thousand men, Soult found his army weakened by the desertion of fifteen hundred or two thousand veteran soldiers.

The Germans had taken up the ground in our immediate front soon after dark on the evening of the 10th; but they were not prepared to abandon the cause of Napoleon at the instant. Messengers were, however, sent in that night, to prepare our general for what was to take place on the morrow, and so to hinder the deserting column from being fired on by our outposts. All was fully arranged. Just before the Portuguese brigade advanced, the advance of which brought on the renewal of hostilities, the German corps began its march; and it was welcomed with cheers by its new allies, who were under arms to receive it. To us it was truly an animating spectacle, and it, doubtless, caused not only annoyance and rage, but alarm and despondency among the ranks of the enemy. But to return to my own personal narrative.

The night of the 11th was spent, as that of the 10th had been spent, round our fires, and in the open air. A supply of beef, biscuit, and rum had, however, been issued out, and the former being broiled over the coals, a substantial supper effectually recruited the strength of those who were really beginning to faint from absolute inanition. Then, the grog being passed round, and pipes and cigars lighted, we lay not down to sleep, till many a rude joke had been bandied about, and many a merry catch chanted. Not that we were altogether insensible to more grave and melancholy feelings. Our ranks were a good deal thinned; of our beloved companions many had fallen; and I speak truly when I say, that we lamented their fall, even in the midst of our mirth. But a state of warfare is productive, and necessarily productive, of more consummate selfishness than any other situation into which man is liable to be thrown; and hence, except some bosom friend have perished, such as Gray was to me, and I to him, it must be confessed that soldiers think less of the dead than of the living. Each man, indeed, is (shall I own it?) too happy to find himself unscathed, to waste many fruitless expressions of sorrow upon those whose fate has been different.

The dawn of the 12th found us, as the dawn of the preceding day had done, under arms. Just before day broke, the battalion, leaving two companies to act as skirmishers, fell back to the rear of a thin hedge-row, for the purpose of keeping an open stubble field in its front, in case the enemy should attack. By this means we hoped to throw in our fire with the better effect, as they moved along this coverless ground, whilst a clear space lying before us, our charge, which must of course follow, would be the more decisive. But the enemy gave us no opportunity of carrying these plans into execution.

The French army was still before us in immense numbers; but it remained perfectly quiet. Hour after hour elapsed without any movement being made on either side, till about eight in the morning his column, which occupied the main road, began to retrograde. An English officer of artillery seeing this, as if determined that the retreat should not be altogether bloodless, fired the two guns which he commanded, I believe, without any orders being given. Whether these shots irritated the Marshal, or whether he was anxious to deceive us into a belief of fresh hostilities on his side, I know not; but they were immediately answered. The column halted, faced about, and made a show of advancing. The piquets came on, and a good deal of skirmishing ensued; but no decided attack was made, though enough was done to keep our attention awake. About noon, however, even this firing ceased, and a sort of pause in hostilities ensued.

Let me take advantage of this pause, to describe the relative positions of the two armies, as far, at least, as my circumscribed opportunities enabled me to judge of them.

The extreme left of the British, and consequently the extreme right of the French army, rested upon the sea. Between the high road and the sea, however, lay a small lake, measuring perhaps a mile in circumference, the ground beyond which was so rugged and so inclosed, that only a few companies were left to guard it. On it no military operations took place. Perhaps, then, I may speak more intelligibly if I say, that the left of our army, and the right of that of the enemy, rested upon the lake. The main road, which was one key of our position, ran along the summit of the high bank above the lake. It was winding, but as nearly level as high roads generally are. To defend it, a battery of three guns had been thrown up a little way to the left, where an inclination of the lake permitted; and where the whole of a long sweep was completely commanded. On the right of the road, again, was the mayor's house, with its out-buildings, gardens, and thick plantations; for the possession of which so much blood had been shed. So far, however, the ground was perfectly even; that is to say, neither the French nor we possessed the advantage of an acclivity; nor could either side boast of superior cover from wood. But about musket-shot from the mayor's house, the case was different, and the general face of the country underwent a change.

In the quarter of which I have last spoken, and where, indeed, my own corps was this morning stationed, the French and English divisions were separated from one another by a ravine. The ground occupied by the enemy was, perhaps, higher than that on which we stood; but then on our side we were better supplied with thickets; and had the contrary been the case, there was an ascent sufficient to give a decided advantage to the defenders over the assailants. In both lines one or two farm-houses stood conveniently enough, as posts of defence; and, on the side of the enemy, a wilderness of furze-bushes covered the face of the hill.

This ravine, after running in a straight direction about three or four hundred yards, wound inwards upon the French hill, so as to place the church of Arcanques rather in front of our station, than the contrary. That building stood, however, upon a detached eminence. It was completely surrounded by ravines, except in the rear, where it sloped gradually down into a woody plain. Beyond Arcanques, it was not possible for me to make any accurate observations; but as far as I could judge, the country appeared flat, with the same sort of inequalities occurring in it, as those already described. There was, however, a great deal of wood scattered here and there, whilst several villages, some in the possession of the French, and others in our possession, could be descried. On the whole, neither position could be pronounced greatly superior in natural strength to the other; nor, perhaps, would ours at least have caught an eye less acute in these matters, than his who selected it for his winter line.

I have said, that a good deal of unconnected firing having been kept up till about noon, a solemn pause ensued throughout the whole line. Not that Marshal Soult had yet resigned all hope of forcing our left, and so gaining the command of the road by which our supplies were brought up; but he appeared satisfied that absolute force would not secure his object, and hence he betook himself to manoeuvring. Of the various changes of ground which now took place among the different divisions of both armies, it is vain for me to attempt any minute description. What I myself beheld, however, may be repeated; though it will convey but a feeble idea of the magnificent operations of these two mighty gamesters.

We had stood, or rather lain, quietly behind a hedge about half an hour, when the arrival of a group of horsemen, on the brow of the French hill, attracted our attention. It was Soult and his staff. The Marshal dismounted, leant his telescope over the saddle of his horse, and swept our line. While he was thus employed, Lord Wellington, followed by about twenty aides-de-camp and orderlies, rode up. The glass of our general was instantly turned upon his adversary, and the two commanders-in-chief gazed at each other for several seconds. Now a mounted Frenchman rode to the rear of his group at full speed; whilst Lord Wellington flew, as fast as his horse could gallop, towards Arcanques; and for about a quarter of an hour all was still.

Soult had departed in the same direction as had Lord Wellington; and we were wondering what was to follow, when the head of a French column suddenly showed itself on the high ground opposite to Arcanques. An attack was of course expected, – but no such thing. As if the two columns had agreed to reach their ground at the same instant, the enemy had hardly appeared, when the wood, in rear of Arcanques, glittered with the bayonets of the seventh division. Again Soult showed himself on the ridge opposite, but a good deal farther to the right, gazing, as if with deep anxiety, upon the advance of these troops. His plan was anticipated, and his newly-formed column melted gradually away.

"Where next?" thought I; but no great time was spent in wondering. The same, or another mass, speedily crowned the hill opposite; and at the same moment, two or three brigades of fresh troops were in our rear. Once more the enemy withdrew. Thus the whole hours of light were spent, the heads of columns appearing and disappearing, at different points; and both armies were guided as the pieces upon a chess-board are guided, when two skilful and tolerably equal players are opposed. Darkness, at length, beginning to set in, an end was put to the manoeuvring, and we again made preparations to spend the night as comfortably as circumstances would permit.

It fell to my lot this evening to mount piquet. As soon as the night had fairly commenced, I put myself at the head of the body of men which was assigned to me, and moved down to the bottom of the ravine which I have already mentioned, as dividing the two armies. There our watch-fire was lighted, and there the main body of the piquet took its ground; whilst the sentinels were posted a little on the rise of the opposite hill. The French, on the other hand, stationed their out-posts on the summit, and placed their sentries opposite to ours, at a distance of perhaps thirty paces. Thus, each man was at the mercy of the other; but both English and French sentinels were too well trained in the school of modern warfare, to dream of violating the sanctity which is happily thrown around them.

It will readily be imagined that this was to me a night of peculiarly high excitement. My friend Gray was with me, so the time passed cheerfully enough, but it was wholly sleepless. We took it by turns to visit our sentinels every half hour, who again were relieved, as sentinels generally are, each at the expiration of a two-hours' watch; and thus, by going our rounds, and examining the state of the men previous to their proceeding to their posts, all inclination to repose was dispelled. The privates, indeed, on whose shoulders no responsibility rested, lay down, with their firelocks beside them, and slept; but we sat by our fire, smoking and conversing, whenever an opportunity of sitting was granted. All, however, passed quietly off. Except the voices of our own and the enemy's sentries, who challenged us as we approached, no sound could be heard in the front; nor did any event occur worthy of notice, till midnight had long past.

It might be, perhaps, about two in the morning of the 13th, when a sentinel, whose post I visited, informed me, that he had heard a more than usual stir in the French lines about ten minutes before, and had seen a blue-light thrown up. "Have any reliefs taken place among them lately?" said I. – "Yes, sir," replied the soldier; "a relief has just gone now." – "We must reconnoitre," rejoined I; and so saying, I stooped down, and, in a creeping attitude, approached the enemy's videttes. One stood directly before me. Though it was very dark, I could distinguish his cap and firelock; so I crept back again, satisfied that all was quiet.

In half an hour I visited the same man. "Has anything occurred since?" asked I. "No, sir," was the answer; "all is perfectly quiet." Repeating my experiment, I found the French sentinel still stationary, and I was again satisfied. The same thing occurred at each successive visitation, till about four in the morning. At that hour, my own sentinel stated that he had heard no relief since he came on duty, neither had the man who was behind heard any. Upon this I returned to consult with Gray; when it was agreed between us that a patrole should go forward and ascertain at once how matters stood. Taking with me four men, I again crept up the hill. The vidette was still there; we approached; he continued silent and motionless. We ran up to him, – it was a bush, with a soldier's cap placed upon the top of it, and a musket leaning against it. The enemy were gone. Not a vestige of them remained, except their fires, on which a quantity of fuel had lately been heaped. Of course, we transmitted to the rear, without delay, intelligence of all that had occurred; when a general recognizance being made along the front of the whole left, it was found that Soult had withdrawn, and that he had carried off with him, not only his artillery and baggage, but all his wounded. We gave him ample credit for the adroit-ness with which his retreat had been conducted.

Chapter 14

Marking Time

It was the battle of St Pierre, just east of Bayonne, which Gleig refers to as taking place on the 13th, in which Soult's casualties numbered some 3,300; those of the Allies were 1,775. No topographical name recognizable as Badarre, as printed by Gleig, appears on a modern large-scale map of the area (can it be a mis-reading of Arbonne or a mis-hearing on his part of Bassussarry?). From cantonments near Guéthary, Gleig revisits scenes of action and ponders on the senseless post-action destruction and pillaging of property wrecked by marauders and camp-followers.

For about two hours after day-break, no movement whatever was made on the left of the army. Parties of cavalry and light infantry were, indeed, from time to time sent forward, for the purpose of guarding against a sudden return of the enemy's columns; but the main body kept its ground as it had done the day before, and the stations of the out-posts were not altered. About nine o'clock in the morning, however, a few changes occurred. My piquet, for example, marched a little to the right, and relieved a body of Brunswickers, which occupied a farm-house near the point where the ravine wound inwards upon the enemy's position; and this body, together with several other battalions, proceeded at a quick pace towards the station of General Hill's corps. The indefatigable Soult, it appeared, had withdrawn his forces from before us, only to carry them against the opposite flank. The whole of the night of the 12th was spent in filing his battalions through the entrenched camp; and by day-break on the 13th, he showed himself in force upon the right of the army. But Sir Rowland was prepared for him. His own division kept the enemy in full play, till reinforcements arrived, when a decided attack was made; and the French, worn out with the exertions of the four preceding days, were totally defeated. They escaped with difficulty within their fortified lines, leaving five thousand men upon the field.

But I must not presume to intrude upon the province of the historian; let me therefore return to myself, and my own little party.

The house of which we now took possession exhibited very unequivocal symptoms of having been the arena of sundry desperate conflicts. The walls were everywhere perforated with cannon-shot; the doors and windows were torn to pieces; a shell or two had fallen through the roof, and bursting in the rooms on the ground-floor, had not only brought the whole of the ceiling down, but had set fire to the wood-work. The fire had, indeed, been extinguished; but it left its usual traces of blackened timbers and charred boarding. Several dead bodies lay in the various apartments, and the little garden was strewed with them. These we, of course, proceeded to bury; but there were numbers concealed by the bushes on the hill-side beyond, on which no sepulture could be bestowed, and which, as afterwards appeared, were left to furnish food for the wolves and vultures. Then the smell, which hung not only about the interior, but the exterior of the cottage, was shocking. Not that the dead had as yet begun to putrefy; for, though some of them had lain for a couple of days exposed to the influence of the atmosphere, the weather was far too cold to permit the process of decomposition to commence; but the odour, even of an ordinary field of battle, is extremely disagreeable. I can compare it to nothing more aptly than the interior of a butcher's slaughter-house, soon after he may have killed his sheep or oxen for the market. Here that species of perfume was peculiarly powerful; and it was not the less unpleasant, that the smell of burning was mixed with it.

Having remained at this post till sun-set, I and my party were relieved, and fell back to join the regiment. We found it huddled into a single cottage, which stood at one extremity of the green field, where we had halted only yesterday, to bring the enemy fairly to the bayonet. Of course, our accommodations were none of the best; officers and men, indeed, laid themselves down indiscriminately upon the earthen floor, and heartily glad was he who obtained room enough to stretch himself at length, without being pushed or railed at by his neighbours. The night, however, passed over in quiet, and sound was the sleep which followed so many dangers and hardships, especially on the part of us, who had spent the whole of the preceding night in watchfulness.

Long before dawn on the morning of the 14th, we were, as a matter of course, under arms. In this situation we remained till the sun arose, when, marching to the right, we halted not till we reached a rising ground in front of the village of Badarre, and immediately in rear of the church of Arcanques. When we set out the sky was cloudy, and the air cold, but no rain had fallen. We had hardly got to our station, however, when a heavy shower descended, which, but for the opportune arrival of our tents, would have speedily placed it out of our power to experience any degree of bodily comfort for the next twenty-four hours. Under these circumstances, the tents, which a few weeks ago we had regarded with horror, were now esteemed dwellings fit for princes to inhabit, whilst the opportunity which their shelter afforded of disencumbering ourselves of our apparel, was hailed as a real blessing. No man who has not worn his garments for five or six days on end, can conceive the luxury of undressing; and above all, the feeling of absolute enjoyment which follows the pulling off of his boots.

As the rain continued during the whole of the day, little inducement was held out to wander abroad. On the contrary, I perfectly recollect, that, for the first time in our lives, we succeeded in lighting a fire in our tent, and escaped the inconvenience of smoke by lying flat upon the ground; and that the entire day was consumed in eating, drinking, smoking, conversing, and sleeping. No doubt, my unwarlike readers will exclaim that the hours thus spent, were spent unprofitably; but I cannot, even now, think so, inasmuch as they were hours of great enjoyment.

We were not without serious apprehension that circumstances had occurred which would compel Lord Wellington to keep us, during the remainder of the winter, under canvass, when the better half of the day following had passed over, and no order arrived for our return into quarters. Nor were these feelings of alarm diminished by witnessing the march of the whole of the 5th division through our encampment, confessedly on their way to comfortable cantonments. As the event proved, however, our dread was perfectly groundless, for, about an hour and a half after noon, we too received orders; two o'clock saw our tents struck, our baggage packed up on the mules, and ourselves in motion towards the high road. Of course, we flattered ourselves that we were destined to return to those rural billets, which, by dint of mechanical skill and manual labour, we had made so snug; but there we were disappointed.

We traversed, almost step by step, the same ground over which we had travelled in the course of the late military operations, till we reached the identical green fields in which it had been our lot to bivouac with so little comfort, on the 10th of the preceding November. I believe I have already mentioned, if not I may state here, that adjoining to these fields were several farm-houses; one of them, indeed, of very respectable size and appearance, but the rest hardly elevated above the rank of cottages. In a mansion of the latter description – in that same mansion, indeed, where I and a host of more active animals had formerly contended for the possession of a bed, were Gray, myself, and our man stationed; nor can I say, though the place was certainly in better plight than when last I beheld it, that we were particularly delighted with our abode.

The room allotted to us was an apartment on the ground-floor. It was furnished with a fire-place, which had been built by the corps that preceded us, and among the members of which it was very evident that there existed no one possessing an equal skill in masonry with ourselves. It smoked abominably. In the construction of their window, our predecessors had, however, been more fortunate, their oiled paper holding out against the wind and rain with much obstinacy; but the quarters were, on the whole, exceedingly comfortless, especially when contrasted, as it was impossible not to contrast them, with those which we had so lately fitted up. Nevertheless, we were too happy in finding ourselves once more under shelter of a roof, to waste many repining thoughts upon unavoidable evils; and we had the satisfaction to know that our abode here would be of no longer continuance than the duration of the winter; if, indeed, it continued so long.

It is an old and a just observation, that the term comfort is one of relative, rather than of direct signification. To the truth of this saying we were speedily compelled to bear testimony, when, about two o'clock in the afternoon of the 18th, we found ourselves once more in line of march, and advancing to the front for the purposes of relieving another brigade in the out-post duty. Everybody, I dare say, recollects the severity of the winter of 1813–14. Even in the south of France, the frost was at times so intense, as to cast a complete coat of ice over ponds and lakes of very considerable depth; whilst storms of cold wind and rain occurred at every interval, when the frost departed. The 18th of December chanced to be one of these wet and windy days, and hence we could not help acknowledging, when we found ourselves once more exposed to the "pelting of the pitiless storm", that our chamber, on the disagreeables of which we had dilated with so much minuteness, was, after all, an abode by no means to be despised.

The corps employed in guarding the front of the left column, consisted of a brigade of three battalions, in other words, of about eighteen hundred men. Of these, six hundred were appointed to furnish the piquets, whilst the remaining twelve hundred acted as a support, in case of need, and busied themselves till the hour of need should arrive, in fortifying their post. The ground on which our tents stood, was the identical green field, where, during the late action, we had bivouacked for two successive nights; whilst our working parties were employed in felling the wood round the mayor's house, in throwing up breast-works contiguous to it, and in constructing a square redoubt, capable of holding an entire battalion in its immediate rear. The redoubt was named after a daughter of the worthy magistrate, who resided, for the present, in the little town of Biaritz, and had already declared himself a partizan of the Bourbons. It was called Fort Charlotte, and gave rise to as many puns, as are usually produced by the appearance of a tongue, or a dish of brains, at a Cockney's table; nor was any one more parturient of such puns, than the father of the young lady himself. Between this gentleman, and the officer commanding the out-posts, a constant intercourse was kept up. The town of Biaritz, where he dwelt, lying upon the sea-shore, and out of the direct line of operations, was not occupied either by the French or allied troops. It constituted, on the contrary, a sort of neutral territory, which was visited, occasionally, by patroles from both armies; but so far retained its independence, that its inhabitants were in the constant practice of carrying their commodities for sale, not only to our camp, but to the camp of the enemy. Though the mayor professed to keep up no such species of traffic, the state of his property, over-run by the invading force, furnished him also with a legitimate excuse for occasionally looking after its preservation; and hence he contrived, from time to time, to make his appearance amongst us, without becoming, as far as I could learn, an object of suspicion to his countrymen.

As the duty in which we were now employed was by no means agreeable, and as any very lengthened exposure to the inclemency of such a season must have proved detrimental to the health of those exposed, it was customary to relieve the advanced corps at the end of three days, by which means each brigade, at least in the left column of the army, found itself in the field, and under canvass, only once in three or four weeks. That to which I was attached, filled what may be termed the stationary outposts, only four times during the entire winter, nor have I any reason to believe that we were, in this respect, peculiarly favoured. Of the events which took place during our present interval of more active service, it is needless to enter into any minute detail. They were such as generally occur on similar occasions; that is to say, our time was passed in alternate watching and labour: whilst an uninterrupted continuance of cold and stormy weather, rendered the arrival of the troops destined to succeed us highly acceptable. Nor was this temporary endurance of hardship and fatigue without its good effect. We learned from it to lay aside what yet remained to us of fastidiousness, and we returned to our quarters perfectly reconciled to those inconveniences and drawbacks, which existed more, perhaps, in our imagination, than in reality.

I should try beyond all endurance the patience of my reader, were I to relate in regular detail, the occurrences of each day, from the 21st of December, 1813, when we returned to our cantonments, to the 2nd of January, 1814, when we again quitted them. Enough is done, when I state in few words, that the ordinary resources against ennui, that is to say, shooting, coursing, and even fishing, were adopted; and that the evenings were spent, for the most part, in convivial parties, to the inordinate consumption of cigars, wine, and sometimes of patience. Nor were other, and more rational employments wanting. On more than one occasion I visited St Jean de Luz, attended high mass, and the theatre; and once I rode as far to the rear as Irun. The effect of the latter ride upon myself, was vivid at the time; and may perhaps be worth conveying to others.

The distance from our present cantonments to the town of Irun might amount to sixteen or eighteen miles. Over the whole of that country, between the two extreme points, the tide of war, it will be recollected, had swept; not boisterously, but with comparative harmlessness, – as when one army rapidly retreats, and another rapidly follows, – but slowly and ruinously; every foot of ground having been obstinately contested, and hence every fold, garden, and dwelling, having been exposed to the ravages inseparable from the progress of hostilities. The spectacle which presented itself on each side of the road, was accordingly distressing in the extreme; the houses and hovels were everywhere in ruins, the inclosures and cultivated fields were all laid waste and desolate, whilst the road itself was strewed with the carcases of oxen, mules, horses, and other animals, which had dropped down from fatigue, and died upon their march. I was particularly struck with the aspect of things in and about the town of Urogne. Of the works on the heights above it, so carefully and so skilfully erected by Marshal Soult, some had already begun to yield to the destructive operation of the elements, and others had been wantonly demolished by the followers of the camp; whilst, in the town itself, where so lately was heard the roar of cannon, and the rattle of musketry, the most perfect silence prevailed. It was wholly tenantless; not even a sutler or muleteer had taken up his abode there; the cavalry were all withdrawn; and of the original inhabitants not one had returned. The reader will easily believe that I looked round, during this part of my journey, with peculiar interest, for the fields across which I had myself skirmished; more especially for a friendly hedge, the intervention of a stout stake in which had saved my better arm; and that I did not pass the churchyard, without dismounting to pay a visit to the grave of my former comrades. Neither was I unmindful of the chateau, in which, to my no small surprise, I had found a letter from my father; and the change wrought in it, since last I beheld it, gave me a more perfect idea of the disastrous effects of war, than any other object upon which I had yet looked.

When a man of peaceable habits, – one, for example, who has spent his whole life in this favoured country, under the shelter of his own sacred roof, – reads of war, and the miseries attendant upon war, his thoughts invariably return to scenes of outrage and rapine, in which soldiers are the actors, and to which the hurry and excitement of battle give rise. I mean not to say that a battle is ever fought without bringing havock upon the face of that particular spot of earth which chances to support it. But the mischief done by both contending armies, to the buildings and property of the inhabitants, is a mere nothing, when compared to that which the followers of a successful army work. These wretches tread in the steps of the armed force, with the fidelity and haste of kites and vultures. No sooner is a battle won, and the troops pushed forward, than they spread themselves over the entire territory gained; and all which had been spared by those, in whom an act of plunder, if excusable at all, might most readily be excused, is immediately laid waste. The chateau of which I am speaking, for example, and which I had left perfectly entire, fully furnished, and in good order, was now one heap of ruins. Not a chair or a table remained; not a volume of all the library so lately examined by me, existed; nay, it was evident from the blackened state of the walls, and the dilapidation of the ceilings, that fire had been wantonly applied to complete the devastation which avarice had begun. To say the truth, I could not but regret at the moment, that I had not helped myself to a little more of Monsieur Briguette's property, than the Spanish Grammar already advertised for redemption.

Having cleared Urogne, and passed through the remains of the barricade which I had assisted in carrying on the tenth of the last month, I soon arrived at the site of the village of which I have formerly taken notice, as being peopled and furnished with shops and other places of accommodation, by sutlers and adventurers. The huts, or cottages, still stood, though they were all unroofed, and many of them otherwise in ruins; but the sign of the "Jolly Soldier" had disappeared. Like other incitements to folly, if not to absolute vice, it had followed the tract of the multitude. I marked, too, as I proceeded, the bleak hill-side on which our tents had so long contended with the winds of heaven; and I could not help thinking, how many of those who had found shelter beneath their canvass, were now sleeping upon the bosom of mother-earth; of course, I paid to their memories the tribute of a regret as unavailing as, I fear, it was transitory.

By and by I reached the brow of the last height on the French border, and the Bidassoa once more lay beneath me. The day on which my present excursion was made, chanced to be one of the few lovely days with which, during that severe winter, we were favoured. The air was frosty, but not intensely so; the sky was blue and cloudless, and the sun shone out with a degree of warmth, which cheered, without producing languor or weariness. High up, the mountains which overhang the river were covered with snow, which sparkled in the sun-beams, and contrasted beautifully with the sombre hue of the leafless groves beneath, whilst the stream itself flowed on as brightly and as placidly as if it had never witnessed a more desperate struggle than that which the fisherman maintains with a trout of extraordinary agility and dimensions. Fain would I have persuaded myself that I was quietly travelling in a land of peace; but there were too many proofs of the contrary ever and anon presented, to permit the delusion to keep itself for one moment in the mind.

Chapter 15

Excursions Behind the Lines

Gleig meets a band of Spanish guerrillas and sees food for fishes. The Spanish infantry he refers to as having just left Irún were presumably the troops of Generals Girón and Longa, among others, which Wellington had sent back across the frontier, as their plundering proclivities and the atrocities some of them had committed the moment they had entered France – and he could not rely on them to desist – would soon turn the whole populous against the Allies: 'would ruin us all', in his words. Only a limited number of Spanish units were allowed to return to the front later. The Nugent referred to was probably George, Baron Grenville, while General Sir Robert Wilson had commanded the Lusitanian Legion in Portugal during 1808–09 before seeing service with both the Russians and Austrians. He revisited the Peninsula in 1823 and was later M.P. for Southwark.

The stone bridge which was wont to connect the two banks of the Bidassoa, and which the French, after their evacuation of the Spanish territory, had destroyed, was not, I found, repaired; but a temporary bridge of pontoons rendered the stream passable, without subjecting the traveller to the necessity of fording. A party of artificers were, moreover, renewing the arches which had been broken down, whilst a new *tete-du-pont* on the opposite side from the old one, was already erected, to be turned to account in case of any unlooked-for reverse of fortune, and consequent retreat beyond the frontier. I observed, too, that the whole front of the pass, beyond the river, was blocked up with redoubts, batteries, and breast-works, and that Lord Wellington, though pressing forward with victory in his train, was not unmindful of the fickleness of the blind goddess.

As I was crossing the pontoon bridge, two objects, very different in kind, but intimately connected the one with the other, attracted my attention almost at the same moment. A body of Spanish cavalry, which appeared to have passed the river at one of the fords a little higher up, presented themselves as they wound up a steep by-path which communicated with the high road just beside the old *tete-du-pont*. They were Guerillas, and were consequently clothed, armed, and mounted, in a manner the least uniform that can well be imagined. Of the men, some were arrayed in green jackets, with slouched hats, and long feathers; others in blue, helmeted like our yeomanry, or artillery-drivers, whilst not a few wore cuirasses and brazen head-pieces, such as they had probably plundered from their slaughtered enemies. But, notwithstanding this absence of uniformity in dress, the general appearance of these troopers was exceedingly imposing. They were, on the whole, well mounted, and they marched in that sort of loose and independent manner, which, without indicating the existence of any discipline amongst them, bespoke no want of self-confidence in individuals. Their whole appearance, indeed, for they could not exceed sixty or eighty men, reminded me forcibly of a troop of bandits; and the resemblance was not the less striking, that they moved to the sound, not of trumpets or other martial music, but of their own voices. They were singing a wild air as they passed, in which sometimes one chanted by himself, then two or three chimed in, and, by and by, the whole squadron joined in a very musical and spirited chorus.

The other object which divided my attention with these bold-looking, but lawless warriors, was about half-a-dozen dead bodies, which the flow of the tide brought at this moment in contact with the pontoons. They were quite naked, bleached perfectly white, and so far had yielded to the operation of decay, that they floated like rags of linen on the surface of the water. Perhaps these were some of our own men who had fallen in the passage of the river upwards of eight weeks ago; or perhaps they were the bodies of such of the French soldiers as had perished in their retreat after one of Soult's desperate, but fruitless efforts, to relieve the garrison of St Sebastian's. Who, or what they were, I had no means of ascertaining, nor was it of much consequence; to whatever nation they had once belonged, they were now food for the fishes; and to the fishes they were left, no one dreaming that it was requisite to pull them to land, or to rob one set of reptiles of their prey only to feed another.

Such is a summary of the events which befell me in a morning's ride from the cantonments at Gauthory, to the town of Irun. After crossing the river, my progress was direct, and of little interest. I journeyed, indeed, amid scenes all of them familiar, and therefore, in some degree, having a claim upon my own notice; but I neither saw nor met with any object worth describing to my reader. It was a little past the hour of noon, when my horse's hoofs clanked upon the pavement of Irun.

I found that city just recovering from the bustle which the departure of a corps of twenty thousand Spanish infantry may be supposed to have produced. This vast body of men had, it appeared, behaved so badly in the action of the ninth of November, that Lord Wellington was induced to order them to the rear in disgrace; and they had remained in quarters in Irun and the neighbourhood, till on the day preceding my arrival, when they were again permitted to join the army. By whom they were commanded on the day of their shame, I have totally forgotten; nor will I cast a slur upon the reputation of any general officer, by naming one at random.

Notwithstanding the departure of so great a multitude, I found the place far from deserted either by military or civil inhabitants. A garrison of two or three thousand soldiers was still there; a corps, I believe, of militia, or national guards; whilst a few of the houses were unoccupied, though whether by their rightful occupants or not, I take it not upon me to determine. One thing, however, I perfectly recollect, and that is, the extreme incivility and absence of all hospitality which distinguished them. Whether it was that the troops so long quartered amongst them had filled them with hatred of my countrymen, or whether that jealousy which the Spanish people have uniformly felt, and which, in spite of all that Lord Nugent and Sir Robert Wilson may assert to the contrary, they feel, even now, towards the English, was, of its own accord, beginning to gather strength, I cannot tell; but I well remember that it was with some difficulty I persuaded the keeper of an inn to put up my own and my servant's horses in his stable; and with still greater difficulty that I could prevail upon him to dress an omelet for my dinner. Nor was this all; my journey, be it known, had been undertaken not from curiosity alone, but in the hope of laying in a stock of coffee, cheese, tea, etc., at a cheap rate. But every effort to obtain these was fruitless, the merchants sulkily refusing to deal with me, except on the most exorbitant terms. I was not sorry, under such circumstances, when, having finished my omelet, and baited and rested my horses, I turned my back upon Irun, and took once more a direction towards the front.

I would lay before my readers a detail of another excursion executed on Christmas-day, to St Jean de Luz, were I not fully aware that there are few among them who are not as well acquainted as myself with the circumstances attending the celebration of that festival in a Roman Catholic country. On the present occasion, all things were done with as much pomp and show as the state of the city, filled with hostile battalions, and more than half-deserted by its inhabitants and priesthood, would permit. For my own part, I viewed the whole not with levity, certainly, but as certainly without devotion; the entire scene appearing to me better calculated to amuse the external senses, and dazzle the imagination, than to stir up the deeper and more rational sensations of piety. I returned home, nevertheless, well pleased with the mode in which the morning had been spent; and, joining a party of some ten or twelve who had clubbed their rations for the sake of setting forth a piece of roast-beef worthy of the occasion, I passed my evening not less agreeably than I had passed the morning.

Among other events during our sojourn at Gauthory, a sale of the effects of such of our brother-officers as had fallen in the late battles took place. On such occasions, the serjeant–major generally acts the part of auctioneer, and a strange compound of good and bad feeling accompanies the progress of the auction. In every party of men, there will always be some whose thoughts, centring entirely in self, regard everything as commendable, or the reverse, solely as it increases their enjoyments, or diminishes them. Even the sale of the clothes and accoutrements of one who but a few weeks or days before was their living, and perhaps favourite companion, furnishes to such men food for mirth; and I am sorry to say, that during the sale of which I now speak, more laughter was heard than redounded to the credit of those who joined in, or produced it. In passing this censure upon others, I mean not to exclude myself – by no means. I fear that few laughed more heartily than I, when shirts with nine tails, or no tails at all, were held up against the sun by the facetious auctioneer; and when sundry pairs of trowsers were pressed upon our notice as well adapted for summer-wear, inasmuch as their numerous apertures promised to admit a free current of air to cool the blood. But, with one or two exceptions, I must say, that there was not a man present who thought of the former owners of these tail-less shirts without affection, and who would not have willingly given the full value, ay, even of the shirts themselves, could that sum have redeemed them from the power of the grave. This sale, however, acted as a sort of warning to me. Though my wardrobe was in as good condition as that of most men, I chose not to have it or its owner made the subject of a joke, so I inserted among my few memoranda, a request that no article of mine should be put up to auction, but that all should be given, in case I fell, as expressly appointed.

I have said, that the usual means of defeating ennui, namely, shooting, coursing, and fishing, were resorted to by Gray and myself, whilst we inhabited these cantonments. Among other experiments, we strolled down one lovely morning towards the sea, with the hope of catching some fish for our dinner. In that hope we were disappointed, but the exquisite beauty of the marine view to which our walk introduced us, amply made amends for the absence of sport. It was one of those soft and enervating days which even in England we sometimes meet with, during the latter weeks of December, and which, in the south of France, are very frequent at that season. The sun was shining brightly and warmly, not a breath of air was astir, and the only sound distinguishable by us, who stood on the summit of the cliff, was the gentle and unceasing murmur of tiny waves, as they threw themselves upon the shingle. The extent of waters upon which we gazed, was bounded on the right by the head-lands at the mouth of the Adour, and on the left by those near Passages. Before us, the waste seemed interminable, and I am not sure that it was the less sublime because not a boat or vessel of any description could be descried upon it. At such moments as these, and when contemplating such a scene, it is hardly possible for any man to hinder his thoughts from wandering away from the objects immediately around him, to the land of his nativity, and the home of his fathers. I do not recollect any hour of my life during which the thought of home came more powerfully across me than the present. Perhaps, indeed, the season of the year had some effect in producing these thoughts. It was the season of mirth and festivity – of licensed uproar and innocent irregularity; and cold and heartless must he be who remembers not his home, however far removed from him, when that season returns. I confess that the idea of mine brought something like moisture into my eyes, of which I had then no cause to be ashamed, and the remembrance of which produces in me no sense of shame even now.

The walk towards the sea became from this time my favourite, but it was not my only one. Attended by my faithful spaniel, (a little animal, by the way, which never deserted me even in battle,) I wandered with a gun across my shoulder over a great extent of country, and in all directions. I found the scenery beautiful, but far less beautiful than I had expected to find it in the south of France. There was no want of wood, it is true; and corn fields, or rather fields lying fallow, were intermixed, in fair proportion, with green meadows and sloping downs. But there was nothing striking or romantic anywhere, except in the bold boundary of the Pyrenees, now twenty miles distant. I observed, however, that there was no want of chateaux and gentlemen's seats. These were scattered about in considerable numbers, as if this had been a favourite resort of those few among the French gentry who prefer the quiet of the country to the bustle and hurry of Paris. Some of these chateaux were, moreover, exceedingly elegant in their appearance, and indicated from that, as well as from their extent, that they belonged to men of higher rank than the Mayor of Biaritz; but the generality were of a description which bespoke their owners as belonging to the class of wealthy merchants, who supported their town-houses and warerooms in Bayonne, or perhaps in Bordeaux. But all were thoroughly ransacked. Over them, as well as over the houses in our rear, the storm of rapine had passed, leaving its usual traces of dilapidation and ruin behind.

It is needless to continue a narrative of such events. Thus passed several weeks, the business of one day resembling, in almost every respect, the business of another. Whenever the weather would permit, I made a point of living out of doors; when the contrary was the case, I adopted the ordinary expedients to kill time within. Nor were we, all this while, without a few occurrences calculated to hinder our forgetting that we really were in an enemy's country, and at the seat of war. The bloody flag was more than once hoisted on the tower of the church of Arcanques, as a signal that the French troops were in motion, and we, in our turn, stood to arms. But of such alarms almost all proved to be groundless, and those which were not intendedly so, might as well have been omitted. The fact was that Soult, having been called upon at this time to detach some divisions of his veteran soldiers to the assistance of Napoleon, already hard pressed by the allies in the north, was under the necessity of impressing into his service every male capable of bearing arms, who was not absolutely required to cultivate the soil. The entire winter was accordingly spent by him in training the conscripts to the use of arms. He marched and countermarched them from place to place, that they might learn to move with celerity and in order. He set up targets for them to fire at, and caused frequent alarms to our piquets when teaching his recruits to take a correct aim; he was, in short, now, as he always was, indefatigable in providing for the defence of the country committed to his care, and in his endeavours to make the most of a force assuredly not adequate for the purpose. But we were not doomed to be continually the dupes of false alarms, nor to be amused for ever with the issuing of orders, which were scarcely issued when they were again retracted. A necessity for a real movement occurred at last, and we bade adieu for ever to the cottage at Gauthory, which we first entered with regret, and finally quitted without reluctance.

Chapter 16

Civilities on Neutral Ground

It was not until the New Year of 1814 that the 85th moved forward to Arcangues, from near which Gleig observed French troops drilling. As many as 14,000 of Soult's veterans had been requisitioned by Napoleon and replaced by raw recruits.

It might be about six or seven o'clock in the morning of the 3rd of January, 1814, when an orderly serjeant burst into our chamber, and desired us to get the men under arms without delay, for that the enemy were in motion. In an instant we sprang from our beds, dressed and accoutred forthwith, ordered the trumpeter to sound the assembly, and our servants to prepare breakfast. The last of these injunctions was obeyed in an incredibly short space of time, insomuch, that whilst the troops were hurrying to their stations, we were devouring our morning's repast; and, in little more than a quarter of an hour from the first signal of alarm, the regiment was formed in marching-order upon the high road. Nor were many moments wasted in that situation. The word was given to advance, and we again pressed forward towards the mayor's house.

When we reached the post, or common, of which so much notice has already been taken, we found, indeed, that the whole of the left column was moving, but that the old battle-ground around the chateau, and in the woods and enclosures near it, was left entirely to the protection of the ordinary piquets. Of the enemy's forces, not a single battalion showed itself here; whilst our own were all filing towards the right, – a rout into which we also quickly struck, as if following the natural current of the stream of war. In this journey we passed over a good deal of ground which was already familiar to us, skirting the brow of the ravine which had separated the hostile armies during the pauses in their late contest, till having reached the meadow where our camp had formerly been pitched, we were turned into a new direction, and led upwards till we gained the top of the hill on which the church of Arcanques stands, and round the base of which the village of Arcanques is scattered. In the maintenance of this post we relieved a section of the light division, which immediately took a rightward course; thus indicating that the whole strength of the army would be mustered at one extremity, and other points of the line left to the protection of a few scattered brigades.

It was evening before we reached our ground, and as yet no provisions had been issued out to us. Of course, our appetites were excellent, indeed the appetites of men who have nothing to eat are seldom sickly; and this we amply demonstrated, as soon as an opportunity of demonstrating the fact was offered. Little time, however, was given for the enjoyment of social intercourse or bodily rest; for we had hardly swallowed a hasty meal, when the better half of the corps was sent forward to occupy a few cottages in front of the village; and the remainder of the night was spent in that state of excitement and anxiety, which necessarily waits upon such as form the outposts or advanced guard of an army.

My own station this night was not exactly at one of the most forward posts, but in a ruinous building at the outskirts of the village, where I was placed, with a body of men, to support the piquets. The thing into which we were ushered had, no doubt, once upon a time been a habitable mansion; at present it consisted of little else than the shell, and a very wretched shell, of a farm-house. Not only were the doors and windows gone, but the ceilings and partitions, which were wont to divide one apartment from another, were all broken down, whilst the roof was in a great measure stripped off, and the fragments which remained of it were perforated in all directions. I well recollect that the night was piercingly cold. The frost had of late set in with renewed severity, and a sharp northerly wind blowing, swept with a melancholy sound through our dilapidated mansion. But we were on little ceremony here. Large fires were lighted in different places upon the earthen floor, round which we gladly crept; whilst an allowance of grog being brought up, and pipes and cigars lighted, we were soon as merry and as light-hearted as men could desire to be. It is true that ever and anon – every half hour, for example – a party of six or eight of us sallied forth, to patrole from piquet to piquet, and to see that all was right between, but we returned from such excursions with increased predilection for our fire-side; and the events of the ramble, be they what they might, furnished food for conversation till another was deemed necessary.

So passed the night of the third; and on the morning of the fourth I expected, as an ordinary matter, to be relieved, and to be withdrawn to the rear; but it was not so. Men, it appeared, were scarce at this part of the line; and hence those who formed it were called upon to perform double duty. Instead of being removed to some place where a sound night's rest might be enjoyed, I and my party found ourselves, on the morning of the fourth, ordered to advance, and to occupy the foremost chain; from which we had the satisfaction of beholding the enemy, in very considerable force, at the distance of little more than a quarter of a mile from our sentries. This sight, however, only gave a spur to our exertions, and hindered us from repining at what we might have been otherwise tempted to consider as an undue exercise of our powers of watchfulness.

The particular piquet of which I was placed in command happened to be detached from all others, and to be nearly half a mile in front of the rest. It was stationed on a sort of sugar-loaf hill, separated from our own regular chain of posts by a deep and rugged glen, and kept apart from the French lines only by an imaginary boundary of hedges and paling. So exposed, indeed, was the spot, that I received positive orders to abandon it as soon as darkness should set in, and to retire across the hollow to the high grounds opposite. The reader will easily believe that, in such a situation, little leisure was given for relaxation either of body or mind. During the entire day, indeed, my occupation consisted in prying closely, with the aid of a telescope, into the enemy's lines; in considering how I could best maintain myself in case of an attack, and retreat most securely in case I should be overpowered.

The view from my piquet-house was, however, extremely animating. Beneath me, at the distance of only two fields, lay the French out-posts, about a quarter of a mile, or half a mile, in rear of which were encamped several large bodies both of infantry and cavalry. Of these, it was evident that vast numbers were raw recruits. They were at drill, marching and countermarching, and performing various evolutions, during the greater part of the day, – a circumstance which at first excited no little uneasiness on my part, inasmuch as I expected every moment that my post would be assaulted; but as soon as I saw a target erected, and the troops practising with ball, I became easy. "There will be no attack to-day," thought I, "otherwise so much ammunition would not be wasted."

I had hardly said so, when I observed a mounted officer advancing from the enemy's camp toward the base of the hill which my party held. He was followed by a cloud of people, in apparent confusion, it is true, but not more confused than French skirmishers generally appear to be, who lay down behind the hedges in the immediate front of my sentinels, as if waiting for an order to fire and to rush on. I had just ordered my people under arms, and was proceeding towards the sentries for the purpose of giving a few necessary orders, when the French officer halted, and a trumpeter, who accompanied him, sounded a parley. Of course I descended the hill, and causing my trumpeter to answer the signal, the Frenchman advanced. He was the bearer of letters from such British officers and soldiers as had been taken in the late actions; and he likewise handed over to me several sums of money and changes of clothing for some of his countrymen who had fallen into our hands.

This being done, we naturally entered into conversation touching the state of Europe, and the events of the war. My new acquaintance utterly denied the truth of Napoleon's reverses, and seemed to doubt the idea of an invasion of France by the armies of the North. He assured me that the whole country was in arms; that every peasant had become a soldier; that bands of partizans were forming on all sides of us; and that it was vain to hope that we should ever pass the Adour, or proceed farther within the sacred territory than we had already proceeded. He spoke of the desertion of the German corps with a degree of bitter contempt, which proved, – the very reverse of what he was desirous of proving, – that the event had greatly shaken the confidence of Soult in his auxiliaries; and, above all, he affected to regard the whole of the recent operations as mere affairs, or trifling contests of detachments, in no way capable of influencing the final issues of the war. Yet he was not displeased when I laughed at his style of oratory; and, after gasconading a good deal, both the one and the other, we shook hands, and parted the best friends imaginable.

I had hardly quitted him, at least I had not reached my station on the top of the hill, when I heard myself called by one of the sentinels, and turned round. I saw the individual with whom I had been conversing sitting in the midst of a little group of French officers, and watching the progress of an old woman, who was coming towards our lines. She held a large bottle in her hand, which she lifted up to attract my notice, and continued to move forward, gabbling loudly all the while. Obeying her signal, I returned, and met her a few yards in front of the sentries, when she delivered to me about a couple of quarts of brandy, as a present from the French officers; who had desired her to say, that if I could spare them a little tea in exchange, they would feel obliged. It so happened that I had brought no such luxury as tea to my post. Of this I informed the female Mercury, but I desired her to offer my best acknowledgments to her employers, and to add, that I had sent to the rear in order to procure it. With this message she accordingly departed, having promised to keep in sight for at least half an hour, and to return as soon as I should make a sign that the tea had arrived.

My bugler made good haste, and soon returned with about a quarter of a pound of black tea, the half of the stock which remained in my canteen. In the meanwhile the French officers continued sitting together, and all rose when I waved my cap to their carrier. The old lady was not remiss in taking the hint. I handed over to her the little parcel, with numerous apologies for its tenuity; and I had the satisfaction to perceive that, trifling as it was, it proved acceptable. The party pulled off their hats as an acknowledgment – I did the same; and we each departed to our respective stations.

There is something extremely agreeable in carrying on hostilities after this fashion; yet the matter may be pushed too far. Towards the close of the war, indeed, so good an understanding prevailed between the out-posts of the two armies, that Lord Wellington found it necessary to forbid all communication whatever; nor will the reader wonder at this, when I state to him the reason. A field-officer, (I shall not say in what part of the line,) in going his rounds one night, found that the whole of the serjeant's piquet-guard had disappeared. He was, of course, both alarmed and surprised at the occurrence; but his alarm gave place to absolute astonishment, when, on stretching forward to observe whether there was any movement in the enemy's lines, he peeped into a cottage from which a noise of revelry was proceeding, and beheld the party sitting in the most sociable manner with a similar party of Frenchmen, and carousing jovially. As soon as he showed himself, his own men rose, and wishing their companions a good night, returned with the greatest *sang-froid* to their post. It is, however, but justice to add, that the sentinels on both sides faithfully kept their ground, and that no intention of deserting existed on either part. In fact, it was a sort of custom, the French and English guards visiting each other by turns.

At the period of which I have spoken above, however, no such extraordinary intimacy had begun. As yet we were merely civil towards one another; and even that degree of civility was for a while interrupted, by the surprisal of a French post by a detachment from General Beresford's division, on the river Nive. Not that the piquet was wantonly cut off, or that any blame could possibly attach to the general who ordered its surprisal. The fact was, that the outpost in question occupied a hill upon the allied bank of the stream. It was completely insulated and detached from all other French posts, and appeared to be held as much out of perverseness, as because it commanded a view of the British lines to a great extent. Lord Beresford had repeatedly dispatched flags of truce, to request that it might be withdrawn, expressing great unwillingness to violate the sacred character which had been tacitly conferred upon the piquets; but Soult was deaf to his entreaties, and replied to his threats, only by daring him to carry them into execution. A party was accordingly ordered out, one stormy night, to cut off the guard; and so successful was the attempt, that an officer and thirty soldiers, with a midshipman and a few seamen, who had charge of the boat by which the reliefs were daily ferried over, were taken. Not a shot was fired. The French, trusting to the storm for protection, had called in their videttes, leaving only one on duty at the door of the house, and he found his arms pinioned, and himself secured, ere the roar of the tempest had permitted him to detect the sound of approaching steps. The unfortunate subaltern who commanded, sent in a few days after for his baggage; but the reply was, that the general would forward to him a halter, as the only indulgence which he merited.

But to return to my own personal narrative. After the adventure of the tea, nothing particular occurred whilst I continued in charge of the post. As soon as darkness had fairly set in, I proposed, in obedience to my orders, to withdraw; and I carried my design into execution without any molestation on the part of the enemy. It was, however, their custom to take possession of the hill as soon as the British troops abandoned it; and hence I had not proceeded above half way across the ravine, when I heard the voices of a French detachment, which must have marched into the courtyard of the house almost at the very moment when I and my men marched out of it. But they made no attempt to annoy us, and we rejoined the corps from which we had been detached, in perfect safety.

The next day was spent in a state of rest in the chateau of Arcanques. It is a fine old pile, and stands at the foot of the little eminence on which the church is built. Like many mansions in England of the date of Queen Elizabeth or Henry VIII, it is surrounded by a high wall; within which is a paved court, leading up to the main entrance. But it, too, like all the buildings near, bore ample testimony to the merciless operation of war, in its crumbling masonry and blackened timbers. There was a grove of venerable old firs round it, from which all the late firing had not entirely expelled a collection of rooks.

Of the church I have a less perfect recollection than I have of the chateau. I remember, indeed, that its situation was highly striking, and that the view from the churchyard was of no ordinary beauty. I recollect, likewise, several statues of knights and ladies reposing in niches round the walls; some with the cross upon their shields, and their legs laid athwart, to show that they had served in Palestine, or belonged to the order of the Sepulchre; and others in the more ancient costume of chain armour. But whether they were worthy of admiration, as specimens of the art of sculpture, I cannot now take it upon me to declare. I remarked, however, that the devices on the shields of most of these warriors, and the crests upon their helmets, resembled the coat and crest which were emblazoned over the gateway of the chateau; and hence I concluded that they were the effigies of the former lords of the castle, and that the family which owned it must have been at one period of some consequence.

It was not, however, in examining these buildings alone, that I found amusement for my hours of idleness. From the churchyard, as I have already stated, the view is at all times magnificent, and it was rendered doubly so to-day by the movements of our army. The tide of war seemed to have taken a sudden turn; and the numerous corps which had so lately defiled towards the right could now be seen retracing their steps, and deploying towards the left. It was a magnificent spectacle. From the high ground on which I stood I could see very nearly to the two extreme points of the position; and the effect produced by the marching of nearly 120,000 men, may be more easily imagined than described. The roads of communication ran, for the most part, in the rear of Arcanques. They were all crowded – cavalry, infantry, and artillery, were moving; some columns marching in eschellon, others pausing from time to time, as if to watch some object in their front; whilst, ever and anon, a grove, or wood, would receive an armed mass into its bosom, and then seem to be on fire, from the flashing of the sun upon the bayonets. Happily for me it was a day of bright sunshine, consequently every object looked to advantage; nor, I suspect, have many of our oldest soldiers beheld a more striking panorama than the combination of the objects around me this day produced.

I stood and watched with intense interest the shifting scene, till it gradually settled down into one of quiet. The various brigades, as I afterwards learned, were only returning from the point towards which the appearance of danger had hurried them, and now proceeded to establish themselves once more in their cantonments. The French general, either awed by the state of preparedness in which he found us, or satisfied with having called us for a few days into the field at this inclement season, laid aside the threatening attitude which he had assumed. It suited not the policy of our gallant leader, to expose his troops wantonly to the miseries of a winter campaign, and hence rest and shelter were again the order of the day. But in these the corps to which I was attached had as yet no participation, our march being directed, on the following morning, to the vicinity of Fort Charlotte, where the charge of the piquets was once more assigned to us.

Chapter 17

Between Bidart and Biarritz

From Bidart (where the 85th was now cantoned), when not supervising the strengthening of their position near 'the Mayor's House' (north-east of Bidart), Gleig and his companions made several escapades to Biarritz, already – but on a very modest scale – a sea-side resort.

The transactions of the three days, from the 8th to the 11th of January, resembled so completely, in all particulars, the transactions of other days, during which it fell to our lot to keep guard beside the Mayor's house, that I will not try the patience of my readers by narrating them at length. He will accordingly take it for granted, that the ordinary routine of watching and labour was gone through; that no attempt was made, on the part of the enemy, to surprise or harass us; and that, with the exception of a little suffering from extreme cold, and the want of a moderate proportion of sleep, we had no cause to complain of our destiny. When we first came to our ground, we found the redoubt in a state of considerable forwardness; quite defensible, indeed, in case of emergency; and we left it on the last day of the month mentioned above, even more perfect, and capable of containing at least a thousand men as its garrison. It was not, however, with any feeling of regret that we beheld a brigade of guards approaching our encampment, about two hours after noon, on the 11th, nor did we experience the slightest humiliation in surrendering to them our tents, our working tools, and the post of honour.

Now, then, we looked forward, not only with resignation, but with real satisfaction, to a peaceable sojourn of a few weeks at Gauthory. We had never, it is true, greatly admired these cantonments, but the events of the last eight or ten days had taught us to set its true value upon a settled habitation of any description; and we accordingly made up our minds to grumble no more. But just as the line of march was beginning to form, intelligence reached us, that the place of our abode was changed; other troops, it appeared, had been placed in our former apartments; and we were, in consequence, commanded to house ourselves in the village of Bedart. I mean not to assert that the order was received with any degree of dissatisfaction; but feeling as at that moment we did, it was, in truth, a matter of perfect indifference where we were stationed, provided only we had a roof over our heads, and an opportunity was granted of resting from our labours.

The village of Bedart is built upon an eminence, immediately in rear of the large common on which the advanced brigade lay encamped. It consists of about thirty houses, some of them of a tolerable size, but the majority are cottages. Into one of the largest my friend and myself were fortunate enough to be ushered; and as we found chimneys and windows already formed, the former permitting us to keep fires alight without the attendant misery of smoke, and the latter proof against the weather, we sincerely congratulated ourselves on our change of abode. Nor was it only on account of the superiority of these over our former quarters, that we rejoiced in this migration. The country around proved to be better stocked with game, especially with hares, than any which we had yet inhabited; and hence we continued, by the help of our guns and greyhounds, not only to spend the mornings very agreeably, but to keep our own and our friends' tables well supplied.

I have mentioned, in a former chapter, that the little town of Biaritz stands upon the sea-shore, and that it was, at the period of which I now write, regarded as a sort of neutral ground by the French and English armies. Patrols from both did, indeed, occasionally reconnoitre it; the French, in particular, seldom permitting a day to pass without a party of their light cavalry riding through it. Yet to visit Biaritz became now the favourite amusement amongst us, and the greater the risk run of being sabred or taken, the more eager were we to incur and to escape it. But there was a cause for this, good reader, and I will tell thee what it was.

In peaceable times, Biaritz constituted, as we learned from its inhabitants, a fashionable watering-place to the wealthy people of Bayonne and its vicinity. It was, and no doubt is, now a remarkably pretty village, about as large, perhaps, as Sandgate, and built upon the very margin of the water. The town itself lies in a sort of hollow, between two green hills, which, towards the sea, end in broken cliffs. Its houses were neatly white-washed; and, above all, it was, and I trust still is, distinguished as the residence of two or three handsome females. These ladies had about them all the gaiety and liveliness of Frenchwomen, with a good deal of the sentimentality of our own fair countrywomen. To us they were particularly pleasant, professing, I know not how truly, to prefer our society to that of any persons besides; and we, of course, were far too gallant to deny them that gratification, because we risked our lives or our freedom at each visit. By no means. Two or three times in each week the favoured few mounted their horses, and took the road to Biaritz, from which, on more than one occasion, they with difficulty returned.

With the circumstances of one of these escapes I may as well make my reader acquainted. We were, for the most part, prudent enough to cast lots previous to our setting out, in order to decide on whom, among the party, the odious task should devolve of watching outside, to prevent a surprisal by the enemy's cavalry, whilst his companions were more agreeably employed within. So many visits had, however, been paid, without any alarm being given, that one morning, having quitted Bedart fewer in number than usual, we rashly determined to run all risks, rather than that one of the three should spend an hour so cheerlessly. The only precaution which we took was to picket our horses, ready saddled and bridled, at the garden gate, instead of putting them up, as we were in the habit of doing, in the stable.

It was well for us that even this slender precaution had been taken. We had sat about half an hour with our fair friends, and had just ceased to joke on the probability of our suffering the fate of Sampson, and being caught by the Philistines, when, on a pause in the conversation taking place, our ears were saluted with the sound of horses' hoofs trampling upon the paved street. We sprang to the window, and our consternation may be guessed at, when we beheld eight or ten French huzzars riding slowly from the lower end of the town. Whilst we were hesitating how to proceed, whether to remain quiet, with the hope that the party might retire without searching any of the houses, or expose ourselves to a certain pursuit by flying, we observed a rascal in the garb of a seaman, run up to the leader of the patrol, and lay hold of his bridle, enter into conversation with him, and point to the abode of our new acquaintants. This was hint enough. Without pausing to say farewell to our fair friends, who screamed, as if they, and not we, had been in danger, we ran with all haste to the spot where our horses stood, and, springing into the saddle, applied the spur with very little mercy to their flanks. We were none of us particularly well mounted; but either our pursuers had alighted to search the house, or they took at first a wrong direction, for we got so much the start of them before the chase fairly began, that we might have possibly escaped, had we been obliged to trust to our own steeds as far as the piquets. Of this, however, I am by no means certain, for they were unquestionably gaining upon us, as a sailor would say, hand over hand, when, by great good fortune, a patrol of our own cavalry made its appearance. Then, indeed, the tables were completely turned. The enemy pulled up, paused for an instant, and took to their heels, whilst our troopers, who had trotted forward as soon as they saw what was the matter, put their horses to the speed, and followed. Whether they overtook their adversaries, and what was the issue of the skirmish, if indeed any skirmish took place, I cannot tell; for though we made an attempt to revenge ourselves upon our late pursuers, we soon found that we were distanced by both parties, and were, perforce, contented to ride quietly home, congratulating each other by the way on our hair-breadth deliverance. From that time forward we were more prudent. Our visits were, indeed, resumed, and with their usual frequency, but we took care not again to dispense with the watchfulness of one, who, on the contrary, took his station henceforth on the top of one of the heights, from which he commanded a view of the surrounding country, to the distance of several miles. Though, therefore, we were more than once summoned to horse, because the enemy's dragoons were in sight, we generally contrived to mount in such time, as to preclude the necessity of riding, as we had before ridden, for life or liberty.

By spending my mornings thus, or in a determined pursuit of game, and my evenings in such society as a corps of gentlemanly young men furnished, nearly a fortnight passed over my head before I was aware that time could have made so much progress. It seldom happens, however, that any period of human existence, whether extensive or contracted, passed by without some circumstance occurring calculated to produce painful sensations. I recollect, in the course of this fortnight, an event, which, though I was no farther concerned in it than as a spectator, made a deep and melancholy impression on my mind. I allude to the loss of a large vessel, during a tremendous storm, on the rocks which run out into the sea off Bedart.

The precise day of the month on which this sad shipwreck occurred, I have forgotten; but I recollect being sent for by my friend during the progress of one of the heaviest gales which we had witnessed, to come and watch with him the fate of a brig, which was in evident distress, about a couple of miles from the land. The wind blew a perfect hurricane on shore; and hence the question was, would the ship succeed in weathering the cape, or would she strike? If she got once round the headland, then her course to the harbour of Secoa was direct; if otherwise, nothing could save her. We turned our glasses towards her in a state of feverish anxiety, and beheld her bending under a single close-reefed top-sail, and making lee-way at a fearful rate, every moment. Presently a sort of attempt was made to luff up, or tack – it was a desperate one. Great God! I cannot even now think without shuddering of the consequence. The sail, caught by a sudden squall, was shivered into a hundred shreds; down, down she went, before the surge; in five seconds she struck against a reef; and in ten minutes more, split into a thousand fragments. One gun only was fired as a signal of distress; but who could regard it? We possessed no boats; and had the contrary been the case, this was a sea in which no boat could live. Powerless, therefore, of aid, we could only stand and gaze upon the wreck, till piece by piece it disappeared amid the raging of the waters. Not a soul survived to tell to what country she belonged, or with what she was freighted; and only one body was drifted to land. It was that of a female, apparently about thirty years of age, genteelly dressed, and rather elegantly formed; to whom we gave such sepulture as soldiers can give, and such as they are themselves taught to expect.

THE SUBALTERN

The impression which that shipwreck made upon me was not only far more distressing, but far more permanent, than the impression made by any other spectacle, of which, during the course of a somewhat eventful life, I have been the spectator. For several days I could think of hardly anything besides, and at night my dreams were constantly of drowning men, and vessels beating upon rocks; so great is the effect of desuetude even in painful subjects, and so appalling is death, when he comes in a form in which we are unaccustomed to contemplate him. Of slaughtered men I have, of course, beheld multitudes, as well when life had just departed from them, as when corruption had set its seal upon their forms; but such sights never affected me, no, not even at the commencement of my military career, as I was affected by the loss of that ship, though she went to pieces at too great a distance from the beach to permit more than a very indistinct view of her perishing inmates. Yet there is nothing in reality more terrible in drowning than in any other kind of death; and a sailor will look upon it, I dare say, with precisely the same degree of indifference which a soldier experiences, when he contemplates the prospect of his own dissolution by fire or steel.

In the course of my narrative, I have not made any regular attempt to convey to the mind of the reader a distinct notion of the peculiar costume and language which distinguish the natives of this country. Two motives have guided me in this. In the first place, it is, now-a-days, known to all who are likely to peruse what I write, that the inhabitants of those provinces, which lie at the immediate base of the Pyrenees, are a race totally distinct, and essentially different in almost all respects, from either the Spaniards or the French. They speak a language of their own, namely Basque, which is said by those who profess to be acquainted with it, to resemble the Celtic more than any other known tongue. The dress of the men consists usually of a blue or brown jacket, of coarse woollen cloth; of breeches or trowsers of the same, with a waistcoat, frequently of scarlet; grey worsted stockings, and wooden shoes. On their heads they wear a large flat bonnet, precisely similar to the Lowland bonnet, or scone, of Scotland. They are generally tall, but thin; and they present altogether an appearance as uncouth as need be fancied. The women, again, equip themselves in many respects as the fish-women of the good town of Newhaven are equipped, with this difference, that they seldom cover their heads at all, and, like the men, wear wooden clogs. They are a singular tribe, and appear to take a pride in those peculiarities, which keep them from coalescing with either of the nations among whom they dwell. But all this, as I said before, is too generally known, to render it imperative upon me minutely to repeat it.

My second motive for keeping, in a great degree, silent on the head of manners and customs, is one, the efficiency of which the reader will not, I dare say, call in question; namely, the want of opportunity to make myself sufficiently master of the subject, to enter, *con amore*, upon it. No man who journeys through a country, in the train of an invading army, ought to pretend to an intimate acquaintance with the manners and customs of its inhabitants. Wherever foreign troops swarm, the aborigines necessarily appear in false colours. The greater part of them, indeed, abandon their homes, whilst such of them as remain are servile and submissive through terror; nor do they ever display their real characters, at least in the presence of a stranger. Hence it is, that nine-tenths of my brethren in arms, who write at all, commit the most egregious blunders in those very portions of their books where they particularly aim at enlightening the reading public; and that the most matter-of-fact tour, spun out by the most matter-of-fact man or woman, who has visited the seat of the late war since the cessation of hostilities, contains, and must contain, more certain information touching the fire-side occupations of the people, than all the "Journals" or "Letters to Friends at Home", which this age of book-making has produced. Frankly confessing, therefore, that any account which I could give of the manners and habits of the Basques, would deserve as little respect as the accounts already given by other military tourists, I am content to keep my reader's attention riveted – if, indeed, that be practicable – upon my own little personal adventures, rather than amuse him with details, which might be true, as far as I know to the contrary, but which, in all probability, would be false.

Proceed we, then, in our own way. From the day of the shipwreck, up to the 23rd of the month, I have no recollection of any occurrence worthy to be recorded. Advantage was taken, it is true, of that period of rest, to lay in a fresh stock of tea, and other luxuries, with the means of accomplishing which an opportune disbursement of one month's pay supplied us; whilst an ample market was established by certain speculating traders, who followed the progress of the army from post to post. Secoa was now the grand mart for the procurement of necessaries, a considerable fleet of English vessels having entered it; and hither I and my comrades resorted for the purchase of such articles as habit, or caprice, prompted us to purchase. Then by coursing, shooting, and riding – sometimes to Biaritz, and the house of our pretty Frenchwomen – sometimes to St Jean de Luz, where, by the way, races were regularly established, and occasionally to the cantonments of a friend in another division of the army, we found our days steal insensibly, and therefore agreeably, away; nor was it without a feeling somewhat akin to discontent that we saw ourselves again setting forth, to take our turn of outpost duty at the old station beside Fort Charlotte.

Chapter 18

Relieving Freezing Piquets

Advances parties are pushed forward and a line of piquets placed east of the Lac de Mouriscot; occupation of a hill is disputed with enemy dragoons.

As the circumstances attending our present tour of duty had in them more of excitation than usual, I shall describe them at greater length.

The air was cold and bracing; it was a fine clear wintry day, when the corps to which I was attached, strengthened by the half of another battalion, began its march to the front. Instead of employing eighteen hundred men at the outposts, nine hundred were now esteemed capable of providing for the safety of the left column of the army; and such was accordingly the extent of the force, which, under the command of a lieutenant-colonel, took the direction of the Mayor's house. On arriving there, we found matters in a somewhat different order from that in which we were wont to find them. The enemy, it appeared, had abandoned the ground, which, up to the preceeding night, their piquets had occupied. Our advanced parties were, in consequence, pushed forward, and the stations of the extreme sentinels were now in front of that ground, upon which so much fighting had taken place in the beginning of last month. The guards themselves, instead of being hutted in and about the chateau, were disposed among a range of cottages, in the very centre of the field of battle; and the objects which were by this means kept constantly before their eyes, were certainly not of the most cheering or encouraging description.

It fell not to my lot to take charge of a piquet guard on the immediate day of our advance. My business, on the contrary, was to superintend the erection of works, which appeared to me to be erected as much for the purpose of giving the soldiers employment, and keeping their blood in circulation, as to oppose an obstacle to the troops of Marshal Soult, from whom no serious attack was now apprehended. On the following morning, however, I led my party to the front; nor have I frequently spent twenty-four hours in a state of higher excitement than I experienced during the progress of those which succeeded the movement.

130

In the first place, the weather had changed greatly for the worse. The frost continued, indeed, as intense, perhaps it was more intense than ever; but the snow came down in huge flakes, which a cold north-east wind drove into our faces. The hut into which the main body of the guard was ushered, presented the same ruinous appearance with almost every other house similarly situated; it furnished no shelter against the blast, and very little against the shower. Intelligence had, moreover, been conveyed to us by a deserter, that Soult, irritated at the surprisal of his post upon the Nive, had issued orders to retaliate whenever an opportunity might occur; and it was more than hinted, that one object of the late retrogression from our front, was to draw us beyond our regular line, and so place us in an exposed situation. The utmost caution and circumspection were accordingly enjoined, as the only means of frustrating his designs; and of these the necessity naturally increased as day-light departed.

That I might not be taken by surprise, in case any attack was made upon me after dark, I devoted a good proportion of the day to a minute examination of the country in front, and on each flank of my post. For this purpose I strolled over the fields, and found them literally strewed with the decaying bodies of what had once been soldiers. The enemy, it was evident, had not taken the trouble to bury even their own dead; for of the carcases around me, as many, indeed more, were arrayed in French than in English uniforms. No doubt they had furnished food for the wolves, kites, and wild-dogs from the thickets; for the flesh of most of them was torn, and the eyes of almost all were dug out; yet there was one body, the body of a French soldier, quite untouched; and how it chanced to be so, the reader may judge for himself, as soon as he has perused the following little story, for the truth of which I solemnly pledge myself.

About the middle of the line covered by my chain of sentries, was a small straggling village, containing a single street, about twenty cottages, and as many gardens. In the street of that village lay about half-a-dozen carcases, more than half devoured by birds and beasts of prey; whilst in several of the gardens were other little clusters similarly circumstanced. At the bottom of one of these gardens a Frenchman lay upon his face, perfectly entire, and close beside the body sat a dog. The poor brute, seeing us approach, began to howl in a very melancholy manner, at the same time resisting every effort, not on my part only, but on the part of another officer who accompanied me, to draw him from the spot. We succeeded, indeed, in coaxing him as far as the upper part of the garden; for, though large and lank, he was quite gentle; but he left us there, returned to his post beside the body, and, lifting up his nose into the air, howled piteously. There are few things in my life that I regret more than not having secured that dog; for it cannot, I think, be doubted, that he was watching beside his dead master, and that he defended him from the teeth and talons which made a prey of all around him. But I had, at the time, other thoughts in

131

my mind; and circumstances prevented my paying a second visit to the place where I had found him.

Among other happy results, the more forward position in which the piquets were now placed, furnished me with an opportunity of obtaining a less imperfect view of the city and defences of Bayonne, than any which I had yet obtained; I say less imperfect, for even from the tops of the houses in the village above referred to, no very accurate survey could be taken of a place situated upon a sandy flat, and still five or six miles distant; but I saw enough to confirm in me in the idea which I had already formed, that the moment of attack upon these entrenchments, come when it might, could not fail to be a bloody one.

Day-light was by this time rapidly departing, and it became incumbent upon me to contract the chain of my videttes, and to establish my party a little in the rear of the cottage where we had been hitherto stationed. By acting thus, I contrived to render myself as secure as a detachment numerically so small can ever hope to be. There were two lakes, or rather large ponds, in the line of my position, one on the left of the main road, and the other on the right; indeed, it was near the opposite extremity of the last-mentioned lake, that we unexpectedly found ourselves exposed to a large charge of cavalry, during the late battle. Of these lakes I gladly took advantage. Planting my people in a large house, about one hundred yards in rear, I formed my sentinels into a curved line, causing the extremities to rest, each upon its own pond, and pushing forward the centre, in the shape of a bow. "Now, then," thought I, "everything must depend upon the vigilance of the watchmen;" and to render that as perfect as possible, I resolved to spend the entire night in passing from the one to the other. Nor did I break that resolution. I may safely say, that I sat not down for five minutes at a time, from sun-set on the 24th till sunrise on the 25th.

The snow, which during an hour or two in the afternoon had ceased, began again to fall in increased quantities after dark. The wind, too, grew more and more boisterous every moment; it roared in the woods, and whistled fearfully through the ruined houses; whilst at every pause I could distinctly hear the wolf's long howl, and the growl and short bark of the wild-dogs, as they quarrelled over the mangled carcases scattered round me. Near the margin of the right-hand lake, in particular, this horrible din was constantly audible. There lay there, apart from each other, about ten bodies, of whom seven wore the fragments of an English uniform, and on these a whole troop of animals from the thickets beyond gorged themselves. Close beside one of these bodies I had been under the necessity of planting a sentinel; and the weakness of my party would not permit me to allow him a companion. He was rather a young man, and had selected the post for himself, in order to prove his contempt of superstition; but he bitterly lamented his temerity, as the situation in which I found him showed.

I visited his post about half an hour after he had assumed it, that is to say, a little before midnight. He was neither standing nor sitting, but leaning against a tree, and was fairly covered with a coat of frozen snow. His firelock had dropped from his hand, and lay across the chest of the dead man, beside whom he had chosen to place himself. When I spoke to the fellow, and desired to know why he had not challenged as I approached, he made no answer; and, on examining more closely, I found that he was in a swoon. Of course, I dispatched my orderly for a relief, and kept watch myself till he returned; when, with the assistance of my comrades, I first dragged the dead body to the lake, into which it was thrown, and then removed the insensible but living man to the piquet-house. There several minutes were spent in chafing and rubbing him before he opened his eyes; but being at length restored to the use of speech, he gave the following account of his adventure.

He said that the corporal had hardly quitted him, when his ears were assailed with the most dreadful sounds, such as he was very certain no earthly creature could produce. That he saw through the gloom a whole troop of devils dancing beside the water's edge, and a creature in white came creeping towards his post, groaning heavily all the way. He endeavoured to call out to it, but the words stuck in his throat, nor could he utter so much as a cry. Just then he swore that the dead man sat up, and stared him in the face; after which he had no recollection of anything, till he found himself in the piquet-house. I have no reason to suspect that man of cowardice; neither, as my reader will easily believe, did I treat his story with any other notice than a hearty laugh; but in the absolute truth of it he uniformly persisted, and, if he be alive, persists, I dare say, to this hour.

Besides this adventure with my fool-hardy, and at the same time superstitious follower, nothing occurred during the entire night calculated to stir up any extraordinary sensation in my own mind, or deserving of particular notice at the distance of nearly twelve years. As I have already mentioned, I took care to visit the sentinels so frequently, that every danger of surprisal was effectually averted. That these constant perambulations would have been undertaken as a matter of choice, I by no means pretend to say; for it was a night of storm and of intense cold: but I felt my situation to be a critical one, and, feeling so, I should have been less at ease by the side of a comfortable fire than I was whilst forcing my way against the wind and snow. Nor had I any reason to find fault with the conduct of my men. They had been warned of their danger in good time, and were now thoroughly on the alert to avert it; and thence I found each sentry more watchful than his neighbour – in other words, one and all of them completely on the *qui vive*.

I recollect, indeed, on one occasion, being put a little upon my mettle. It was about two in the morning, when I was informed by a soldier, who kept watch at the extremity of the hamlet already described, that he had heard within the last ten minutes a more than usual noise, in a large house about a hundred and fifty yards in front of his post. He described it to me as if people were tearing up the boards, or thumping down heavy weights upon the floor; and he himself seemed to think, that a body of the enemy's infantry had newly arrived, and had established themselves within the building. I listened attentively, in order to catch any sound which might proceed from that quarter, but none reached me. He persisted, however, in his story, and added, that if the noise which he had heard proceeded not from men, it must come from spirits. "And why not from dogs or wolves?" said I. "Because dogs and wolves cannot split wood," said he; "and I will swear, that if ever I heard planks torn asunder, I heard it now." Being little inclined to leave the matter in doubt, I remained with the sentinel, and dispatched my orderly to bring up half a dozen men for the purpose of making a recognizance.

The reader has probably anticipated that I found the house empty. It was so; for after stealing through the street with the utmost caution, stopping every two minutes, and applying my ear to the ground in order to catch the slightest noise, – after peeping over the garden-wall, listening at the entrance, and creeping up the front steps with the pace of a burglar, – I found that the chateau was wholly tenantless; and what was more, that not a trace of its having been recently visited, at least by human tenants, could be discovered. Nevertheless, I commended the soldier for his watchfulness, advised him to continue equally watchful as long as he should remain on duty; and leaving it to himself to decide whether the sounds which he had reported proceeded from ghosts or more tangible creatures, I quitted him.

It may not be amiss if I state here, what I have already more than hinted, that on all these occasions I was accompanied by a little spaniel bitch. I had brought the creature with me from England, when she was a puppy of only nine months old, and she became attached to me in a degree such as would not in all probability have been the case, had my mode of life been more settled, and she in consequence less my companion. Nor was it only because I was fond of the animal that I taught her to follow my fortunes thus closely. A well-trained dog is no bad help-mate to an officer who has charge of an out-post; indeed, I was never greatly alarmed, notwithstanding the communications of my videttes, unless my little four-footed patrol confirmed their statements. If she barked or growled, then I felt assured that something dangerous was near; if she continued quiet, I was comparatively easy. To that dog, indeed, I owe my life; but the circumstance under which she preserved it occurred in a different quarter of the world, and has no right to be introduced into my present narrative.

In this manner was the night of the 24th of January spent. About an hour before day-break on the 25th I mustered my piquet, according to custom, and kept them standing under arms, in front of the house, till dawn appeared. This measure was necessary, not only because it is a standing order in the British army for advanced corps to get under arms thus early, but because experience has proved that the first of the morning is the favourite moment of attack, inasmuch as, by commencing hostilities at that young hour of the day, good hopes are held out of effecting something decisive before the day shall have ended. On the present occasion, however, no attack was made; and hence, after waiting the usual time, I prepared again to shift my ground, and to take post at the more advanced station which I held yesterday, and which I had evacuated solely for the purpose of making myself less insecure during the hours of darkness.

We had returned to our day-light position about a quarter of an hour, when a patrol of light cavalry arrived, and proposed to plant a vidette upon the top of an eminence, about a mile in our front. The person who commanded the party appeared, however, to be a little in doubt as to the practicability of performing the orders which he had received. He said, that the enemy were not willing to allow that height to be occupied by us; that the last relief which had attempted to establish itself there was driven off, and that he was not without apprehension of an ambuscade, and of being taken, with his whole party; in a word, he begged that I would allow a portion of my men to follow him, and that I would support him in case he should be attacked either by infantry or cavalry.

To say the truth, I was a good deal puzzled how to act, for nothing had been communicated to me on the subject; nevertheless, I determined to lend as much assistance as I could spare, and accordingly commanded about a dozen men to follow the dragoons. Not deeming it right, however, to intrust a detachment of my own people entirely to the charge of a stranger, I resolved to accompany them, and, perhaps, it was well I did.

We were yet a half musket-shot from the hill which the cavalry were desired to occupy, when we observed a superior force of French dragoons advancing from the lines towards the the same point. The push now was for the high ground. We foot-soldiers could not of course keep pace with our mounted comrades, but we followed them at double quick time, and arrived at the base just as they had crowned the height. They were hardly there, however, when a discordant shout, or rather yell, told us that the French were ascending by the opposite side. Our dragoons, I observed, instantly formed line; they discharged their pistols, and made a show of charging; but whether it was that the enemy's numbers overawed them, or that their horses took fright at the report, I cannot tell, but before the caps of their opponents were visible to our eyes, their order was lost, and themselves in full retreat. Down they came, both parties, at full speed; and now it was our turn to act. I had already placed my men behind a turf fence, with strict orders not to fire till I should command them. It was in vain that I stood upon the top of the wall, and shouted and waved to the fugitives to take a direction to the right or left. They rode directly towards the ditch, as if their object had been to trample us under foot; and, what was still more alarming, the enemy were close behind them. In self-defence, I was therefore obliged to give the pre-concerted signal. My people fired, – one of our own, and three of the French dragoons dropped. The latter, apparently astonished at the unlooked-for discharge, pulled up. "Now, now," cried we, "charge, charge, and redeem your honour!" The dragoons did so, and we rising at the same instant with loud shouts, the enemy were completely routed. Two of their troopers were taken, and of all who escaped, hardly one escaped without a wound.

After this trifling skirmish, the French no longer disputed with us the possession of the hill. Leaving the cavalry, therefore, to maintain it, I fell back with my men to the piquet-house, and, about an hour after my return, was by no means displeased to find another party arrive to relieve us. Having given to the officer in command of that party as much information as I myself possessed, I called in my sentries, and marched to the rear.

Chapter 19

Hares and Woodcocks

In mid-February, Hill's 'Corps', forming the Right Wing, advanced east, at the commencement of the final campaign of the war, which was to take them to Orthez, where, after heavy fighting, Soult was defeated on the 27th of the month. Meanwhile, on the 21st, Aylmer's Brigade was marched closer to the outworks of Bayonne, taking up a position between Anglet and the Nive, with Colonel Archibald Campbell's Portuguese troops between them and the river; a Spanish contingent commanded by General Carlos de España was placed to their left. The Major Dalgetty referred to was 'Dugald Dalgetty', a garrulous soldier of fortune in Sir Walter Scott's 'A Legend of Montrose', published in 1819. Dr William Kitchiner, author of 'Apicius Redivivus, or the Cook's Oracle' (1817), which went into several editions, was well-known for his culinary skill. Sir William Curtis was Lord Mayor of London in 1795–96.

From the 26th of January up to the 20th of the following month, nothing occurred either to myself individually, or to the portion of the army of which I was a member, particularly deserving of notice. During that interval, indeed, a fresh supply of wearing-apparel, of flannels, stockings, and shoes, reached me, being a present from kind friends at home; and seldom has any present proved more acceptable, or arrived more opportunely; but the reader is not, I dare say, over anxious to know whether the articles in question were too large, too small, or whether they fitted to an hair's breadth. Neither would it greatly amuse him were I to detail at length how ships freighted with corn reached Secoa; how fatigue-parties were ordered out to unload them; and how the loads, being justly divided, were issued as forage for the horses, which stood much in need of it. It may, however, be worth while to state, that previous to the arrival of these corn-ships, even the cavalry and artillery were under the necessity of feeding their horses chiefly upon chopped furze, and hence that disease had begun to make rapid progress among them, many dying almost every day, and all, even the most healthy, falling rapidly out of condition. But for this providential supply of wholesome oats and barley, I question whether we should have been able to take the field, at least effectively, till later in the season.

On the 16th of February, 1814, the allied troops may be said to have fairly broken up from their winter quarters. The corps to which I belonged continued, indeed, under cover till the morning of the 21st; but we were already, in a great measure, at our posts; seeing that our cantonments lay immediately in rear of the piquets. Such divisions as had been quartered in and about St Jean de Luz began, however, to move towards the front on the 16th, and pitching their tents on the crest of the position, they waited quietly till their leader should see fit to command a farther advance. On these occasions, no part of the spectacle is more imposing than the march of the artillery. Of this species of force, six, sometimes eight pieces, form a brigade, each gun is dragged by six or eight horses; by six, if the brigade be intended to act with infantry, by eight, if it belong to what is called the flying artillery. In the former case, eight gunners march on foot beside each field-piece, whilst three drivers ride *a la postilion*; in the latter, the gunners are all mounted and accoutred like yeomanry cavalry. Then the tumbrils and ammunition-waggons, with their train of horses and attendants, follow in rear of the guns, and the whole procession covers perhaps as much ground as is covered by two moderately strong battalions in marching order.

The great part of the infantry attached to the left column had passed, when brigade after brigade of guns wound through our village. These halting just after they had cleared the street, diverged into some open fields on the right and left of the road, where the whole park, amounting to perhaps thirty pieces, was established. In another green field at the opposite side of Bedart, four heavy eighteen-pounders took their station, to be in readiness, in case of need, to be transported to Fort Charlotte. Last of all came the cavalry, consisting of the 12th and 16th light dragoons, and of two regiments of heavy Germans; nor could we avoid remarking, that though the 12th and 16th dragoons are both of them distinguished corps, the horses of the foreigners were, nevertheless, in far better order than those of our countrymen. The fact, I believe, is, that an Englishman, greatly as he piques himself on his skill in farriery, never acquires that attachment for his horse which a German trooper experiences. The latter dreams not, under any circumstances, of attending to his own comfort till after he has provided for the comfort of his steed. He will frequently sleep beside it, through choice, and the noble animal seldom fails to return the affection of his master, whose voice he knows, and whom he will generally follow like a dog.

There was another striking difference in the two brigades of cavalry which I remarked. The English rode on, many of them silent, some chatting of a thousand things, others whistling or humming those tuneless airs in which the lower orders of our countrymen delight. The Germans, on the contrary, sang, and sang beautifully, a wild chorus – a hymn, as I afterwards learned, to the Virgin, different persons taking different parts, and producing altogether the most exquisite harmony. So great an impression did this music make upon me, that I caught the air, and would note it down for the benefit of my reader, were I sufficiently master of the art of notation; but as this happens not to be the case, he must wait till we become personally acquainted, when I promise to play it for him, in my very best style, upon the flute.

Nor was it only on the left that warlike movements occurred. The whole army took the field; and that a serious campaign was already commenced, the sound of firing at the extreme end of the line gave notice. I had wandered abroad with my gun on the morning of the 18th, not indeed venturing to proceed far from home, but trying the neighbouring copses for a hare or woodcock, when my farther progress was arrested by the report of several cannons in the direction of Lord Hill's division. These were succeeded by a rapid but short discharge of musketry, and my sport was immediately abandoned; but I found on my return that no alarm was excited, and that every description of force which I had left in a state of inaction continued still inactive.

The same degree of suspense prevailed amongst us during the 19th and 20th. On the latter of these days my mind, at least, was kept employed by a journey to the harbour, for the purpose of bringing up a fresh supply of corn for the horses; though it was a species of employment with which I would have readily dispensed, inasmuch as the day chanced to be particularly cold, with snow. But our anxiety was destined not to be of long continuance; an order reaching us that night, at a late hour, to be accoutred and in line of march by three o'clock in the following morning. Now then, at length, we applied ourselves to the task of packing the baggage. The tents were once more summoned into use; their condition closely examined; such rents as appeared in the canvass were hastily repaired, and every deficiency in pegs and strings made good. Then the ordinary supply of *provend*, as Major Dalgetty would call it, being put up, we threw ourselves down in our clothing, and fell asleep.

It was still dark as pitch, when the well-known sound of troops hurrying to their stations roused me from my slumber. As I had little to do in the way of accoutring, except to buckle on my sabre, and to stick my pistols in a black leathern haversack, which on such occasions usually hung at my back, abundance of time was given for the consumption of as much breakfast as at that early hour I felt disposed to consume; after which I took post beside my men. The reader will have doubtless noted, that, like the good soldier already named, I never set out upon any military expeditions, without having, in the first place, laid in a foundation of stamina to work upon. And here I would recommend to all young warriors, who may be gathering laurels when nothing of me shall remain except these Memoirs, invariably to follow my example. They may rely upon it, that an empty stomach, so far from being a provocative, is a serious antidote to valour; and that a man who has eaten nothing previous to either an advance or a retreat, runs no little risk of finding his strength fail at the very moment when its continuance is of vital importance to him. No, no; your hot-brained youth, who is too impatient to eat, is like your over-anxious hunter, which refuses its corn because the hounds pass the stable. Neither the one nor the other will go through a hard day's work.

The troops being formed in marching order, the word was given, and we advanced in the direction, now so familiar to us, of the Mayor's house. As we passed the park of artillery, we heard, rather than saw the drivers limbering up, and preparations busily making for service. The tramp of many feet, too, could be discerned, as well as the clattering of horses' hoofs, the jingling of steel scabbards, and the rattle of canteens and cartouch-boxes; but it was not till these various sounds had been faint and distant that day-light began to break upon us. We had, however, been conscious of having struck into a sort of by-lane, and of having proceeded for some time in a direction towards the right; and hence, when objects became visible, we were not surprised to find that we had passed even the village of Arcanques; and that all the country hitherto traversed by us, was left behind. As may be guessed, this circumstance alone excited pleasurable feelings; for we were weary of the eternal Mayor's house and Fort Charlotte, and anxious to reach some other fields on which to prove our courage.

The point towards which our steps were turned, was a lofty eminence, distant about a quarter of a mile from the banks of the Nive, and commanding an extensive view of a country extremely beautiful. The height had been occupied during the preceding day by a part of the 5th division, which now resigned the charge to us, and descending into the plain, crossed the river, and pushed off in a direction to the right. For ourselves, we were commanded to halt here; and as neither the tents nor baggage had arrived – as indeed we soon learned that they were not to follow – we sedulously set about lighting fires, and prepared to bivouack. These were, however, as yet early days for bivouacking; and hence arrangements were made for getting us under cover during the night; in accordance with which, we descended soon after sunset to a large chateau, close beside the advanced sentries, where ample accommodation was found for all of us. There the night was passed, not altogether free from apprehension, seeing that no piquets – only a chain of sentinels, were between us and the enemy – but as everything remained quiet, without any attempt being made to molest us, no evil consequences resulted from the adoption of a plan, agreeable enough, it is true, but savouring perhaps of rashness, rather than excess of caution.

As soon as the morrow's early parade was dismissed, and I perceived that no indication was given of further movements, I took my gun, and set off to the woods, where I hoped to find game enough to furnish out a comfortable repast in the evening. Nor was I disappointed. Hares and woodcocks abounded here; there were moreover numerous flocks of golden plover; and of these I contrived to bring home a sufficient number to satisfy my own wants, and the wants of others. But it was not alone because I chanced to be particularly successful in shooting, that the day's excursion gave me pleasure. The country around was more romantic and striking than any which I had yet seen, and came nearer to a realization of my previous notion respecting the scenery in the south of France, of what it really was, or rather what it ought to be. All was hill and dale, sweeping groves and green meadows, with here and there a vineyard, already beginning to give signs of vegetation, and to put forth its delicate fibres, like our hop plant in the month of May. The proximity of the Nive, too, added not a little to the beauty of the prospect, as it flowed gently and quietly on, winding for a while between sloping grassfields, and then eluding the eye amid the thick groves which overhung its banks. It would have been altogether as sweet and pastoral a landscape as the imagination can very well picture, but for the remote view of the entrenched camp, which from various points might be obtained, and the nearer glimpse of numerous watch-fires, round which groups of armed men were swarming. To me, however, these were precisely the most interesting objects in the panorama, and those upon which I chiefly delighted to fix my attention.

The game which the sporting members of the corps contrived this day to pick up was so abundant, that we resolved to admit the whole of our brother officers to a participation in it, and to spend an evening together after the fashion of an evening at home. For this purpose, all the culinary utensils within reach were put in requisition, and all the individuals skilled in the gastronomic art were invited to give proof of their abilities. Beef – lean beef – that everlasting and insipid food of soldiers – was disguised in every imaginable form, whilst hares were melted down into soup, woodcocks stewed, golden plovers roasted, and sundry rabbits curried. In a word, we sat down, in number about five-and-twenty, at six o'clock, to a dinner which would have done no discredit, in point of cookery, to the favourite disciple of Dr Kitchener, and which even Sir William Curtis himself would not have deemed unworthy of his notice. Good cheer, moreover, is generally the parent of good-humour, and good-humour is the source of benevolence; nor would it be easy to point out in this selfish world of ours, five-and-twenty persons whose hearts overflow more richly with the milk of human kindness, than did ours, as we took our seats by the well-filled board. Fervently did we wish that every corps in the British army, ay, and in the French army too, could that day fare as well; whilst we proceeded to prove, in the most satisfactory of all manners, that delicate viands were not thrown away, at least upon us.

These praise-worthy expressions had hardly ceased, and we had just begun to pay our addresses to the well-boiled soup, when the tread of horses' hoofs attracted our notice. It would have been a positive sin had the enemy come on at such a moment as this; and I verily believe, that we in our wrath would have given him no quarter. Nevertheless, sins are daily committed; nor were we by any means at ease, touching this important matter, till the cause of the alarm appeared. It was a wounded officer who had been shot in a skirmish this morning, and was now slowly travelling to the rear, being with difficulty held on his horse by a couple of attendants. Our dinner was instantly abandoned, and we all ran to offer such assistance as it lay in our power to offer. But the poor fellow was too seriously hurt to accept of our invitations to eat. The surgeon accordingly took him in charge, and having amputated the arm which one ball had broken, and striven in vain to extract another from his side, he left him to the care of his servant. The man was dead before morning.

It is impossible to describe the chilling effect of this adventure upon all of us. Steeled, as men necessarily become, in a continued state of warfare, against the milder and more gentle feelings of our nature, they must be hardened indeed, if they can behold a dying fellow-creature arrive among them, in an hour of jollity and mirth, without viewing the contrast in so strong a light as to damp, if it be unable utterly to destroy, their hilarity. For our own parts, we returned, indeed, to table, and we chatted, or rather endeavoured to chat, as if no such guest had come among us. But it would not do. Our party, which we had designed to keep together till dawn, broke up soon after ten o'clock, and we lay down to sleep with minds more full of our suffering brother-in-arms, than of our joviality.

The wounded officer belonged to a regiment of the fifth division. He had acted, with a small party, as one of the flank patrol, during an oblique movement of his brigade, along the front of the enemy's line, and falling in with a body of their skirmishers, had been wounded in a wood, where the rapid advance of the column left him. His servant and another man, having procured a horse from one of his friends, returned to his assistance. But before they could discover him the division was too far on its way to be overtaken, consequently they took with him a direction to the rear, which brought them to our house. He had received his wounds at an early hour in the day, and had been preserved from bleeding to death only by the cold; but the long period which elapsed ere his hurts could be dressed, rendered them doubly severe. Our surgeon, indeed, assured us, that no care, however speedily bestowed, could have saved him; and therefore it was perhaps as well that the absence of medical assistance shortened his misery, by protecting him from the torture necessarily attendant upon useless dressings.

We had just begun to drop into a forgetfulness of all causes, both of joy and sorrow, when a dragoon arrived with orders for the commanding officers, by which it appeared that we were to be under arms at three o'clock next morning, and to follow where the bearer – a soldier of the corps of guides – should lead. Something, too, was whispered about a general attack upon the enemy's lines; of passing the Adour, and investing Bayonne; but these were mere surmises, naturally following upon such vague directions. For myself, I permitted them not to occupy much of my attention, or to keep their places long in my mind; but philosophically concluding that I had no choice submitted to me, and that I must go wherever I should be sent, and act exactly as I should be desired to act, I once more threw myself on the floor, and closed my eyes. Sleep was not long a stranger to my eyelids.

Chapter 20

Tightening the Knot

Several topographical names may require further identification: for Hilletre, see Helette (south-east of Cambo); Arriverente, is now Osserain-Rivareyte (south-west of Sauveterre); Oyergave is Œyregave, south-east of Payrchourade, or rather Peyrehorade; and Villenueve is presumably Viellenave-de-Navarrenx. While Aylmer's Brigade were closing in on Bayonne, General the Hon. Edward Stopford's Brigade of the 1st Division was moving through pine-woods to a position on the south bank of the Lower Adour opposite Boucau ready to cross the river and isolate Bayonne. There, General Pierre Thouvenot commanded a garrison of about 12,000, to which it had been reduced by sickness and desertion. The initial crossing took place at noon on the 23 February by means of pontoons and rafts only, as the vessels carrying the planks and beams collected during previous weeks at St Jean-de-Luz and Ciboure to form the bridge of boats had been blown out to sea by a gale, and their belated arrival at the river-mouth had delayed the operation planned. The rockets, erratic and inaccurate projectiles in which Wellington had little faith, had been invented some eight years earlier by Colonel Sir William Congreve. The loud hiss they made effectively frightened troops encountering them for the first time, as they did on this occasion, bursting over an approaching enemy column, which retired to the safety of their citadel.

Of the appearance of the country through which we marched, on the morning of the 23rd of February, I can say but little, the greater part of the journey having been performed in the dark. When day dawned, however, we perceived that we had been defiling by a new road towards the left; and at eight o'clock we found ourselves in a green field, about a musket-shot from the high-road, and within three miles of the works in front of Bayonne. At the other end of the field was a piquet of the enemy, which instantly turned out, and lined the ditches, whilst we contented ourselves with forming into column; and then piling our arms, we stood still till farther instructions should arrive. In the meanwhile, I was not unemployed. By the help of my telescope I took as accurate a survey of the stupendous fortifications before me as circumstances would permit, and the following is, as nearly as I recollect, the aspect which they presented:–

The position which Marshal Soult had taken up, and which has long been justly regarded as one of the most formidable positions in the south of France, ran parallel, or nearly parallel, for about four miles, with the Ardour. Its right rested upon the strong and extensive fortifications of Bayonne, its left upon the small river Joyeuse, and the formidable post of Hilletre. When I state this as being the position of Marshal Soult's army, I mean to say, that such was the line which that army occupied, previous to the renewal of hostilities on our part. Towards his right no change had, indeed, taken place; but on his left he had been driven back, first from Hilletre upon St Martin, and then through St Palais, as far as the village of Arriverente. From this again he was dislodged on the 17th by the 92nd regiment, under the command of Colonel Cameron; till, finally falling back from post to post, the strength of his forces became divided; the entrenched camp near St Jean Pied de Pont was abandoned, and Soult, after defending as long as they were defensible, his strongholds, principally at Hastingues and Oyergave, retired with his extreme left within the *tete-du-pont* at Payrchourade. When I glanced my eye, therefore, along the entrenchments this morning, I was able to take in only so much of the formidable line as extended from the city to the hamlet of Villenueve, on the Gave d'Oleron; and of the last-mentioned of these places I obtained a view so indistinct, that had I not previously known that it formed one key of the position, I should not have been aware of its vast importance.

It is not my design to attempt an accurate detail of the eventful operations of this and the following day. On the left of the centre, (the point where I chanced to be stationed,) comparatively little fighting took place. We made, indeed, from time to time, demonstrations of attack, drove in a few piquets, and ever and anon sent out a body of skirmishers, just by way of keeping the attention of the enemy awake; but it was on the right of our line that the most important proceedings occurred. Lord Wellington's plan was to cut off the army of Soult entirely from Bayonne, and to draw him, if possible, from the works which he had thrown up; and in the execution of that plan, he was as successful as he generally proved to be in all his schemes. Whilst, therefore, we were thus amusing ourselves on the heights above Bayonne, Sir Rowland Hill, with the light, the second, and a Portuguese division, passed the Gave d'Oleron at Villenueve; Sir Henry Clinton crossed, at the head of the sixth division, between Montfort and Laas; and Sir Thomas Picton, with his own favourite third division, threatened the bridge of Sauveterre, and obliged the enemy to blow it up. The effect of these numerous attacks was to break the line which Soult had formed, in no less than three points, and to oblige him to draw off the main body of his army from his entrenched camp, and to establish himself on the heights above Orthes.

In the meanwhile, the first division, on the extreme left, was not inactive. It formed a part, and a prominent part, in this stupendous plan of operations, to take possession of both banks of the Adour, as well below as above the city; and to place Bayonne in a state of blockade, at the very moment when the army which covered it should be driven from its position. To render that scheme effectual, it was necessary to push a detachment of infantry across the Adour on rafts, for the purpose of protecting the formation of a bridge, which Lord Wellington had resolved to erect. This was effected at a part three miles from the sea, where the river is full eight hundred yards wide; and so little was the movement anticipated, that six hundred men, under the command of Major-General Stopford, were actually ferried over before the enemy exhibited any symptom of alarm or of consciousness that an attempt of the kind had been made.

The bridge itself was destined to be composed of small vessels, decked boats, and chasse marees, placed at the distance of twenty or thirty yards from one another, and connected by strong cables and deals laid transversely across. The vessels had, indeed, been collecting in the harbour of Secoa during the last ten days; and now only waited for a favourable breeze to effect their entrance into the Adour. Nor is that an easy matter, even for a vessel of forty or fifty tuns burthen. At the mouth of the Adour is a bar or bank of sand, quite impassable at low water; which, even at ordinary full tides, is so little covered, that nothing larger than a large fishing-boat can float. During the season of spring-tides, I believe ships of a considerable size may enter; but nothing approximating a ship can hope to cross at any other season.

When the army broke up from winter quarters, it was not the season of spring-tide; neither could military operations be delayed till that season should arrive. It was accordingly determined by Rear-Admiral Penrose, who commanded the squadron cruising off the coast, to force his way up the stream at all hazards, as soon as a breeze should spring up; and the command of the boats dedicated to this perilous service was intrusted to a gallant officer from the sister isle, by name O'Reily. No man could be better cut out for such an enterprize. Brave, impetuous, perhaps somewhat rash, Captain O'Reily was not a little galled when he found his progress delayed, during the whole of the 23rd, by a dead calm; but he was not therefore useless. Perceiving that nothing could be done on his own element, he came to land, and was not a little serviceable in constructing the rafts, and putting the soldiers in proper order for crossing.

It was about ten in the morning, when the posts which the enemy occupied in and near Anglette, as well as among the sand hills on the left banks of the Adour, being carried, General Stopford's little corps began to pass the river. To facilitate this operation, or rather to hinder the enemy from observing it at all, our brigade, which had hitherto remained idle upon the brow of the identical rising ground, where, after the action of the 9th of the preceding November, we had halted, was directed to execute various manoeuvres. We first deployed into line, then extended our files into skirmishing order; next threw out half a dozen companies, who rushed forward at double quick time, and with loud shouts, as if an assault were seriously intended. Nor were our movements unnoticed. In less than five minutes, several batteries and breast-works in our immediate front, which had previously remained almost empty of defenders, were crowded with soldiers, whilst three pieces of light artillery came galloping from the right, and took post in a field, across which our route, had we pursued it, must have lain.

To meet the detached companies, a body of tirrailleurs advanced, and a very entertaining skirmish began. For myself, I was, during the entire day, in a place of perfect safety; out of reach even of the light cannon, which were turned against us; and hence I had every opportunity of observing, with an easy mind, the progress of those about me. Immediately on our left was a division of Spanish infantry, which, occupying the village of Anglette, kept up the communication between us and the guards. On our right again was a Portuguese corps; and it is curious enough, that whilst the French were satisfied with watching us, and of giving proof that they were determined to oppose any attack on our part, they made several spirited assaults upon our allies. By the Portuguese they were met with as much gallantry, and in as good order, as they would have been met by ourselves; towards the close of the war, indeed, the Portuguese infantry were inferior to none in the world. From the Spaniards, on the contrary, they received no very determined opposition; and but for the sight of our column on one side, and of a column of guards and the German legion on the other, they would have made there, in all probability, a breach in the line. As it was, they contented themselves with driving the troops before them, ever and anon, from the village; and then fell back, as soon as they found themselves in danger of being taken in flank, by us, or the Germans.

It was a positive relief to avert my eyes from the operations of the Spanish corps, and to turn them towards the Portuguese. The latter consisted of three battalions of caçadores, and two of heavy infantry; of which the caçadores alone could, in strict propriety, be said to be engaged. Covering the front of the others, and communicating with our skirmishers, they spread themselves in extended order over the fields, and kept up a steady, cool, and well-directed fire, upon the cloud of tirrailleurs which vainly endeavoured to drive them back upon the reserve. In looking at such a scene as this, you generally fix your eye upon one or two individuals, whose progress you watch so long, that you become at last as much interested in their safety, as if they were personal acquaintances of your own. I recollect that one Portuguese soldier, in particular, attracted my notice that day. He seemed, if I might judge from his proceedings, to be animated with a more than ordinary degree of hatred towards the French; that is to say, he looked neither to his right nor to his left – paid no attention either to the momentary retrogression or advance of his comrades; but steadily kept his ground, or varied it only for the purpose of obtaining a better aim at his opponents. He had posted himself considerably in advance of his own line, behind a large furze-bush, or rather in the middle of a furze-bower, from which I saw him deliberately pick off three Frenchmen, one after another. At length he was noticed by the enemy, and six or seven of them turned towards his place of ambuscade. Nothing daunted, the Portuguese remained perfectly steady; he crouched down, indeed, to load, but the moment his rifle was charged, he leant over the bush, and fired. One of his assailants fell whilst the rest, pointing their pieces to the spot from whence the smoke issued, gave him a volley; but it was harmless; he had darted to the other side of the bush, and every shot missed him. He knelt down and loaded again; the enemy were now within twenty yards of him; he fired, and an officer who accompanied them, walked off the field, grasping his left arm in his right hand. The rest of his adversaries, as if panic-struck, retreated; and there he staid, till the close of the affair; after which, he returned to his ranks, apparently unhurt. That man killed and wounded not fewer than eight French soldiers during the day.

It was now drawing towards evening, when our attention was powerfully, and somewhat painfully, attracted to the little corps which had crossed the Adour upon rafts, and now occupied a position among the sand hills on the opposite bank. Hitherto, they had been either unnoticed, or disregarded by the enemy. The only serious fighting, indeed, which had as yet taken place, on the extreme left of our line, was a sort of struggle between a French frigate, assisted by two gun-boats, and a British battery of eighteen-pounders, well supplied with red-hot shot. The result of that struggle was, as it may be anticipated, the complete destruction of the gun-boats, and the compulsory retreat of the ship; but to the passing of our infantry, no regard seemed to have been paid – at least no endeavour was made to cut them off, or to hinder them from strengthening their post. At length, however, the French general appeared to have discovered his error. A column of five thousand infantry, with several pieces of cannon, was accordingly formed, and marched in firm array to the attack of only six hundred soldiers of the British guards, supported by a small detachment of rockets.

The ground which General Stopford held, was, happily for him, extremely favourable. It was full of inequalities; each of which formed, as it were, a natural parapet, behind which troops could shelter themselves. Perceiving the approach of his assailants, the general formed his people to the best advantage in rear of one of the sand hills; and causing them to lie down, so as to be completely concealed, he waited patiently till the head of the attacking column had arrived within twenty yards of him. Then the word was given to start up; and the rocket men throwing in their diabolical engines with extraordinary precision, at the very instant when the infantry fired a well-directed volley, the confusion created in the ranks of the enemy beggars all description. I saw and conversed with a French serjeant who was taken in this affair. He assured me, that he had been personally engaged in twenty battles, and that he had never really known the sensation of fear till to-day. A rocket, it appeared, had passed through his knapsack without hurting him; but such was the violence with which it flew, that he fell upon his face, and the horrible hissing sound produced by it was one which he declared that he never could forget. Nor is it the least appalling part of a rocket's progress, that you see it coming, and yet know not how to avoid it. It skips and starts about from place to place in so strange a manner, that the chances are, when you are running to the right or left to get out of the way, you run directly against it; and hence the absolute rout, which a fire of ten or twelve rockets can create, provided they take effect. But it is a very uncertain weapon. It may, indeed, spread havock among the enemy, but it may also turn back upon the people who use it, causing, like the elephant of other days, the defeat of those whom it was designed to protect. On the present occasion, however, it proved materially serviceable, as every man can testify who witnessed the result of the fire.

Having thus briefly detailed the issue of the engagement, it may appear almost superfluous to state, how we were affected by the expectation of its occurrence. We knew well that a mere handful of our fellow-soldiers were unavoidably thrown into such a position, that, let their case be what it might, no succour could be afforded them. We saw by the dense and lengthened mass which was moving down, and by the guns and horses which accompanied it, that this little corps was about to sustain an assault from a force capable of overwhelming it by absolute bodily weight; and feeling that we could render no other aid, than that which empty wishes supply, we cast no imputation upon the bravery of our comrades, when we trembled for their safety. All eyes were directed to the sand-hills; scarce a word was spoken by the spectators, and the greater number absolutely held their breath, till the shock was given.

The battery of eighteen-pounders, of which I have already spoken, failed not to salute the enemy's column as it passed. The range was a long one; but our gunners were skilful, and it was consolatory to see, from the occasional checks and disorders in various parts of the advancing corps, that its salute was more than honorary. But what had become of our own people? – they had all disappeared; and it seemed as if the French troops might march without molestation to the margin of the sea. The problem was speedily solved; and the very first discharge, given as I have described above, decided the business. It was followed, as such a fire is generally followed in the British service, by a charge with the bayonet, and we, who, but a moment before, had been breathless with apprehension, now shouted in triumph, as we beheld the mass, of late so formidable, scattered and put to flight by a single battalion.

Darkness was by this time setting in so rapidly, that objects could no longer be discerned at any distance, and hence, farther military operations were put a stop to on both sides. The French, by way, I presume, of wishing good night to their invaders, made one more spirited attack upon the Spanish and Portuguese posts, which they supported by a demonstration in our front, and by a discharge of cannon upon our skirmishers. Being, as usual, successful on one part, and defeated on the other, they called in their stragglers, and fell back within their lines, leaving us to push forward our piquets, and to keep quiet possession of all the ground that we had gained. For our parts, having been informed, about an hour ago, that we should be required to march to the left as soon as the night could screen the movement, we stood, or rather lay down, inactively, on the brow of the hill, where we had spent the day; till a division of Spaniards coming up, – the same division which had so feebly defended the village of Anglette during the morning, – we resigned to them the care of a post abundantly defensible, and took the direction of the sand hills and the Adour.

Whether it was the intention of Sir John Hope to carry us farther towards his left this night, I cannot tell; but on arriving in rear of Anglette, we were by no means displeased at being told that we were destined to remain there until the morrow. The roads were all choked up with tumbrils, ammunition-waggons, baggage, and troops, filing to different points, apparently in not the best of order. Around the village, in particular, a vast bivouack, chiefly of Spanish infantry and muleteers, had been formed, insomuch that it was not without some difficulty that we made our way into the street. Then the sounds which saluted us as we passed – the Babel-like confounding of all languages – the laugh, the cry, the oath, and here and there the low moan or wild shriek of the wounded, – formed altogether a species of concert which certainly gave no evidence of strict discipline or accurate arrangement. It was, however, altogether a wild and a striking scene; and a sort of wavering and dull light which the fires of the bivouack shed over it added not a little to its sublimity.

At length we reached the houses which were set apart for our accommodation, and truly they were far from being over commodious. About three hundred men were ushered into a cottage consisting of two apartments, or, as they say in the north, of "a but and a ben"; and here, upon the earthen floor, we were fain to cast ourselves down, in order to obtain in sleep an escape from the cravings of hunger, which for several hours past had been somewhat urgent. We had eaten nothing since three o'clock in the morning, nor had any supply of provisions arrived. The poor cottage was, as may be imagined, wholly unfurnished with viands; indeed, we were as much surprised as pleased when the peasant to whom it belonged, and who had remained to keep possession, produced us a bottle of very bad brandy, called, in the language of the country, *aquadent*. This we divided among us as far as it would go; and having wished in vain for the arrival of the quarter-master and commissary, we wrapped our cloaks about us and lay down. Sleep soon came to our relief.

Chapter 21

The Bridge of Boats

On the 24 February, between thirty and forty chasse-marées *(a local variety of lugger), after sailing with difficulty through the surf and over the sand-bar at the mouth of the Adour, were anchored parallel to each other a short distance up river, with planks then lashed across them to form a gangway. The construction of the bridge, contrived by Major Sturgeon and Captain Todd, and supervised by Colonel Elphinstone, now Wellington's chief engineer, advised by Admiral Penrose, was completed by the afternoon of the 26th. Gleig's memory was unreliable at this point. On the 20th Wellington had written to Bathurst in London that 'the weather is so unfavourable that it is impossible to attempt the operation at the present moment. I therefore return to Sir Rowland Hill's corps tomorrow morning . . . and I leave it to Sir John Hope to cross the Adour when the weather will permit.' Captain Browne's 'Journal' states that Wellington was on the banks of the Gave de Pau on the 26th, surveying Soult's positions at Orthez prior to the following day's battle, and that Hope had passed the Adour below Bayonne: 'A further concerted operation was then decided on. Ld. Wellington rode to the Head Quarters of Sir John Hope, from the right of the Army, & expressed in strong terms, his approbation of Sir John's measures & their great facility which their successs had given to his future operations. He then left Hope and returned to the right . . .' Doubtless, the confusion was caused by Gleig having caught sight of Wellington on an earlier occasion, when he was discussing with Hope the most convenient site for the future placement of the bridge of boats.*

The night of the 23rd passed by in quiet, and long before dawn on the 24th we stood, as usual, in our ranks and under arms. Thus passed about half an hour, when orders were given to form into marching order, and to file towards the left in the direction of the Adour. These orders were promptly obeyed; and, after a journey of about a league, we found ourselves commanded to halt upon a sandy plain, at the distance of perhaps a couple of miles from the walls of Bayonne, and half that distance, or something less than half, from the outworks. Though thus placed within point-blank range of the enemy's advanced batteries, we were nevertheless amply secured against their fire; for a little sand-hill stood in our immediate front, of height sufficient to shut out not only the soldiers, but the tops of the tents, from the gaze of the besieged.

Though we reached our ground at an early hour in the morning, a considerable space elapsed ere the baggage and provisions came up. The reader will therefore imagine that the setting forth of a substantial breakfast, which immediately ensued, proved a source of no trifling gratification to men who had fasted for upwards of forty hours, and whose appetite, though stifled by sleep, had revived of late in a very troublesome degree. It consisted, I well recollect, of slices of beef, hastily and imperfectly broiled, with mouldy biscuits, and indifferent tea; but the coarsest viands are sweet to the hungry, and we were in no humour to find fault with the quality of ours.

Having finished our meal, we were by no means displeased to learn that, for the present at least, we were doomed to be stationary. The camp was accordingly pitched in due form; sundry ruinous dwellings in its vicinity were taken possession of, chiefly as stables for the horses. Guns, fishing-rods, and greyhounds were desired to be put in serviceable order; and every disposition was made to secure comfort. The sole subject of complaint, indeed, was found to be in the unfavourable state of the weather, which had become since yesterday boisterous, with heavy showers of rain and hail; but this very circumstance, at which we were disposed to murmur, chanced to be of all others the most favourable to the operations of the army. By means of these squalls, the boats and chasse-marees, which had hovered about the mouth of the Adour for several days, were enabled to pass the bar, and the ground-work of the floating bridge (if such an Irishism be admissible) was laid.

As the passage of the bar was an operation of considerable difficulty, and as I was fortunate enough to be an eye-witness of the daring intrepidity and nautical skill of those who effected it, I shall take the liberty of describing the occurrence more at length.

My friend and myself, having seen a little to the comforts of our men, and added in an important degree to our own by a change of habiliments, walked forth, with no other view than that of whiling away certain hours, which might have otherwise hung heavy on our hands. We took the direction of the river's mouth, because there a dark pine-wood promised to shelter us from the blast; and because we were anxious to see how far the engineers had proceeded in the construction of the bridge. At this time, be it observed, we were wholly ignorant of the kind of bridge which was about to be formed. We knew not so much as that it was to consist of sailing vessels at all, but concluded that pontoons would be anchored, as had been the case at the Bidassoa. Our astonishment may therefore be conceived, when, on mounting an eminence, we beheld a squadron of some thirty craft, bearing down with all sail set towards the bar; over which the waves were dashing in white foam, being driven inwards by a strong gale from the north-east. But we were not the only anxious spectators of this animating show. The bank of the river, and all the heights near, were crowded with general and staff officers, conspicuous among whom were Sir John Hope, and, if my memory fail me not, Lord Wellington himself. The groups were, one and all of them, speechless. The sense of sight appeared to be the only sense left in full vigour to the individuals who composed them, and even from it all objects were apparently shut out, except the gallant squadron.

Down they came before the breeze with amazing velocity; but the surf ran so high, and there seemed to be so little water upon the sands, that I for one felt as if a weight had been removed from my heart, when I beheld them suddenly put up their helms and tack about. The prospect from the sea was indeed by all accounts appalling; and even British sailors hesitated, for once in their lives, whether they could face the danger. But the hesitation was not of long continuance. A row-boat, Spanish built, but manned by Lieutenant Cheyne, and five seamen from the Woodlark, threw itself, with great judgment, upon a wave. The swell bore it clear across the shoal, and loud and reiterated were the shouts with which it was greeted as it rushed proudly through the deep water. The next which came was a prize – a large French fishing lugger, manned by seamen from a transport, closely followed by a gun-boat, under the command of Lieutenant Cheshire. They, too, were borne across; but the fourth was less fortunate. It was a schooner-rigged craft, full of people, and guided by Captain Elliot. I know not how it came about, whether a sudden change of wind occurred, or a rope unfortunately escaped from its fastening, but at the instant when the schooner took the foam, the mainsail of her hinder mast flapped round. In one second her broadside was to the surf, in another she was upset, and her gallant captain, with several of his crew, perished among the breakers. The rest were dashed by an eddy towards the bank, and happily saved.

The horror which we experienced at contemplating this event, though extreme for the moment, was necessarily of short duration; for our attention was immediately attracted to other vessels, which, one after another, drew near. Of these, all except one particular chasse maree, succeeded in making good the passage; – it shared the fate of the schooner. It was upset upon the curl of a wave, and went down, with the whole of its crew. This last was even a more awful spectacle than the former. The little vessel, after being tossed around, rocked for a moment, as it were, upon the surf, just long enough for us to see the despairing gestures of the sailors, and to hear their shriek of consternation – and then a huge wave striking her, she fell, not upon her broadside, but absolutely with bottom upwards. Not a man escaped of all who had conducted her; and several fine promising midshipmen were among them.

154

Five-and-twenty vessels having now entered the Adour, besides four or five gun-boats destined to protect them, no time was lost in running them up to their proper stations, and in bringing them securely to anchor, at equal distances from one another. The whole were then strongly bound together by cables, the ends of which were made fast to winches prepared for the purpose on each bank; and which, running both by the bows and sterns, kept the craft tolerably steady, notwithstanding the violence of the current. I need not add, that no economy was exercised in the matter of anchors, of which two were dropped from each bow, and a like number from each stern.

The boats being thus rendered sufficiently secure, half a dozen strong ropes were extended along their centres, at equi-distances of about two feet from one another. These were so disposed as not to bear any continual weight upon the smaller vessels. They were indeed steadied as they passed over each other, by being fastened to capstans, and so kept from swinging too widely; but it was upon four or five of the largest class only that they were made to lean, the intervals between being in reality so many hanging bridges. Across these ropes again were laid down planks, made fast by ties only; and the whole was so nicely balanced, that the tread of a single passenger caused it to swing backwards and forwards, whilst an entire army might pass with the most perfect safety. Such was the famous bridge of boats across the Adour, which connected the two banks of the river where it measures eight hundred yards in width, and which, in itself, including ground-work on both sides, covered a space little short of nine hundred yards.

Ahead of the bridge, with their broadsides towards the town, were moored five gun-boats, each armed with six long twenty-four pounders. These again were in part defended by a slight boom; whilst a boom in-finitely stronger, capable of repelling any substance which might be floated down by the tide, hung between them and the bridge. A boom somewhat similar, but more in the shape of a break-water, was placed behind the bridge, to shelter it from any sudden swell of the sea, such as might be apprehended during spring-tides; and each boat being manned by a party of seamen, well skilled in the management of such craft, the fabric was justly regarded as abundantly secure. To complete its construction, however, gave employment to the artificers of the army during two whole days, though they contrived to render it passable for infantry in less than half that space of time.

In the meanwhile, neither the right nor the centre of the allied army were inactive. The operations of the 23rd, – of which I have already said as much, and perhaps more, than one who professes not to speak from personal observation is entitled to say, – having been concluded, Soult, alarmed at the determined advance of his enemies, and confounded by the celerity of their movements, retired in the night of the 24th from Sauveterre across the Gave du Pau, and destroying all the bridges in his flight, assembled the strength of his army, on the morning of the 25th, near the village of Orthies. Hither Lord Wellington immediately followed. Pushing forward a numerous body of Spaniards, so as to cut off all communication between the French Marshal and the garrison of Bayonne, he manoeuvred with the 3rd, 4th, 5th, 6th, and 7th British divisions, during that and the succeeding days, and finally on the 27th, fought the glorious battle of Orthies, of which, as I had no share in it, I shall attempt no description. The result of it, as everybody knows, was the hasty and disastrous retreat of Marshal Soult upon Toulouse; the capture of Bourdeaux, and the first public declaration which had yet been made by any part of the French nation, of the renewal of their allegiance to the house of Bourbon.

Whilst these great deeds were performing elsewhere, a corps, consisting of the 1st and 5th British divisions, of two or three brigades of Portuguese, and a crowd of Spaniards, proceeded, under the command of Sir John Hope, to invest the town and citadel of Bayonne. As the rest of my journey will consist entirely of such occurrences as befell during the progress of the siege, it may not be amiss if I endeavour to convey to the mind of my reader something like a correct idea of the important city against which our efforts were turned, and of the general face of the country immediately around it.

The city of Bayonne stands upon a sandy plain; the citadel, upon a rock or hill which closely overhangs it. Between them runs the river Adour, with a sluggish current, resembling, in the darkness of the water, and the sliminess of its banks, the Thames, near Gravesend or Blackwall, but considerably narrower, and more shallow. Both town and fortress are regularly and strongly fortified; and, on the present occasion, a vast number of field-works, of open batteries, flesches, and redoubts, were added to the more permanent masonry which formed the ramparts. Nor was the erection of these the only method adopted by the enemy to give unusual strength to this most important place. Various sluices were cut from the river, by means of which, especially in our immediate front, the whole face of the country would be inundated at pleasure to the extent of several miles; whilst ditches, deep and wide, were here and there dug with the view of retarding the advance of troops, and keeping them exposed to the fire from the walls, as often as the occurrence of each might cause a temporary check. The outer defences began, in all directions, at the distance of a full mile from the glacis. The roads were everywhere broken up and covered with abattis and other incumbrances; nothing, in short, was neglected, which promised in any degree to contribute to the strength of a city, which is justly regarded as the key of the southern frontier of France.

Such was the condition of the works about Bayonne. With respect to the country which these works commanded, it varied considerably both in its nature and general appearance, the soil being in some directions tolerably fruitful, in others little better than usual. It was, however, universally flat, and very slightly wooded or broken, to the distance of three or four miles in every direction from the ditch. A few hamlets were, indeed, scattered here and there, (and wherever there is a French hamlet, a certain quantity of foliage will be found,) the largest of which was Anglette, where we had spent the night of the 23rd, and through which runs the great road to Bourdeaux and Paris; but, in general, the desolate aspect of things seemed to indicate, that the labours of the builder and planter were prohibited, lest a village or a grove might shelter the assailants, or furnish a point of establishment within cannon-shot of the walls. In the direction of the sea, again, and parallel with the left bank of the river, deep sands prevailed. These were, for large patches, totally bare of verdure, but thick woods of dark short pine more frequently overspread them, which, rising and falling, as the sands had broken up into little eminences and valleys, gave a very striking and romantic appearance to that side of the panorama. As I afterwards learned, the Llandes, those vast forests which stretch all the way to Bourdeaux, and which, according to the tradition of the natives, were originally planted to render firm what had previously been an huge moving quicksand, begin here.

The description which I have hitherto given of Bayonne, and the scenery near it, applies only to the city and to the track of country situated on the southern, or Spanish side of the Adour. The citadel, being built upon a hill, or, rather, upon the crest of a range of heights which rise gradually from the sea, and extend upwards in a sort of inclined plane for about eight miles, differs entirely from the preceding sketch, both in its style of fortification, and in the nature of the prospect which it presents to the gaze of a traveller. Like all hill-forts, its works are constructed rather as the natural inequalities of the ground permit, than after any scientific plan or model. One of its fronts, that which faces the village of St Etienne, and the mouth of the river, presents, indeed, the regular appearance of being part of an octagon; but, in other directions, the abrupt and uneven course of the rock has compelled the engineer to draw his wall around without any respect to form or figure. Yet it is a place of prodigious strength; the only assailable point in it being that which the regularity of the ground has permitted to receive the most perfect kind of fortification.

The view from the ramparts of that pile is extremely pleasing. Vast woods of pine are seen in the distance, whilst nearer the face of the country is beautifully diversified, by the intermingling of corn fields, meadows, groves of magnificent cork trees, vineyards, cottages, and several chateaux. Close beneath the wall, moreover, lies the romantic village of St Etienne, with its neat church and churchyard, sloping along the side of a ravine, and having all its cottages surrounded by pretty gardens, well stocked with fruit trees and shrubs. This village was completely commanded, not only by the guns from the citadel, but by a redoubt which General Thouvenot, the French governor, had caused to be erected on a sort of table land near it, and which, though no addition to the beauty of the landscape, added greatly to the general strength of the castle, by occupying the only level spot across which the besiegers might hope to push a sap with any success.

Though Bayonne was already, to all intents and purposes, invested – that is to say, though the garrison and inhabitants were fairly cut off from holding any open intercourse with other parts of the country, nothing of the confinement of a siege was yet felt by them. The besiegers had, indeed, drawn an extended line around the works; but the French piquets were still posted at the distance of three, four, and some of them five miles from the glacis; whilst their patrols continually broke the chain of connexion, and made excursions as far as the camp of Marshal Soult at Orthies. This was the case, at least, up to the evening of the 24th. There being no direct or safe communication between the two banks of the Adour below the town, Sir John Hope could not venture to tighten the cord, or to convert the investment into a strict blockade. As yet, all reinforcements to the little corps, which, under the command of General Stopford, had passed on the 23rd, were floated across by means of rafts; the men and guns sitting upon the beams of wood, and leading the horses, which swam after them. Yet even in this rude way, so great a force contrived to establish itself among the sand hills, by evening on the 24th, that all apprehension of a renewed attack from the enemy was laid aside. Nevertheless, the artificers were anxiously pressed to render the bridge trust-worthy, with as little delay as possible; and they strenuously exerted themselves to meet the wishes of the General.

In the meanwhile, about forty thousand men of the Spanish army were posted along those faces of the town and citadel which looked towards Helletre and the Joyeuse. The left of this semi-circular line resting upon the heights, where, during the late affair, I stood in safety to watch the progress of the skirmishers on both sides of me, swept round, through the abandoned entrenchments, to the brink of the river. Here the stream being narrow, a pontoon-bridge was already formed, and the line recommencing on the opposite bank, wound on till it formed a junction with a corps of Portuguese, at the back of the citadel. But as yet, the chain was continued from that point, only by occasional patrolling parties; and through this opening the enemy daily sent out his foragers, and brought in supplies. Such a state of things, however, could not be long permitted to exist. It was essential to the prosecution of Lord Wellington's future operations that the gap should be filled up previous to the renewal of hostilities between his army and that of Soult; nor was much time wasted in making preparations for driving in the garrison within the walls.

Working parties laboured hard, not only during the day, but during the whole night of the 24th; and at dawn on the 25th, it was declared that infantry might cross the floating-bridge with safety. This was the signal for action; and hence the 25th was again, at least to part of the army, a day of hostile employment.

Chapter 22

Bayonne is Invested

By 27 February the investment of Bayonne was completed, with some 15,000 men on the north side of the Adour, and 16,000 on the south bank, among whom remained Aylmer's Brigade. Gleig is incorrect in referring to Thouvenot as having previously defended Burgos: it had been General Dubreton. Casualties in storming the fortifications in the northern suburb of St Etienne had been heavy: 328 among the five battalions of King's German Legion alone, which, led by their commander, General Heinrich von Hinüber (who was wounded), had borne the brunt.

A direct communication between the opposite banks of the river being thus established, the remaining battalions of the Guards, the chief part of the King's German Legion, together with a proportionate force of cavalry, and of artillery, marched, at day-break on the twenty-fifth, to join their comrades among the sand hills. The whole of the besieging army being at the same time put in motion, the gap which, prior to this date, had existed in the line of investment, was filled up. Little or no fighting took place on that occasion. The enemy perceiving our design, offered no serious resistance to its accomplishment, but evacuating the village of Boucaut, after having exchanged a few shots with the skirmishers, established their piquets about half a mile in its rear. As yet, therefore, a good deal more of open space was granted to them than they could long hope to enjoy; but all opportunity of corresponding with Marshal Soult, as well as of adding to the stock of grain and provisions already in their arsenals, was cut off.

The running and irregular fire which had been maintained throughout the morning, gradually died away, and ceased altogether about noon. From that hour till after night-fall, everything continued quiet. A feverish excitement, necessarily consequent even upon a trifling skirmish, prevailed indeed amongst us; nor did we venture to take off our accoutrements, or return to our usual employments during the remainder of the day. But we might have done so, had we felt disposed, with the most perfect safety, for the enemy were too well satisfied with being permitted to retain what they did retain, of territory beyond the glacis, to endanger its loss by a useless attempt to regain what had been wrested from them. Still we were anxious, and the anxiety which pervaded us all the day, ceased not to operate at night.

The garrison of Bayonne, we were well aware, was at once numerically powerful, and composed of the best troops in the French army. From all that we could learn, Soult had by no means calculated upon the plan of operations adopted by Lord Wellington. Concluding that his Lordship would halt after the passage of the Adour, and invest that important place with the whole of his forces, he had thrown into it no fewer than fifteen thousand picked men, assigning the command to General Thouvenot, an officer, who, by his successful defence of Burgos, on a former occasion, appeared worthy of so delicate a trust on the present. Lord Wellington was, however, too conscious of the advantages which arise in war from celerity of movement, to waste his time before the walls of Bayonne. He accordingly left Sir John Hope to mask the city with the two British divisions, which composed the left column, a force somewhat inferior in point of numbers to that which it blockaded; whilst he himself, with the remaining five divisions, hung upon the rear of the retreating army. It is true, that our little *corps d'armée* was supported by thirty or forty thousand Spaniards, who, if they served no other purpose, made at least a show, and hindered weak foraging parties from traversing the open country; but upon their efforts little reliance could be placed, in case a bold sally should be made; whilst the scattered order of our encampment hindered us from opposing, at any given point, a force at all competent to meet at least with decisive superiority, that portion of the garrison which the governor might at any time employ in such a service. The circumference of Bayonne, measuring it from the exterior of the works, cannot be computed at less than four miles. Our line again, which encircled it at a distance of three miles from the ditch, would of course greatly exceed this; and when it is remembered that not more than fifty thousand men at the utmost, and of these something less than fifteen thousand who were trust-worthy, occupied that line, it will be seen that our situation was not such as to render caution unnecessary, or apprehension groundless.

We had, however, retired to rest at the usual hour, on the night of the 25th; all things continuing in apparent security; when sleep, which was beginning to assert its dominion over our senses, was suddenly dispelled, by the report of a musket-shot, in the direction of the piquets. The battalion to which I was attached, still kept its ground behind the sand hill, whither it had moved, after the affair of the 23rd. Its outposts were divided from the camp only by the hill; consequently, little time could be given to prepare and accoutre in case an attack should be made. Not a moment was therefore wasted in surmises, not a hint was thrown out as the propriety of waiting till a little more firing should bespeak cause of serious alarm; but every man sprang from his pallet, and casting about him as much of his garments as could be found on the instant, seized his arms, and ran to the place of muster. And now another and another shot was fired; the bugles began to sound, the baggage was hastily packed, the horses saddled, and all the bustle and hurry attendant upon the preparations for battle took place. For myself, having seen that my men were in their ranks, I ran to the top of the hill, from whence I beheld the flashes of several muskets, half way between our sentinels and those of the enemy; but no sound of advancing columns met my ear, neither were these flashes returned by our own soldiers. The degree of surprise excited by all this was not, however, of long continuance. The officer in command of the outposts dispatched a messenger to inform us, that no symptom of an attack was discernible; but that several deserters had come into his lines, at whom the French sentries fired as they fled. This account was speedily confirmed by the arrival of the deserters in the camp; and the troops accordingly laid aside their weapons, and returned to their tents.

The alarm in that direction had hardly subsided, when another and a not less serious one arose in a different quarter. A sentry who was posted by the bank of the river, reported to his officer, when visiting him, that boats were moving, and oars splashing in the water. Apprehensions were immediately excited for the safety of the bridge, against which we naturally concluded that some attempt was about to be made. To oppose it as far as possible, of whatever nature it might be, three field-pieces which were attached to our brigade, limbered up, and galloped to the water's edge; these I accompanied, and certainly the splash of oars was very audible, though the darkness would not permit us to distinguish from whence the sound proceeded. A shot or two were, however, fired in the direction of the sound, just by way of hinting to the enemy that we were awake; and whether it was that the hint was not lost upon them, or that they never seriously entertained the idea of assailing the bridge, an immediate cessation of rowing was the consequence. Having watched, therefore, for half an hour, and neither hearing nor seeing anything indicative of danger, I left the gunners to themselves; and returning to my cloak and blanket, I wrapt myself closely up, and slept soundly and securely till the morning.

The whole of the 26th passed over, without the occurrence of any event worthy of mention. By myself it was spent, not very profitably, in sauntering about among the pine-woods, where little or no game was to be found; whilst for the troops in general, as well within as without the walls of the beleaguered city, it might be accounted a sort of armed truce. Hardly a cannon-shot was fired from sun-rise till sun-set, on either side; but matters were drawing fast to a crisis. Stores and ammunition were continually conveyed across the river in large quantities, and it was manifest, that even the few miles of open country which the garrison still held, would, before long, be taken away from them. It was, therefore, no unexpected communication which I received, on the morning of the 27th, that the corps was to stand to its arms forthwith, and that the enemy were to be driven in all directions within their works.

Having, in a former chapter, described the nature of the ground in our immediate front, the reader will readily understand why no serious advance on our part was intended. We were already within point-blank range of the guns on the ramparts; whilst between the ramparts and the camp, no broken ground, nor village, nor any other species of cover, existed. We could not, therefore, hope to establish ourselves, had we even pushed on, whilst the French general, by opening the sluices from the river, might, at any moment, lay the whole level under water. On the opposite side of the Adour, however, the case was different. There the most forward British piquets were very little in advance of the village of Boucaut, and the village of Boucaut is full four miles from the citadel. The face of the country, too, between these points, being rugged and broken, numerous positions could be taken up by the besiegers, in which, whilst they were themselves secure from the fire of the place, they could easily prevent the garrison from venturing beyond the ditch; whilst the relative situations of the town and fortress, rendered the one secure against active annoyance, till after the other should have fallen into our hands. Though, therefore, it was understood that the whole of our line was to be drawn somewhat more tightly round the city, we were all aware that the trenches would be opened, and breaching batteries thrown up against the citadel alone.

The men being accoutred, and the baggage packed, we stood quietly in our ranks, behind the sand hill, till a gun, from the opposite bank of the stream, sounded the signal of attack. Upon this we extended our files, so as to give to a single weak battalion the appearance of an entire brigade, and ascending the heights, we stopped short where the tops of our bayonets, and the feathers of our caps, just showed themselves over the ridge. Similar demonstrations were likewise made by the corps which filled Anglette and crowned the rise in connexion with it; whilst occasionally a shout was raised, as if at length the order of attack had been given, and we were preparing to rush on. All this was done, for the purpose of drawing the attention of the enemy to many different points at the same time, and thus hindering them from opposing, with the total strength of the garrison, the forward movements of those who were appointed to invest the castle.

Whilst we, and the divisions near us, were thus amusing ourselves and the enemy with the pomp and circumstance, rather than with the reality of war, the guards and light Germans, with a corps of Portuguese infantry, were very differently occupied on the other bank of the river. As our situation was a commanding one, it enabled us to obtain a tolerably distinct view of their proceedings. We saw one column of British troops form on the sands beside Boucaut. In front of it was a body of German riflemen, who pressed leisurely forward in skirmishing order, till they reached the piquets of the French troops. Of the enemy, on the other hand, a heavy column showed itself upon the high ground, where it halted, and continued to send out numerous parties to support the outposts; between whom and the Germans, a hot skirmish soon began, nor could it be said that any decided advantage was gained by either party during several hours.

The column which we descried upon the sands beside Boucaut, was not of great strength; indeed, the numbers of our own people, discernible by us, were very inconsiderable. The fact, as I afterwards learned, was, that the side of the hill visible to us, was by far the most rugged and the least assailable of any; consequently, the main attack was to be made in another direction, the attack in this waiting till the other should have in part succeeded. Hence the trifling progress made by our skirmishers, who seemed to be kept back rather than animated forward by their officers, and hence the apparently obstinate resistance of the French piquets. But it was, nevertheless, an exceedingly interesting spectacle, to the beauty of which, the uneven and picturesque nature of the scenery around added not little.

I wish I could convey to the mind of the reader some notion of the scene as it then appeared, and is still remembered by myself. Let him imagine himself, then, lying with me upon the brow of a sand hill, and looking down, first upon the broad and deep waters of the Adour, and over them, upon a sandy bank, which speedily ends, and is succeeded by a green hill: having in its side, the side upon which we are gazing, frequent cuts or gullies, or glens, some of them bare, others wooded, with here and there a white cottage showing itself from among the trees. Let him imagine that he sees, on the summit of the heights, and immediately in a line with himself, a portion of an armed mass, with a single field-piece pointed towards the river's mouth. About a mile to the rearward, again, let him figure to himself a green field, more level than any other part of the hill-side, a sort of table-land, as it were, having a hedge along that face of it which is turned towards Boucaut, and a precipitous red bank under the hedge. In this field he will observe about three hundred infantry soldiers, dressed in grey great-coats and broad caps, or chacauts, who carry hairy knapsacks on their backs, and are armed with long clear muskets, which have bayonets screwed to their muzzles. These are Frenchmen. Under the red bank, let him farther suppose that there is a picturesque valley, stocked with tall and shadowy cork-trees, about the middle of which is a neat mansion, something larger than a farm-house, and yet hardly deserving the name of a chateau. That house is full of light Germans, and almost every tree about it affords cover to a rifleman, who fires, as a good aim is presented to him, at the persons behind the hedge. From the windows of the house, too, many shots are from time to time discharged, whilst the sudden flash, and uprising of smoke, from the various parts of the hedge, show that the French tirailleurs are not less active than their assailants, or disposed to receive their salute without returning it. In this skirmish little change of ground takes place. Occasionally, indeed, a single rifleman will steal on, running from tree to tree, till he has reached a convenient spot; whilst a Frenchman will as often rise, and having watched him through a brake, or over a bush, will fire whenever he exposes himself to his observation. But no grand rush is made on either side, nor any decided loss is sustained, either of ground or in men.

All this while the exertions of our people were, as far as might be, aided by a well-served cannonade from the three pieces of artillery, which had kept their station near the bank of the river since the evening of the 25th. The fire of these guns was directed chiefly against a large house – apparently some public work or manufactory – which stood by the brink of the water, and was filled with French troops. Neither were the enemy's batteries opposite to us idle. Having wasted about twenty or thirty round shot without effect, they brought a couple of mortars, with a howitzer or two, to bear upon us, from which they threw shell after shell among our ranks; but from the effects of the cannonade, the nature of the soil secured us, the shells either burying themselves in the sand to the extinction of the fuze, or exploding when we were all snugly laid flat, and therefore safe from their fragments.

Matters had continued thus for several hours, and we were beginning to fear that some part of our General's plan had gone wrong, or that the enemy were in too great force to be driven in by the divisions opposed to them, when a sudden stir in the French column which had hitherto stood quietly upon the heights, attracted our attention. The field-piece was all at once wheeled round, and turned in the direction of the opposite country – the infantry collected into compact order, and were gradually hidden from us by the brow of the hill. By and by, a few musket-shots were fired, then about a dozen more, then came the report of one, two, or three field-pieces, and lastly a roar of cannon and small-arms was heard. This was kept up hot and rapid for half an hour. Every moment it came nearer and nearer. Now the smoke which had at first followed each report after the interval of a few seconds, rose at the same instant with the noise – then the glancing of arms over the high ground was distinguishable – next came the French troops, some retiring slowly, and firing as they fell back, others flying in extreme confusion. Mounted officers were galloping over the ridge, and apparently exerting themselves to restore order, but all would not do. The enemy were in full flight. Down they rushed towards the river, and away along the sands in the direction of the citadel, whilst our three guns poured in round shot amongst them, many of which we could distinctly perceive take effect; and now the green field, on which my reader and I have so long looked, was abandoned. The tirailleurs fled, the riflemen pursued, the little column in scarlet pushed on in good order and with a quick pace, whilst on the brow of the height above, a British ensign was held up as a signal for our battery to cease firing. The signal was obeyed, and we had nothing farther to do during the remainder of the day, than to watch, which we eagerly did, the progress of our victorious comrades.

The enemy having fled as far as the manufactory, were there joined by reinforcements from the garrison. Here, then, the battle was renewed with great obstinacy, but, desperate as was the resistance offered, it became every hour less and less effectual. At length the building took fire – it was abandoned, and its defenders fled; after which, the entire scene of action was hidden from us, and we were enabled to guess at the state of affairs only by the sound of the firing, and the direction which it took. That inclined every moment more and more towards the ramparts; but it was ceaseless and awful till darkness had set in, and both parties were compelled to desist, because they could not distinguish friends from foes.

In this affair the loss on both sides was severe, but we were completely successful. The enemy were driven within their works, and our advanced posts were established in the village of St Etienne, about half pistol-shot from the nearest redoubt. In other directions, little change of ground occurred. Some Spanish divisions took up a position, I believe, somewhat less distant than formerly from the walls of Bayonne; but neither we, nor the divisions in communication with us, were in any degree affected by it. We returned, on the contrary, to our tents, having lost by the cannonade only one man killed, and three wounded.

I recollect having stated, in another part of my narrative, that, except on one occasion, I could not tax my memory with any symptom of violent or permanent grief on the part of a soldier's wife at the death of her husband. How to account for this I know not, unless it be that a camp seldom fails to destroy all the finest feelings of one sex, if it leave those of the other uninjured. The occasion to which I then alluded occurred to-day. A fine young Irishman, the pay-serjeant of my own company, had brought his wife with him to the seat of war. He married her, it appeared, against the wish of her relations, they considering themselves in a walk of life superior to his. To what class of society they belonged I cannot tell, but she, I know, was a lady's-maid to some person of rank, when the handsome face and manly form of M'Dermot stole her heart away. They had been married about a year and a half, during the whole of which time she had borne the most unblemished character, and they were accounted the most virtuous and the happiest couple in the regiment. Poor things! they were this day separated for ever.

M'Dermot was as brave and good a soldier as any in the army; he was, at times, even fool-hardy. Having observed a raw recruit or two cower down in no very dignified manner, as a cannon-ball passed over them, M'Dermot, by way of teaching them to despise danger, threw himself at his ease on the summit of the sand-hill, with his head towards the enemy's guns. He was in the very act of laughing at these lads, assuring them that "every bullet has its billet", when a round shot struck him on the crown of the head, and smashed him to atoms. I shall never forget the shriek that was raised. He was a prodigious favourite with all ranks; and then all of us thought of his poor young wife, so spotless, and so completely wrapped up in him. "O, who will tell Nance of this?" said another non-commissioned officer, his principal companion. – "Poor Nance!" cried the soldiers, one and all; so true is it that virtue is respected, and a virtuous woman beloved, even by common soldiers. But there was no hiding it from Nance. The news reached her, Heaven knows how, long before we returned to our tents, and she was in the midst of us in a state which beggars all description, in five minutes after the event took place.

I cannot so much as attempt to delineate the scene which followed. The poor creature was evidently deranged, for she would not believe that the mangled carcase before her was her husband; and she never shed a tear. "That, O that is not he!" cried she; "that M'Dermot – my own handsome, beautiful M'Dermot! O no, no – take it away, or take me away, and bring me to him!" She was removed with gentle violence to the camp, and the body was buried; a young fir tree being planted over it.

Several days elapsed before Mrs M'Dermot was sufficiently calm to look her situation in the face. But at length the feeling of utter desolateness came over her; and instead of listening, as women in her situation generally listen, to the proposals of some new suitor, all her wishes pointed homewards. To her home she was accordingly sent. We raised for her a handsome subscription, every officer and man contributing something; and I have reason to believe that she is now respectably settled in Cork, though still a widow.

Chapter 23

Crossing the Adour

At dawn on 4 April the 85th were marched across the bridge of boats and encamped above Boucau, before advancing south to approach closer to the citadel of Bayonne. The precise site of the château – the 'blue house' – in which Gleig was stationed, is uncertain, although the church of St Etienne survives.

From the above date, namely, the 27th of February, the siege of Bayonne may be said to have fairly commenced. To follow, in regular detail, the occurrences of each day, as it proceeded, would not, I am sure, greatly interest my readers, whilst to lay such detail before them, would be to myself an occupation little less irksome than it sometimes was to kill the tedious hours of a ten weeks' blockade. I may be permitted, then, to state generally, and in few words, that the strictest investment was continued all the while, and that an extremely harassing kind of duty was imposed upon us till the siege and the war were brought to a conclusion together, by the hoisting of the white flag on the 28th of the following April. Premising this, I shall merely take the liberty of narrating, without regard to dates or natural order, such events and adventures as appeared to myself best deserving of record.

In the first place, then, it may be observed, that whilst on our side of the river no other works were erected than such as appeared absolutely necessary for strengthening our own position, and rendering the bridge, and the high road, and the stores brought up by them, safe from molestation, the Guards and Germans on the other side were busily employed in digging trenches, and in pushing forward active operations against the citadel. These, as may be imagined, they were not permitted to carry on without being annoyed, in every practicable manner, by the besieged. A continual, or rather a dropping and irregular fire of cannon, was kept up upon their parties from the ramparts, to which even the darkness of the night brought no cessation; for blue lights were ever and anon thrown out where the people were at work, by the flame of which the artillery-men were guided in taking their aim; nor were we wholly exempt from that species of entertainment. On the contrary, as the erection of a three-gun battery on the top of our hill was deemed necessary, we worked at it by turns till it was completed; and, as a matter of course, we worked under the fire of all the cannon and mortars which could be brought to bear upon us. These working parties are by far the most unpleasant of all the employments to which a soldier is liable. There is in them nothing of excitement, with a great deal of danger; and danger, where there is no excitement, no man would voluntarily choose to incur, for its own sake. Let me describe one of these mornings' amusements.

It fell to my lot frequently to superintend the people when at work. The spot on which we laboured was high, and therefore completely exposed to the view of the enemy. It was the top of the hill opposite to them. Immediately on our arrival, a four-gun battery, with one howitzer, and two nine-inch mortars, began to play upon us. They were admirably served, and the balls hit apparently in every quarter, excepting the particular spots on which each of us stood. On such occasions, if there be no very pressing demand for the completion of the work, you generally station one of your party to watch the enemy. As soon as he perceives a flash, he calls out – "Shot", or "Shell", as the case may be. If it be simply a cannon-shot, you either toil on without heeding it, or, having covered yourselves as well as you can till the ball strike, you start up again, and seize your tools. If it be a shell, you lie quite still till it burst. The unmilitary reader may perhaps question whether it be possible to tell the nature of the missile which is coming against you, when as yet it has barely escaped from the muzzle of the gun, and is still a mile or two distant; but he who has been in the habit of attending to these matters will entertain no such doubt. Not to mention the fact, that an experienced eye can trace, by means of the burning fuze, the whole journey of a shell through the air, from its expulsion till its fall; the more perpendicular flight of the smoke may of itself inform him who watches it when it issues from a mortar; whilst there is a sharpness in the report of a gun which the firing of a mortar produces not, and which will effectually distinguish the one from the other, even if the sense of sight should fail. I have heard men assert, that they can trace not only a shell, but a cannon-ball through the air. This may be possible, but if it be, it is possible only to those whose sense of sight is far more acute than mine.

Though abundantly annoying, it is really wonderful how harmless this cannonade proved, continued, as it was continued, day after day, during the course of several weeks. I do not believe that it cost us, in all, above five men. Neither were the enemy more successful in an attempt which they made to harass us by throwing shells into the camp. As our tents were hidden from their view, they, of course, fired at random, and their ammunition was wasted; But the sound of shells falling around us, both by night and day, was not exactly the kind of music which we should have selected. We became, however, accustomed to it, so as in a great degree to disregard it; even the dogs, which at first would run up and apply their noses to each

169

as it alighted, gradually ceased to take any notice of them, till the enemy guessing, or perhaps judging, from the absence of all commotion amongst us, that their fire was not very destructive, gradually omitted, and at last left it off.

Unless my memory greatly deceive me, the chief subject of complaint amongst us was, that we were fettered to one spot, and that, without there being in our situation enough of peril, or of excitation, to hinder us from feeling the confinement as a restraint. Though tolerably secure, from the very nature of the ground, our post was one of vast importance; that is to say, had the enemy succeeded in forcing it, they might have easily made their way to the bridge ere any fresh troops could be brought to oppose them. Under these circumstances, it was considered imprudent to wander far, or frequently, from the tents; and hence even the resource of fishing and shooting was, in a great measure, denied to those who would have gladly availed themselves of it. My friend and I did, indeed, occasionally venture into the woods; but these excursions were too rare to be very profitable, and our limits too confined to furnish an abundance of game.

All our days and all our nights were not, however, of the same tame character. Independently of the usual round of out-post duty, (a duty which, to me at least, was never irksome, because it always served to keep my interest awake,) a deserter would, from time to time, come over, and bring with him rumours of sorties intended. One of them I particularly recollect as having in it a more than ordinary degree of excitement. We were sitting one Sunday evening, Gray and myself, in the upper loft of an old mill, where, by way of an indulgence, we had established ourselves; our commanding officer had read prayers to the battalion about half an hour before, and the parade had just been dismissed, when a serjeant clambered up the ladder to inform us, that the servants and batmen were commanded to sleep accoutred; that the horses were to be saddled, and the baggage in readiness to move, at a moment's notice. On inquiring the cause of this order, we learned, that a French officer had arrived in the camp, that he had brought with him intelligence that a sally would certainly take place a little before midnight; and that the garrison were already making preparations for the attack. As may be supposed, we put everything in a proper trim forthwith; and having seen that our men lay down, with knapsacks buckled up, and pouches and bayonets slung on, we, too, threw ourselves on the floor, in our clothes.

It might be about eleven o'clock, when we were startled from our repose by the firing of cannon. The sound was, however, distant; it evidently came from the opposite side of the river, and it was followed by no musketry. We watched it, therefore, for a while, anxiously enough, and sat up prepared to issue forth as soon as our presence might be wanted. But no bugle sounded, nor was any other summons given; so we lay down again, and the night passed by in peace. I have reason to believe, however, that the French officer deceived us not. An attack upon our position had been seriously intended, and the plan was abandoned, only, because this very officer being missed, it was conjectured that we should be fully prepared to repel it.

Another little affair took place soon after. Whether our advanced posts on the left of Anglette had been, of late, pushed somewhat more in advance than formerly, I cannot tell; but the enemy sent a message, one morning, by a flag of truce, to the officer in command, desiring that he would fall back, otherwise they would compel him. To such a message a direct refusal was the reply; and they having allowed him an hour to change his mind, proceeded, at the expiration of that time, to carry their threat into execution. A considerable body of light troops attacked the post, and a sharp skirmish ensued. The sound of firing soon drew assistance to our piquet; and the result was, that the French once more retired within their works, leaving us in possession of the disputed ground. This event, with many others which I have not recorded, because they have in them even less of interest, occurred during the remaining days of February, and the whole of March. On the first of April our position was changed, and we took, from that period, a more active part in the conduct of the siege.

The change of ground to which I now allude, proved, at least for a day or two, extremely agreeable to the corps in general. My friend and myself had indeed, as I have already stated, fixed our abode in an old mill close to the camp, and yet sufficiently apart from it to be freed from the bustle. It was a ruinous and dilapidated mansion, I admit; our living and sleeping chamber consisting simply of one half of a loft; and only of one half, because the flooring of the other half had given way; to which we ascended by means of a ladder or trap-stair, and from which we looked down upon our horses and mules that occupied the basement story. But in that old mill, the tiling of which was unsealed, and can hardly be said to have been proof against the weather, I spent some weary and many more pleasant evenings, whilst, ruinous as it was, it appeared comfortable to men who repaired to it from the sandy ground on which they had previously spent several days and nights, under cover of the canvass. Though therefore I cannot accuse myself of murmuring at the removal of the camp, it is quite certain that I partook not in the general rejoicing which the occurrence produced among my comrades; or that the beauty of the spot, to which my tent was transferred, at all compensated for the loss of a boarded floor, and a detached habitation.

It was, however, a delightful change to the majority. During the last week or ten days, the heat of the sun had become exceedingly oppressive, beating, as it did, through the white canvass, and having its rays reflected back, on all hands, from a grey sandy soil. Not a tree grew near to shelter us; nor was there a blade of grass within sight, on which the weary eye could repose. On the 1st of April we retired about a couple of miles, into the heart of a pine-wood, and left the sand hill to be guarded by the piquets alone. Our tents were pitched in a sweet little green vale, overshadowed with the dark foliage of the fir trees; and near the margin of a small lake or pond of clear water. Here we remained in a state of comparative idleness and enjoyment for three days; running and leaping, and causing the men to run and leap, for rewards; till an order arrived in the evening of the 3rd, that we should be under arms at day-break on the morrow, and cross the bridge, to take part in the fatigues and dangers of the trenches.

At an early hour on the 4th, we formed into marching order, and took the direction of the bridge. This we crossed, the planks waving and bending beneath us, as the cables to which they were fastened swung to and fro with our tread, and then filing to the right, we halted in an open field above the village of Boucaut, where the ground of encampment was marked out. It was a day of heavy rain, so we were thoroughly saturated by the way; and as several hours elapsed ere the baggage came up, we were compelled to continue in that uncomfortable plight all the while. It came at length, however, and our tents were pitched; after which, having substituted dry for wet apparel, I spent the rest of the evening in lounging among the numerous stalls and booths which surrounded the market-place.

The village of Boucaut presented at this period a curious spectacle. It was not deserted by its inhabitants; all, or the greater number, of whom remained quietly in their houses. Their little shops were not closed; the inns, for there were two in the place, so far from being abandoned, were continually crowded with customers; cooks, waiters, landlady, and mine host, were all in motion from morning till night; whilst the country people came in in crowds, with eggs, butter, cheese, poultry, and other luxuries. These articles of merchandize were exposed for sale in the centre of the market-place, a large square, surrounded by lofty walls; whilst along the sides of these walls, sutlers' tents, porter booths, confectioners' stalls, and even tables loaded with hardware, shoes, stockings, etc., were laid out in regular order. The place was, moreover, full of people, soldiers, camp followers, villagers, peasants, male and female; and much laughing and much merriment prevailed in every direction. To a mere spectator, there was constant food for amusement; in the fruitless endeavours of an English soldier, for example, to make love to a pretty French girl – or, in the vain efforts of a staid German to overreach some volatile, but mercenary villager – whilst the ceaseless gabbling in all European tongues – the attempts made on all hands to carry on by signs that conversation to which the faculty of speech lent no assistance, – to watch these, and a thousand other extravagances, furnished ample and very agreeable employment to one who was willing to find amusement where he could. Yet, with all this apparent confusion, the greatest regularity prevailed. Not a single instance of violence to a native, either in person or property, occurred; indeed, both men and women scrupled not to assure us, that they felt themselves far more secure under our protection, than they had been whilst their own countrymen were among them.

It was our business, whilst the camp stood here, to march up every morning to the front, and to work, in turns, at the erection of batteries and redoubts, within half-musket-shot of the walls of the citadel. The spot where I invariably found myself stationed, when my turn of duty came round, was a chateau, situated upon the brow of an eminence; from the windows and garden of which I obtained a distinct view of one flank of the castle. Upon this building an incessant fire of round shot, shells, grape, and occasionally of musketry, was kept up. The enemy had upon their walls a number of long swivel guns, which they could elevate or depress, or turn in any direction, at will; and with which as perfect an aim could be taken as with an ordinary fuse. These threw, with great force, iron balls of about a quarter of a pound weight. Beside them men were always stationed, who watched our movements so closely, that it was impossible to show so much as your head at a window, or over the wall, without being saluted by a shot, whilst ever and anon a nine-inch shell would tumble through the roof, and burst sometimes before we had time to escape into another apartment. – Then the crashing of the cannon balls as they rushed through the partitions – the occasional rattle of grape and cannister, which came pouring in by the windows – all these things combined produced a species of feeling, of which no words can convey an adequate notion to him who has not experienced it. It was not terror, it can hardly be called alarm – for we followed our occupations unceasingly, and even our mirth was uninterrupted; but it kept the mind wound up to a pitch of excitation, from which it was by no means an unpleasant matter to relieve it.

Ours was a mortar battery. It was formed by heaping up earth against the interior of the garden wall, and proceeded with great rapidity. We likewise cut down trees, and constructed out of their branches fascines and gabions; but we had nothing to do in the trenches. Of these, indeed, not more than a couple were dug; the uneven nature of the ground producing numerous valleys and hollows, which saved us a great deal of toil, and very sufficiently supplied their place.

Besides working parties, it came occasionally to my turn to command a piquet. The post of which I was put in charge, was the village of St Etienne, and the church formed the head-quarters of the guard. It was a small building, but, fortunately for us, constructed with great solidity, inasmuch as it stood under the very muzzles of half-a-dozen field-pieces, which the enemy had placed in a redoubt about a short stone's throw distant. To add to its strength, and to render it more tenable in case of an attack, an embankment of earth – of earth carried from the churchyard, and so mixed with the mouldering bones of "the rude forefathers of the village", was raised inside, to the height of perhaps four feet; above which ran a line of loop-holes, cut out for the purpose of giving to its garrison an opportunity of firing with effect upon their assailants. When I say that the church formed the head-quarters of the guard, I mean that the guard took up its station there during the night. Whilst daylight lasted, it kept itself as much as possible concealed behind a few houses in the rear of the building, and left only a single sentinel there to watch the movements of the enemy.

A little to the right of my post was a couple of barricades; the one cutting off the main road, the other blocking up the entrance to a cross-street in the village. Beside these respectively stood a six-pounder gun. They were, I should conceive, about pistol-shot from the walls of the castle, and formed our most advanced stations. Our sentinels again ran through the churchyard and streets, winding away by the right and left, as the shape of the place required; and they were planted as close to one another as the occurrence of trees, or other species of cover, would permit. For the French were no longer the magnanimous enemy which we had found them in the open field. Every man, no matter whether a sentry or a lounger, who could be seen, was fired at; nor could the ordinary reliefs proceed as in other situations they had been wont to proceed. No corporal's party could march round here, but the men themselves stole up, one by one, to the particular spot allotted to them, whilst those whom they came to relieve stole away after a similar fashion. Yet even thus, we seldom returned to the camp without bringing a wounded man or two back with us, or leaving a dead comrade behind.

At night, again, the very utmost vigilance was necessary. The enemy were so close to us, that the slightest carelessness on our part would have given them free and secure access through our chain, whilst that very proximity rendered it utterly impracticable for the videttes to give sufficient warning to men who should not be at every moment in a state of preparation. No man slept, or so much as lay down. The privates stood round the embankment within the church, as if they had been all on watch, whilst the officer crept about from place to place in front of it, or listened, with deep anxiety, to every sound. In these wanderings, the conversation of the French soldiers could be distinctly overheard, so near were the troops of the two nations to each other; and so perilous, or rather so momentous, was the duty which we were called upon to perform.

Chapter 24

The Sortie from Bayonne

After a brief respite on the south bank of the Adour, the 85th recrossed the Adour to their former camp near Boucau on 12 April, two day before Thouvenot's fruitless and unjustified sortie took place. Although warned by a deserter that an attempt to break out was certainly to be made, General James Hay chose to disbelieve him and took no additional precautions. Luckily, General Hinüber suspected that there might well be some truth in it, and it is probable than neither the Guards nor the K.G.L. would have reacted as rapidly as they did had he not alerted them. The entire reponsibility of causing the needless death of 150 men and almost 700 wounded among the Allies – largely among the Guards (over 500) and the K.G.L. (190) – together with some 900 of his own men, was Thouvenot's. He had been advised two days earlier of Napoleon's abdication on the 6th, although, admittedly, no official confirmation had reached him, and did not surrender until the 26th, after receiving a copy of the armistice dated the 17th. Included among the British casualties were Sir John Hope, who had been wounded and captured in the sortie, and General Hay, killed. Also among the wounded were Colonel the Hon. Horatio ('Bull') Townsend, General the Hon. Edward Stopford (1st and 3rd Foot Guards respectively). Command of the Allies before Bayonne devolved on General the Hon. Charles Colville of the 5th Division, who enjoined that unremitting vigilance should be observed on the part of the outposts until the cessation of hostilities.

The blockade of Bayonne being now decidedly converted into a siege, Sir John Hope very justly determined, that every brigade of British and Portuguese troops – in other words, every brigade upon which he could at all depend – should take by turns a share in the fatigue and danger attendant upon the progress of operations. The tour of duty allotted to each was accordingly fixed at three days. In consequence of this arrangement, we, who had assumed the care of the works and outposts on the 4th, were relieved on the evening of the 7th; and at an early hour on the morning of the 8th, once more turned our faces in the direction of the pinewood. The tents which we had pitched in the vicinity of Boucaut were not, however, struck. These we left standing for the benefit of a brigade of Portuguese, which crossed the river to succeed us; and hence, instead of halting where we had formerly sojourned, beside the pond, and under the shadow of the fir-trees, we pushed on as far as the outskirts of Anglette. The morning of the 8th chanced to be uncommonly dark and foggy. It so happened, more-over, that a man, who had got drunk upon duty the night before, was doomed to suffer punishment, as early as circumstances would allow, and the battalion having reached what was supposed to be its ground, formed square in a green field for the purpose. Partly in consequence of the density of the fog, which rendered all objects at the distance of fifty yards invisible, and partly because the country was altogether new to us, we lost our way. Our astonishment may therefore be conceived, when, on the clearing away of the mist, we found ourselves drawn up within less than point-blank range of the enemy's guns, and close to the most advanced of our sentinels in this part of the line.

For a moment or two we were permitted to continue thus unmolested, but not longer. The breast-works in front of us were speedily lined with infantry; mounted officers arrived and departed at full speed; a few field-pieces being hurried through a sally-port, were posted upon the exterior of the glacis; and then a sharp cannonade began. It was quite evident that the enemy expected an assault; and the accidental appearance of two other British brigades, which chanced at the moment to pass each other in our rear, added strength, without doubt, to that expectation. The scene was highly animating; but the enemy's guns were too well served to permit our continuing long spectators of it. A ball or two striking in the centre of the square warned us to withdraw; and as we were clearly in a situation where we were never meant to be, as well as because no act of hostility was on our part intended, we scrupled not to take the hint, and to march some-what more to the rear. There a certain number of houses was allotted to us, and we again found ourselves, for the space of four days, under cover of a roof.

We were thus situated, when a messenger extraordinary arrived at the quarters of the commanding officer, about midnight on the 11th of April, with intelligence that the allies were in possession of Paris, and that Buonaparte had abdicated. It would be difficult to say what was the effect produced upon us by the news. Amazement – utter amazement – was the first and most powerful sensation excited. We could hardly credit the story; some of us even went so far for a while as to assert, that the thing was impossible. Then came the thought of peace, of an immediate cessa-tion of hostilities, and a speedy return to our friends and relatives in England; and last, though not with the least permanent influence, sprang up the dread of reduction to half-pay. For the present, however, we rather rejoiced than otherwise at the prospect of being delivered from the irk-some and incessant labour of a siege; and we anticipated with satisfaction a friendly intercourse with the brave men against whom we had so long fought, without entertaining one rancorous feeling towards them. I fear, too, that the knowledge of what had passed in Paris, caused some diminution in the watchfulness which we had hitherto preserved; at least, I cannot account upon any other principle for the complete surprisal of our outposts in the village of St Etienne, a few nights after.

The messenger who conveyed this intelligence to us went on to say, that Sir John had dispatched a flag of truce to inform the Governor of Bayonne that there was no longer war between the French and English nations. General Thouvenot, however, refused to credit the statement. He had received, he said, no official communication from Marshal Soult; and as he considered himself under the immediate command of that officer, even a dispatch from the capital would have no weight with him, unless it came backed by the authority of his superior. Under these circumstances, no proposals were made on either side to cease from hostilities, though on ours the troops were henceforth exempted from the labour of erecting batteries, in which it was very little probable that guns would ever be mounted. In other respects, however, things continued as they had previously been. The piquets took their stations as usual; all communications between the garrison and the open country was still cut off, and several families of the inhabitants, who sought to pass through our lines, were compelled to return into the town. This last measure was adopted, as it invariably is adopted when a city is besieged, in order not to diminish the number of persons who must be fed from the stores laid up in the public arsenals.

Though there was peace in Paris, there was no peace before Bayonne. Our brigade having enjoyed its allotted period of rest, accordingly prepared to return to its camp beside Boucaut, for which purpose a line of march was formed on the morning of the 12th; and we again moved towards the floating-bridge. As yet, however, our services at the out-posts were not required; and as working parties were no longer in fashion, we spent that and the succeeding day peaceably in our camp. Not that these days were wholly devoid of interesting occurrences. During the latter, a French officer arrived from the north, bearing the official accounts of those mighty transactions, which once more placed his country under the rule of the Bourbons; and him we sent forward to the city, as the best pledge for the truth of our previous statements, and of our present amicable intentions. Still General Thouvenot disbelieved, or affected to disbelieve, the whole affair; but he returned an answer by the flag of truce which accompanied the aide-de-camp, "that we should hear from him on the subject before long".

It will be readily believed, that the idea of future hostilities was not, under all these circumstances, entertained by any individual of any rank throughout the army. For form's sake, it was asserted that the blockade must still continue, and the sentinels must still keep their ground; but that any attack would be made upon them, or any blood uselessly spilled, no man for a moment imagined. The reader may therefore guess at our astonishment, when, about three o'clock in the morning of the 14th, we were suddenly awoke by a heavy firing in front; and found, on starting up, that a desperate sortie had taken place, and that our piquets were warmly engaged along the whole line. Instantly the bugles sounded. We hurried on our clothes and accoutrements, whilst the horses came galloping in from their various stables, and the servants and bat-men busied themselves in packing the baggage; and then hastily taking our places, we marched towards the point of danger, and were hotly and desperately in action in less than a quarter of an hour.

The enemy had come on in two columns of attack, one of which bore down upon the church and street of St Etienne, whilst the other, having forced the barricade upon the high road, pressed forward towards the chateau where our mortar-battery was in progress of erection. So skilfully had the sortie been managed, that the sentries in front of both these posts were almost all surprised ere they had time, by discharging their pieces, to communicate an alarm to those behind them. By this means, and owing to the extreme darkness of the night, the first intimation of danger which the piquets received was given by the enemy themselves, who, stealing on to the very edge of the trench within which our men were stationed, fired a volley directly upon their heads. In like manner, the serjeant's guard which stood beside the guns in the village was annihilated, and the gun itself captured; whilst the party in the church were preserved from a similar fate, only in consequence of the care which had been taken to block up the various door-ways and entrances, so that only one man at a time might make his way into the interior. It was, however, completely surrounded, and placed in a state of siege; but it was gallantly defended by Captain Forster of the 38th regiment and his men.

Just before the enemy sallied out, a French officer, it appeared, had deserted; but unfortunately he came in through one of the more remote piquets, and hence those which were destined to receive the shock reaped no benefit from the event. His arrival at head-quarters had, however, the effect of putting Sir John Hope on his guard; and hence greater preparations to meet the threatened danger were going forward than we, on whom it came unexpectedly and at once, imagined. A corps of five hundred men, for example, which was daily stationed as a sort of reserve, about a mile in rear of the out-posts, was in full march towards the front when the firing began; and the enemy were in consequence checked before they had made any considerable progress, or had reached any of our more important magazines. The blue house, as we were in the habit of naming the chateau, was indeed carried; and all the piles of fascines and gabions, which had cost us so much labour to construct, were burned; but besides this, little real benefit would have accrued to the assailants, had the state of affairs been such as to render a battle at this particular juncture at all necessary, or even justifiable.

Immediately on the alarm being given, Sir John Hope, attended by a single aide-de-camp, rode to the front. Thither also flew Generals Hay, Stopford, and Bradford, whilst the various brigades hurried after them, at as quick a pace as the pitchy darkness of the night, and the rugged and broken nature of the ground, would permit. Behind them, and on either hand, as they moved, the deepest and most impervious gloom prevailed; but the horizon before them was one blaze of light. I have listened to a good deal of heavy firing in my day; but a more uninterrupted roar of artillery and musketry than was now going on, I hardly recollect to have witnessed.

As the attacking party amounted to five or six thousand men, and the force opposed to them fell somewhat short of one thousand, the latter were, of course, losing ground rapidly. The blue house was carried; the high road, and several lanes that ran parallel with it, were in possession of the enemy; the village of St Etienne swarmed with them; when Sir John Hope arrived at the entrance of a hollow road, for the defence of which a strong party had been allotted. The defenders were in full retreat. "Why do you move in that direction?" cried he, as he rode up. "The enemy are yonder, sir," was the reply. "Well then, we must drive them back – come on." So saying, the general spurred his horse. A dense mass of French soldiers was before him; they fired, and his horse fell dead. The British piquet, alarmed at the fall of the general, fled; and Sir John, being a heavy man, – being besides severely wounded in two places, and having one of his legs crushed beneath his horse, lay powerless, and at the mercy of the assailants. His aide-de-camp, having vainly endeavoured to release him, was urged by Sir John himself to leave him; and the French pressing on, our gallant leader was made prisoner, and sent bleeding within the walls.

Of this sad catastrophe none of the troops were at all aware, except those in whose immediate presence it occurred. The rest found ample employment, both for head and hand, in driving back the enemy from their conquests, and in bringing succour to their comrades, whose unceasing fire gave evidence that they still held out in the church of St Etienne. Towards that point a determined rush was made. The French thronged the street and churchyard, and plied our people with grape and canister from their own captured gun; but the struggle soon became more close and more ferocious. Bayonets, sabres, the butts of muskets, were in full play; and the street was again cleared, the barricade recovered, and the gun retaken. But they were not long retained. A fresh charge was made by increased numbers from the citadel, and our men were again driven back. Numbers threw themselves into the church as they passed, among whom was General Hay; whilst the rest gradually retired till reinforcements came up, when they resumed the offensive, and with the most perfect success. Thus was the street of St Etienne, and the field-piece at its extremity, alternately in possession of the French and allies; the latter being taken and retaken no fewer than nine times, between the hours of three and seven in the morning.

Nor was the action less sanguinary in other parts of the field. Along the sides of the various glens, in the hollow ways, through the trenches, and over the barricades, the most deadly strife was carried on. At one moment, the enemy appeared to carry everything before them; at another, they were checked, broken, and dispersed, by a charge from some battalions of the Guards; but the darkness was so great that confusion everywhere prevailed, nor could it be ascertained, with any degree of accuracy, how matters would terminate. Day at length began to dawn, and a scene was presented of absolute disorder and horrible carnage. Not only were the various regiments of each brigade separated and dispersed, but the regiments themselves were split up into little parties, each of which was warmly and closely engaged with a similar party of the enemy. In almost every direction, too, our men were gaining ground. The French had gradually retrograded; till now they maintained a broken and irregular line, through the churchyard, and along the ridge of a hill, which formed a sort of natural crest to the glacis. One regiment of Guards, which had retained its order, perceiving this, made ready to complete the defeat. They pushed forward in fine array with the bayonet, and dreadful was the slaughter which took place ere the confused mass of fugitives were sheltered within their own gates. In like manner, a dash was made against those who still maintained themselves behind the churchyard wall; and they, too, with difficulty escaped into the redoubt.

A battle, such as that which I have just described, is always attended by a greater proportionate slaughter on both sides, than one more regularly entered into, and more scientifically fought. On our part, nine hundred men had fallen; on the part of the enemy, upwards of a thousand; and the arena within which they fell was so narrow, that even a veteran would have guessed the number of dead bodies at something greatly beyond this. The street of St Etienne, in particular, was covered with killed and wounded; and round the six-pounder they lay in heaps. A French artilleryman had fallen across it, with a fuse in his hand; there he lay, his head cloven asunder, and the remains of the handle of the fuse in his grasp. The muzzle and breech of the gun were smeared with blood and brains; and beside them were several soldiers of both nations, whose heads had evidently been dashed to pieces by the butts of muskets. Arms of all sorts, broken and entire, were strewed about. Among the number of killed on our side was General Hay; he was shot through one of the loop-holes, in the interior of the church. The wounded, too, were far more than ordinarily numerous; in a word, it was one of the most hard-fought and unsatisfactory affairs which had occurred since the commencement of the war. Brave men fell, when their fall was no longer beneficial to their country, and much blood was wantonly shed during a period of national peace.

A truce being concluded between General Colville, who succeeded to the command of the besieging army, and the Governor of Bayonne, the whole of the 15th was spent in burying the dead. Holes were dug for them in various places, and they were thrown in, not without sorrow and lamentations, but with very little ceremony. In collecting them together, various living men were found, sadly mangled, and hardly distinguishable from their slaughtered comrades. These were, of course, removed to the hospitals, where every care was taken of them; but not a few perished from loss of blood ere assistance arrived. It was remarked, likewise, by the medical attendants, that a greater proportion of incurable wounds were inflicted this night than they remembered to have seen. Many had received bayonet-thrusts in vital parts; one man, I recollect, whose eyes were both torn from the sockets, and hung over his cheeks; whilst several were cut in two by round shot, which had passed through their bellies, and still left them breathing. The hospitals accordingly presented sad spectacles, whilst the shrieks and groans of the inmates acted with no more cheering effect upon the sense of hearing, than their disfigured countenances and mangled forms acted upon the sense of sight.

It is unnecessary to remind the reader, that whilst our column of the army was thus engaged before Bayonne, Lord Wellington, following up his success at Orthies, had gained the splendid victory of Toulouse. As an immediate consequence upon that event, the important city of Bourdeaux was taken possession of by Lord Dalhousie, and declared for Louis XVIII; whilst farther conquests were prevented only by the arrival of Colonels Cook and St Simon, the one at the head-quarters of Lord Wellington, the other at those of Marshal Soult. By them official information was conveyed of the great change which had occurred in the French capital. An armistice between the two generals immediately followed; and such an order being conveyed to General Thouvenot, as he considered himself bound to obey, a similar treaty was entered into by us and the governor. By the terms of that treaty all hostilities were to cease. The two armies were still, however, kept apart, nor was any one from our camp allowed to enter Bayonne without receiving a written pass from the adjutant-general. Foraging parties only were permitted to come forth from the place at stated periods, and to collect necessaries from any point within a circle of three leagues from the walls. Yet the truce was regarded by both parties, as an armed one. After so late an instance of treachery, we felt no disposition to trust to the word or honour of the French governor; whilst the enemy, guessing, perhaps, that our bosoms burned for revenge, exhibited no symptoms of reposing confidence in us. On each side, therefore, a system of perfect watchfulness continued. We established our piquets, and planted our sentinels, with the same caution and strictness as before; nor was any other difference distinguishable between the nature of those duties now and what it had been a week ago, except that the enemy suffered us to show ourselves without firing upon us. So passed several days, till, on the 20th, the war was formally declared to be at an end.

Chapter 25

Looking Back

Residual antagonism is displayed by the French. On 8 May the 85th strike its tents and are marched away from Bayonne to await further orders. Gleig moralizes on his youthful enthusiasm for the profession of arms – he was only just eighteen when embarking for his second and last campaign, in America; but, as he later admitted in the dedication to the Duke, the year as subaltern under Wellington's command was 'the happiest in his life'.

Little now remains for me to add. My tale of war, and its attendant dangers and enjoyments, is told; and I have nothing left to notice, except a few of the most prominent of the adventures which befell, between the period of my quitting one scene of hostile operations, and my arrival at another. These are quickly narrated.

Early on the morning of the 28th of April, 1814, the whole of the allied troops encamped around Bayonne, drew up, in various lines, to witness the hoisting of the white flag upon the ramparts of that city. The standards of England, Spain, Portugal, and of the Bourbons, already waved together from the summit of every eminence in our camp. Up to this date, however, the tri-color still kept its place upon the flag-staff of the citadel; to-day it was to be torn down, and the "drapeau blanc" substituted in its room. To us, no doubt, the spectacle promised to be one of triumph and rejoicing; for we thought of the gigantic exertions of our country, which alone, of all the nations in Europe, had uniformly refused to acknowledge the sovereignty of the usurper; but by the French, it was very differently regarded. Even among the country-people, not a spark of enthusiasm could be traced; whilst by the garrison, no secret was made of their abhorrence of the new state of things, and their undiminished attachment to their former master. But there was no help for it. "*La fortune de la guerre,*" said a French officer to me one day, as we talked of these matters; but he shrugged his shoulders as he spoke, and gave no proof that he was satisfied with its results.

We had stood in our ranks about an hour, dressed in our best attire, and having our muskets loaded with powder only, when a signal-gun was fired from one of the batteries of the town, and a magnificent tri-coloured flag which had hitherto waved proudly in the breeze, was gradually lowered. For perhaps half a minute the flag-staff stood bare; and then a small white standard, dirty, and, if my eyes deceived me not, a little torn, was run up. Immediately the guns from every quarter of the city fired a salute. By such of our people as kept guard at the out-posts that day, it was asserted that each gun was crammed with sand and mud, as if this turbulent garrison had been resolved to insult, as far as they could insult, an authority to which they submitted only because they were compelled to submit. On our parts, the salute was answered with a feu-de-joie, from all the infantry, artillery, and gun-boats; and then a hearty shout being raised, we filed back to our respective stations, and dismissed the parade.

From this period, till the general breaking up of the camp, nothing like friendly or familiar intercourse took place between us and our former enemies. We were suffered, indeed, by two at a time, to enter the city with passports, whilst some half-dozen French officers would occasionally wander down to Boucaut, and mingle in the crowd which filled its market-place. But they came with no kindly intention. On the contrary, all our advances were met with haughtiness, and it seemed as if they were anxious to bring on numerous private quarrels, now that the quarrel between the countries was at an end. Nor were these always refused them. More duels were fought than the world in general knows anything about; whilst vast numbers were prevented, only by a positive prohibition on the part of the two generals, and a declaration, that whoever violated the order would be placed in arrest, and tried by a court-martial.

We were still in our camp by the Adour, when various bodies of Spanish troops passed through on their return from Toulouse to their own country. Than some of these battalions, I never beheld a finer body of men; and many of them were as well clothed, armed, and appointed, as any battalions in the world. But they were, one and all, miserably officered. Their inferior officers, in particular, were mean and ungentlemanly in their appearance, and they seemed to possess little or no authority over their men. Yet they were full of boasting, and gave themselves, on all occasions, as many absurd airs, as if their valour had delivered Spain, and dethroned Napoleon; such is the foolish vanity of human nature.

Like my companions, I neglected not any opportunity which was afforded of visiting Bayonne, or of examining the nature of its works. Of the town itself, I need say no more, than that it was as clean and regularly built, as a fortified place can well be; where the utmost is to be made of a straitened boundary, and houses obtain in altitude what may be wanting in the extent of their fronts. Neither is it necessary that I should enter into a minute description of its defences, sufficient notice having been taken of them elsewhere. But of the inhabitants, I cannot avoid remarking, that I found them uncivil and unfriendly in the extreme, as if they took their tone from the troops in garrison, who sought not to disguise their chagrin and disappointment.

Besides paying occasional visits to the city, much of my time was passed in fishing, and in taking part in the public amusements which began to be instituted amongst us. The sands, for example, were converted into a race-course, upon which we tried the speed of our horses day after day. Balls were established in the village, which were attended by ladies of all classes, and from all parts of the surrounding country; and, in a word, all the expedients usually adopted by idle men, were adopted by us, to kill time, and make head against ennui.

Such was the general tenor of my life, from the 20th of April, till the 8th of May. On the latter day, the regiment struck its tents, and marched one day's journey to the rear, where it remained in quiet, till the arrival of the order, which sent it first to the neighbourhood of Bourdeaux, and afterwards to North America.

Thus ends the narrative of the adventures of a single year in the life of a Subaltern Officer. Whatever may be thought of it by the public, it has not been compiled without considerable satisfaction by the narrator; for the year referred to is one on which I now look back, and probably shall ever look back, with the feeling of melancholy satisfaction, which invariably accompanies a retrospect of happiness gone by. If ever there existed an enthusiastic lover of the profession of arms, I believe that I was one; but the times were unfavourable, and he must live for very little purpose, who knows not that enthusiasm of any kind rarely survives our youth. I loved my profession, as long as it gave full occupation to my bodily and mental powers; but the peace came, and I loved it no longer. Perhaps, indeed, the kind of feeling which I had taught myself to encourage, was not such as, in the present state of society, any prudent person is justified in encouraging; for I care not to conceal, that the brightest hopes of my boyhood have all faded, and that manhood has produced none capable of taking their place. The friend who shared with me so many dangers and hardships, fell at my side, by the hand of an unworthy enemy. The walk of life which I pursued, for a while, so merrily, has been abandoned; my sabre hangs rusty upon the wall; and my poor old faithful dog is gathered to her fathers. She lies under the green sod before my window; and morning and evening as I walk past her grave, if I shed no tear to her memory, I at least pay to it the tribute of a kindly thought. Well, well, all this is as it ought to be; it is quite right that we should learn the folly of fixing our affections too strongly upon anything in a scene so shifting and uncertain as human life; and I suspect there are few persons who are not taught that lesson, at least occasionally, long before their prime be past.

Let it not, however, be supposed, that he who thus expresses himself must therefore be discontented with his lot, or that he murmurs against the Providence which has cast it for him. By no means. If in my new mode of existence there can be less of excitement and of wild enjoyment than in my old, at least there is more of calm and quiet gratification. Other ties, likewise, are around me, different in kind, indeed, but not less tender, than those which time has severed; and if there be nothing in the future calculated to stir up ambitious longing, there is still sufficient to defend against discontent. At all events, I am certain that my present occupations are such as will prove more permanently and vitally beneficial to others, than those which preceded them; and let me add, that a man need not be accused of fanaticism who is convinced, that to look back upon a life, not uselessly spent, is the only thing which will bring him peace at the last.

But enough of moralizing, when, in the words of our greatest living poet, I wish to such as have honoured my tale with a perusal,

> "To each and all, a fair good night,
> And rosy dreams, and slumbers bright."

THE END.

Index

Gleig's erratic interpretation of topographical names have been retained in the text and index, but their conventional spellings, together with the correct spellings of surnames, are added in bold. This selective index, while concentrating on persons and places referred to in the scenes of actions described, also includes those mentioned in the preliminary paragraphs to each chapter.

INDEX